SERENITY

A WALK With The SERENITY PRAYER

Daily Devotions for People in Recovery

THOMAS NELSON PUBLISHERS
Nashville

Acknowledgments

Drs. Meier and Minirth wish to express their appreciation to their fellow faculty members at Dallas Theological Seminary for producing *The Bible Knowledge Commentary,* edited by John F. Walvoord and Roy B. Zuck (Victor Books, 1987). It was a great help in the preparation of this devotional book. We would also like to thank Jan Meier, Cheryl Meier, and Mark and Marie Verkler for their research, typing and editorial assistance.

Copyright © 1991 by Paul Meier, Dr. David Congo, Jan Congo, and Dr. Frank Minirth

Published in Nashville, Tennessee, by Thomas Nelson, Inc., and distributed in Canada by Lawson Falle, Ltd., Cambridge, Ontario.

Library of Congress Cataloging-in-Publication Data

A Walk with the Serenity prayer / Paul Meier . . . [et al.].
    p.   cm. — (Serenity meditation series)
    ISBN 0-8407-3236-8
    1. Devotional calendars. 2. Consolation—
    Meditations. I. Meier, Paul D. II. Series.
BX4810.W34 1991
242′.4—dc20   90–20577
                                    CIP

Printed in the United States of America
1 2 3 4 5 6 7 — 96 95 94 93 92 91

Introduction

All of us suffer from time to time as we sojourn through life. Some of us honestly admit it, serenely accept inevitable pain, courageously change unnecessary pain, and humbly ask God for wisdom to know the difference. This is what the Serenity Prayer is all about. It is a prayer for honest sojourners—a family of fellow sufferers:

> *God, grant us the serenity to accept the things we cannot change, courage to change the things we can, and wisdom to know the difference.*

The principles of the Serenity Prayer have, by now, transformed the lives of literally millions of people. And like a seed that grows into a beautiful plant, these benefits have been extended to millions of their descendants. The real power behind this beautiful metamorphosis has not come directly from the Serenity Prayer itself but from the cooperative teamwork of God, His Word, and honest companions.

A loving, all-knowing, all-powerful God continues to plant the principles found in His Word (His love letter to us) in the hearts of a unique family of humble human spirits. They are eternal sons and daughters of God, made in the image of God, and given authority by the Creator-God to subdue the earth. They acknowledge the three major truths found in the Serenity Prayer:

Truth #1: Many of the pains and personal struggles we experience are *unavoidable*. In eternity, God will wipe away all tears, but in the meantime He instructs His followers to "weep with those who weep." Reality really hurts sometimes. Reality includes some very significant losses and grief. Victorious travelers are those who grieve the pain and learn to serenely accept the things they cannot change.

Truth #2: Many of the pains and personal struggles we experience *seem* unavoidable, but are actually avoidable by courageously taking individual responsibility to change the things we can change, with God's power. Recovery requires us to bond in love to honest fellow seekers who will accept us the way we are, while we speak the truth to each other in love.

Truth #3: We humans tend to get a little puffed up from time to time with our own "wisdom." That is why psychiatrists are jokingly referred to as "head shrinkers." God's wisdom is so much higher than ours! God even tells us to study the behavior of ants so we can learn how to store up for the "tough winters" of life.

To be successful sojourners, we must humbly kneel before an all-knowing God and ask Him for wisdom. We need wisdom to know the difference between avoidable and unavoidable pain and personal struggles. And we need His divine wisdom to somehow *apply* what we have learned to improve behavior patterns in our lives. It is not easy to serenely accept the unavoidable and courageously change the avoidable, even after God grants us the wisdom to know the difference. It takes *hard work:* very hard work. That is why we need the love and support of others who know the truth about us and choose to love us anyway.

This devotional contains 365 powerful passages from God's letter to His beloved sons and daughters. Each passage is examined for behavioral applications that can actually transform our lives. Each week's journey through this devotional book will take the reader on a mini-tour through the seven key principles of the Serenity Prayer. Each day's passage has the potential to become a transforming seed for a searching soul.

Every positive application of God's principles ultimately benefits both us and others. Every sin we commit somehow, sooner or later, hurts us and others. Think about that. Accepting God's wisdom as being higher than our own, then courageously changing our behavior to fit in with His loving plans for us, transforms us into successful sojourners. Not *perfect* sojourners, but successful ones. We will still fail from time to time. We will still be human. We will still suffer. But we will learn to decrease our pain: the avoidable pain that we can courageously change. And all the rest, including our suffering, will benefit us in the long run. It will mature us. It will help us grow into beautiful people who are actually brothers and sisters in the family of God. Life will not be perfect! But life will have value and meaning. What more could we ask for?

If we have comprehended the security found in God's accepting and forgiving love, if we can grasp that God loves us just as much whether we succeed or fail, then we can set aside fear and be free to risk. Fear can be replaced with trust and courage to face new challenges.

If you want to break a habitual pattern of worry and fear, why not try the following:

1. Take a 3 x 5 card and write the word *stop* in big letters on one side.

2. On the other side, write "Perfect love casts out fear."

3. Each time you find yourself starting to worry or

be fearful, pull out the card and read the word *stop* aloud. Then turn it over and refocus your thinking on God's love and acceptance of you.

Are you so secure in God's love that you are able to risk rather than retreat? To have faith rather than fear? Dare to trust Him today.

Yet as we see ourselves in the mirror, we get discouraged and can easily develop a negative spirit or attitude. We must ask God, therefore, to renew a right spirit within us.

Give yourself permission to review your life and write a list of the areas you feel need to change. Remember, you can only change yourself.

God calls us to love, not change, those significant other persons in our life. God challenges us to dare to grow, and He keeps on loving us in the process.

A father of the fatherless, a defender of widows,
Is God in His holy habitation.
God sets the solitary in families;
He brings out those who are bound into prosperity;
But the rebellious dwell in a dry land.

—PS. 68:5–6

One of the most common problems articulated in therapy is a feeling of being isolated, alone, or cut off from others. There are many reasons for this.

Sally can still remember with horror the night her dad left. He never again contacted Sally's mother, or the children, and failed to support them financially. Steve remembers waiting for his dad to come and cheer him on at his baseball games, but his dad was at the local bar having another beer. Alice remembers the helpless, isolated feeling when her husband of 28 years died in a motorcycle accident.

Each of these people felt abandoned and alone. Each wanted to be loved, accepted, and supported. Each one wanted to feel connected.

God does want us to be in spiritual supportive families. In Northern California grow the majestic, tall redwood trees. The redwood tree has a very shallow root system. How do these trees withstand the strong winds that would blow them over? They grow in groves and the roots of one tree branch out and intertwine with the roots of another tree. Together they stand. Seldom do you ever see a large redwood standing alone. Neither were we meant to go it alone.

God meant for you to have support. Join an AA group, an ACA group, a mini-church, or a therapy group where you can be loved.

Oh, keep my soul, and deliver me;
Let me not be ashamed, for I put my trust in You.
—PS. 25:20

Shame is the driving force behind all addictions. It is the belief in the very core of our being that we are not okay, that we were a mistake, that we're worthless. No one could possibly love us; we can't even love ourselves. No one can fix us; we are defective. How lonely and abandoned our shame makes us feel. How can we ever escape?

Escaping is an unhealthy way to alter our mood. We may think it's easy. All we have to do is eat, drink, have sex, pop pills, get more money, or work harder. The trouble is, the more we do these things the more shame we feel. This downward spiral seems darker every day. We are powerless.

Step Two of the Twelve Step Program states, "We came to believe that a Power greater than ourselves could restore us to sanity." Step Three states, "We made a decision to turn our will and our lives over to the care of God as we understood Him."

God knew that there was no escape from our shame unless He provided it. That's what he did through Jesus Christ. Jesus was the final answer to our shame and the final victory over our sin. All He asks of us is that we admit our powerlessness and abandon ourselves to Jesus' loving care.

Regardless of our past mistakes or failures, God looks at each of us and says, "You are my beloved child and I am pleased with you." It's time to take on a new identity. We are forgiven, accepted and loved.

My son, do not forget my law, but let your heart keep my commands: for length of days and long life and peace they will add to you.
—PROV. 3:1–2

At the suggestion of the rabbi, a Jewish boy made a list of the great values he would pursue during his lifetime. He included fortune, fame, and physical health. When he finished his list, he excitedly gave it to the rabbi. With his years of experience and wisdom, the rabbi looked over the list in search of one particular word. It wasn't there. He turned to the boy and said, "You have missed one of the most important values of life, and that is peace of mind. What good is fame, what good are money and fortune, and what good is physical health, if you do not have peace at the core of your life?"

The Jewish people continue to use the same greeting they have used for centuries: "Shalom"—which means peace.

Peace is an ingredient of life all of us desire.

Solomon, in talking to his son, shares that he will have peace plus long productive days and a long life if he will determine to focus on God's Word and follow God's commands. God's Word contains principles that can make life more fulfilling, meaningful, and characterized by peace. God has our best in mind. The intent of his commands is not to control us, but to enrich our lives.

Peace is not something I seek. It is the by-product of following God's commands.

> *Therefore we do not lose heart. Even though our*
> *outward man is perishing, yet the inward man is*
> *being renewed day by day.* —2 COR. 4:16

It's been said that young people look forward, old people look back and the middle aged just look tired. There's truth in that statement, isn't there! How much better it would be if each age group would look at their present reality from a new perspective.

All of us are aging. We cannot avoid it no matter how hard we try. Yet how frantic we get trying to be younger, thinner, and wealthier. All we can see is ourselves.

If we viewed our aging process with an eternal perspective, we wouldn't be so quick to forget how important inner beauty is. We would be the kind of people who didn't forget to count their blessings even if it became a necessity to also count calories. We would be aware that once we get to know good people, they all become beautiful. We, as older people, would build our lives into younger people so that when we die all our wisdom wouldn't die with us. We would live each day with compassion knowing that it is a precious, never to be repeated, gift.

The next time you feel as if you're experiencing "midlife crisis," remember that learning to accept your realities is a sign of your eternal hope.

*"With us is the LORD our God, to help us
and to fight our battles."*
—2 CHRON. 32:8

Twenty-two years ago she began her first battle against cancer. Cures were infrequent then, particularly for the type of cancer her doctors had diagnosed. Still she hoped God would heal her, either by the skill of physicians or by a private miracle.

With extensive treatment, God did heal her! Years passed and then she was diagnosed with another cancer of an entirely different type. She believed God for restoration once again, and her Father answered.

Then, Mary Beth contracted a third cancer. For four years she battled the awful pain. If friends asked how she was, she replied, "Oh, I'm just fine!" And she was! In spite of the pain, she lived those four years radiantly. Everyone around her was inspired by her faith.

How did she face such incalculable odds without fear? Two weeks ago I talked with Mary Beth in the hospital. "How are you dealing with this business of dying?" I asked. She replied, "Oh. I'm not afraid of dying—I dealt with that years ago. Besides, God has promised to heal me—one way or the other! Either here or over there!"

Last Wednesday we celebrated her home-going. God had kept His promise.

No adversary in life need send fear to the heart of God's children. He promises to deliver us.

Lord, when circumstances look so threatening and overwhelming, grant that we may look first to You and Your promises.

> *Do you not know that those who run in a race all run, but one receives the prize? Run in such a way that you may obtain it.*
> —1 COR. 9:24

Winning in life does not come automatically. It usually involves setting aside certain privileges and pleasures for a time in order to achieve a goal.

A dear friend was brought to the hospital following a mild stroke. At the age of sixty he was overweight and out of shape. The doctor was kind, but direct, "Herb, unless you change your eating habits and get into a walking or swimming program, I'm afraid you might soon have a serious heart attack."

Herb decided to make some changes. He began to walk for a short distance several times a day. He cut sugar out of his diet and began eating smaller portions at meals. He set a goal to participate in a ten kilometer run in five years.

Little by little, his short walks were extended. He began jogging intermittently. He lost weight too. After one year he was able to walk and jog in a 5K run. Four years into the program, he had built up his stamina until he could run, not walk, the 10K course.

Like Paul in this passage, Herb did not let his body master him, but he disciplined himself. He denied himself of some pleasures in order to achieve what would be best for him.

———————

What do I need to change in order to achieve a personal goal?

A wise man will hear and increase learning.
And a man of understanding will attain wise counsel.
—PROV. 1:5

The secret of growing in wisdom is centered in how we respond to consultation and confrontation. These verses point out that the fool thinks he knows it all. He shuns any input or advice. He holds on to his viewpoint in a bull-headed way.

The wise man responds so differently. He embraces input from others and seeks counsel from individuals more experienced than himself. The wise man listens to and learns from the advice and information.

The trouble is, not all confrontation is motivated by love. For this reason, I evaluate all criticism through the acrostic, THANKS:

T   Take the time to listen.
H   Honestly evaluate the input.
A   Ask God and yourself if this is an area in which you need to grow.
N   Nullify it, if it is false. Make needed adjustments if it is true.
K   Know God loves you anyway.
S   Select a new goal!

The next time you are criticized, look your critic right in the eye and say "thanks." You might catch him or her off guard.

The way of a fool is right in his own eyes.
But he who heeds counsel is wise. (Prov. 12:15)

> *Let this mind be in you which was also in Christ*
> *Jesus, who, being in the form of God, did not*
> *consider it robbery to be equal with God, but made*
> *Himself of no reputation, taking the form of a*
> *servant, and coming in the likeness of men. And*
> *being found in appearance as a man, He humbled*
> *Himself and became obedient to the point of death,*
> *even the death of the cross. Therefore God also has*
> *highly exalted Him and given Him the name which*
> *is above every name. . . .*   —PHIL. 2:5–9

How do people see God, who is intangible and invisible? We may be the closest experience of God some will have. Therefore if we rightly relate to others, following God's example, we enable them to have a clearer and bigger understanding of God.

In this passage, Paul gives us a picture of Jesus Christ and His attitude toward us. Jesus was equal with God.

What did Christ do so as to relate to us? "He humbled Himself." He didn't try to be the hot-shot, the hero, the big guy. He chose rather to come alongside us, to love and to serve us. He washed the disciples feet, living out the responsibility of a servant.

Love, not power, was Christ's way of relating. Serving rather than expecting to be waited on was His choice for relationships. Christ chose to be a host rather than a guest; to give rather than to get.

Are you controlled by the love of power or are you living out the power of love?

I can be God's eyes, hands, and arms to the needy and hurting people around me.

Behold, the eye of the LORD is on those who fear Him,
On those who hope in His mercy,
To deliver their soul from death,
And to keep them alive in famine.
Our soul waits for the LORD;
He is our help and our shield.
For our heart shall rejoice in Him,
Because we have trusted in His holy name.
Let Your mercy, O LORD, be upon us,
Just as we hope in You. —PS. 33:18–22

Victor Frankl, known for his writing and position as head of the Department of Psychiatry in Vienna, Austria, was captured by the Nazis during the Second World War. At the concentration camp, the guards took his shirt, cap, belt and shoes. Next they took his slacks and underwear. There he stood naked before them. Frankl says they all began to laugh. They stripped him of his wrist watch, his wedding ring, and his dignity.

While all this was going on, Frankl was thinking, "There is one thing you cannot take. You cannot take from me my power and freedom to choose my attitude." The reality is the Nazis never did, even though Frankl suffered through years in the concentration camp.

Three thousand years ago, King David also prayed for mercy and chose a victorious attitude. We can come to God with our petitions, large and small. We can ask the Lord to deliver our souls from death, to keep us alive in whatever kind of "famine" we face.

Don't hesitate to ask God for His help in your time of need.

> *. . . having faith and a good conscience, which*
> *some having rejected, concerning the faith have*
> *suffered shipwreck. . . .*   —1 TIM. 1:19

One day my wife was baking cookies. She had to run to the corner market to get a few ingredients to finish off her project.

As she dashed out the front door, she told our five-year-old son to stay out of the cookies and she would give him some when she was finished.

You guessed it! The temptation was too great and he and his little friend succumbed.

When Jan returned, he and his friend anxiously ran to the back corner of our property. He was on edge as my wife approached him. He did not even want to look her in the eye.

Why? His conscience was bothering him. He knew he had disobeyed, and he certainly was not at peace.

Serenity comes from having a clear conscience, from knowing we have nothing to hide. Serenity comes from being real and honest.

My wife realized what had happened. My son confessed that he had disobeyed, and was able to thereby clear his conscience with Mom. His normal carefree spirit and peace returned.

I don't have to be perfect, but I do need to be honest. A clear conscience leads to serenity.

This is my comfort in my affliction.
For Your word has given me life.
—PS. 119:50

It's not what happens to you that's most important; it's what happens within you.

I can still hear that doctor's words as he evaluated a large mark on our son's leg: "Either this is melanoma or an unusually textured birthmark."

Talk about afflictions. My wife and I felt overwhelmed. This isn't fair. How could a child of six have cancer? "What are you trying to do, God?" were our thoughts.

We were faced with a choice. Did we believe God is good only if things are positive? Were we going to turn our backs on God because of this turn of events in our son's life? It wasn't what had just happened to us that was most important, but what was going to happen within us. We could either become bitter or better. We could accept the affliction or reject God. As we prayed that night, we told God we were going to trust Him no matter what happened.

We drew closer to Him because of this affliction. Like the psalmist, we can now say that it is good that we were afflicted, so that we could learn more of His promises. Those promises sustained us in the following months.

The Lord touched our son. He is now fourteen and growing into a fine young man.

I may not be able to choose my circumstances, but I can choose my response.

Jesus wept.
—JOHN 11:35

One of the tragedies of our western culture is an idea that has been passed down particularly to men. It is this: if you cry, you are a sissy and you are weak. Instead be strong; be a man; be courageous and "stuff" your feelings. The Scripture passage contradicts this philosophy. In fact it shows Jesus, the most courageous man who ever lived, showing His feelings. The passage succinctly says, "Jesus wept."

He was real. He was free to feel. He was not ashamed of letting His feelings out, and apparently did so publicly. Jesus showed us that courage does not mean stuffing our feelings or not grieving when we experience loss.

Grieving is normal, following a loss of any kind. It could be the loss of a family member or friend, a financial loss, the loss of a job. Whatever the loss, allow the feelings to come, and have the courage to grieve and let the tears come. It will take some time, but grieving allows us to face reality and in time, move on in spite of the loss.

May God grant me the serenity to be real, and the courage to let my true feelings out.

Your word is a lamp to my feet
And a light to my path.
—PS. 119:105

The other night I went into my son's room to tell him good night. His light was already out and our hall light was burned out. He had gone to bed a little while before, but I didn't know whether or not he was asleep yet. Therefore, I opted not to turn on his bedroom light. In the darkness I proceeded toward his bed only to stumble and fall over the chair he had left in the path.

I picked myself up after the noise and clatter of my fall. I thought to myself, "I should have had a light." Even a small pocket light or night-light would have helped me avoid my tumble and my skinned knees and ankles.

God's Word is a light to my path. Its purpose is not to be restricting or negative, but rather to keep me from falling—to help me see the way. His Word provides direction to my life. The more I learn of His Word the more chance I have of staying on track.

Learn God's Word.

Live God's way.

Love God's light.

> *"Abide in Me, and I in you. As the branch cannot bear fruit of itself, unless it abides in the vine, neither can you, unless you abide in Me. I am the vine, you are the branches. He who abides in Me, and I in him, bears much fruit; for without Me you can do nothing."*
>
> —JOHN 15:4–5

True wisdom is found in establishing a balance in teamwork with God. It seems so often there is a tendency to go to one extreme or the other.

We can adopt the philosophy of "Let go and let God" and sit back and expect God to do everything. However, I have found that if I'm lazy, God won't do it for me. On the other hand, there have been times when I have gone to the other extreme of trying to do it all on my own and proceeding almost as if God was not around. That too, has usually ended in failure.

Philippians 4:13 brings these two contrasting extremes into balance: "I can do all things through Christ who strengthens me." The verse is not saying I can do it all, period. Nor is it saying Christ does it all. It is a joint project, a teamwork relationship, a partnership.

Today's passage uses an example from nature to illustrate the same point. The branch without the vine or trunk soon withers and dies and produces no fruit. The trunk provides nourishment to the branches, which produce the fruit. Teamwork is God's mode of operation.

Be wise and team up with God. Watch excitedly for the results of your partnership in your daily accomplishments.

Blessed be the Lord.
Who daily loads us with benefits.
The God of our salvation!
—PS. 68:19

I had the privilege of meeting the well-known speaker, Karen Mains. She relayed a game her family has played together, an uncommon form of "I spy."

Anytime anyone in the family was aware of some blessing or benefit the Lord was giving them, they would say "I spy." If they were alone at the time, they would jot it down in their "I spy" notebook. On Saturday evenings in preparation for worship on Sunday, each family member would share the week's 'I spy."

We have tried this in our family, and it encourages us to be alert to those things God does on our behalf.

After a long drive through an unpopulated area on a hot day, we found ourselves in a little town. As we drove down the street looking for a parking space, our seven-year-old daughter said "I spy" and excitedly pointed to one directly in front of an ice cream parlor.

Several years ago when we moved to a new area, my son did not seem to have any boys his age in the area to play with. We prayed each night about this. After two weeks, my son came through the front door saying "I spy." He had just met a boy who lived one block away, who was going into the same grade.

Along with the psalmist we can say God daily loads us with benefits.

Try playing "I spy." Record God's benefits in a notebook at the end of each day this week.

> *And He was withdrawn from them about a stone's throw, and He knelt down and prayed, saying, "Father, if it is Your will, remove this cup from Me; nevertheless not My will, but Yours, be done." Then an angel appeared to Him from heaven, strengthening Him.*
>
> —LUKE 22:41–43

God answers our requests in various ways. He can say yes, no, or grow, depending on the request, the circumstances, and how it fits in His overall plan.

When He chooses to answer yes, most of us are overjoyed. However if He chooses to say no or grow, our reaction may be quite different. It is easy to interpret a no response as *He does not really care* or *maybe He didn't really understand what I asked for.*

In this passage, Jesus asked if He could forego having to drink the cup of death and be placed on the cross. God's answer to His Son was no. God the Father knew Jesus had to die to take our place, so we wouldn't have to pay for our own failures and sins.

However, notice the next verse. When God said no, He sent an angel to strengthen Jesus. When God says no, He has a reason, but He also desires to be supportive.

The angels God sends to us often come in the form of another person who can help to sustain us. "Angels" can be found in a Twelve Step group, in therapy or support groups. Sometimes the "angel" is a family member or close friend. Sometimes it is also our guardian angel.

May God grant me the serenity and courage to not fear His answer to my prayers but help me to grow when confronted with a "no".

The curse of the LORD is on the house of the wicked,
But He blesses the habitation of the just.
—PROV. 3:33

Each time something replaces the love for Christ within us, inner conflict is the result. We can't have habitual, willful sin and also experience serenity.

Sin is much like a splinter in our unconscious mind. Unless sin is removed through confession and repentance, it will fester just as a splinter festers. It will lead to feelings of inadequacy and inferiority. It's not as easy to stand tall and tell ourselves we're okay when we know we have violated God's standard. Inner conflict rages. Still, we ignore it and the sin continues to fester. There is a loss of creativity and perhaps even lowered efficiency. If we continue to ignore sin, we will experience a sense of failure. After all, we have been unfaithful to ourselves and to Jesus. Even ill health can be a result if we refuse to acknowledge the presence of sin in our lives.

The fourth step of the Twelve Step program is to make a searching and fearless moral inventory of ourselves. Have you done that yet?

Becoming a Christian isn't merely fire insurance. It's a relationship with a loving God that affects every area of our lives. It transforms our values, our lifestyles, our will, and even our sexuality. It involves obedience; unconditional love compels us to obey. Wholeness, serenity, and health are the result.

Habitual, willful sin freezes me; obedience and confession free me.

> *Concerning this thing I pleaded with the Lord three times that it might depart from me. And He said to me, "My grace is sufficient for you, for My strength is made perfect in weakness."* —2 COR. 12:8

Paul had "a thorn in the flesh" that kept bothering him. He did three things with it.

1. He faced it head-on. He didn't pretend and deny that it was part of his life.

2. He placed it at God's feet in prayer. He petitioned God to take it away three times. For some reason, God chose not to do that. Therefore Paul took another step.

3. He embraced it. He accepted this obstacle that made him feel weak, since it made him more aware of his need for the Lord in his life.

Many theologians have tried to guess what Paul's thorn was. Some of the suggestions are that it was a personal temptation. Others say it was an unresolved interpersonal conflict, or a chronic physical illness such as malaria, migraine headaches, or an eye disease. Whatever the problem, Paul's principles for dealing with it also apply to us today with our personal thorns in the flesh.

We need to face them squarely, place them at God's feet, and finally, embrace them. The result of this action is that Christ's power is best displayed against the background of human weakness.

My weakness is God's opportunity to demonstrate His power.

Then he said to them, "Go your way, eat the fat, drink the sweet, and send portions to those for whom nothing is prepared; for this day is holy to our LORD. Do not sorrow, for the joy of the LORD is your strength."
—NEH. 8:10

Another source of courage for us is joy. There are lots of things in life that bring us good, clean, moral joy. We should take note of them and remember what they are. The things that brings us joy also give us the courage to keep fighting during the painful times in life.

In our passage for today, Ezra the priest brought the Bible before a large congregation of Jews in front of the Water Gate. He read it for several straight hours, from morning until lunchtime.

Assistants helped explain to small groups of this huge crowd what was being read as they stood in their places. The people wept—probably for guilt and for joy—as Ezra read and explained God's Word to them. Have you found yourself weeping after reading God's Word and learning what it means for you? I hope so.

But Nehemiah, Ezra, and the Levites told the people to put aside their tears that day and celebrate, because it was a special day for the Lord. They told them to allow the joy of knowing God to strengthen their courage.

_____

Look for ways to find pure joy today from various sources. But make one of those sources the joy of knowing Jesus Christ.

*When I was a child, I spoke as a child, I
understood as a child, I thought as a child; but
when I became a man, I put away childish things.
For now we see in a mirror, dimly, but then face to
face. Now I know in part, but then I shall know just
as I also am known. And now abide faith, hope,
love, these three; but the greatest of these is love.*
—1 COR. 13:11–13

One of the exciting aspects of parenting is to observe
your children slowly, progressively changing their behavior. In contrast, one of the most upsetting and scary
experiences is to realize that your child appears to be
blocked in a physical or emotional aspect of normal
development.

I had a sister who had a cerebral palsy due to a birth
injury. My parents have shared the feelings and fear
that grew within them as they realized that she was not
moving as other children did, or talking as other much
younger children were.

Paul addresses three particular behaviors in which
he challenges us all to keep growing and changing:
talking, thinking, and reasoning.

He challenges us to develop three qualities needed
in maturing individuals. These are faith, hope and love.

*What childish behaviors do I need to change? How can I develop my
faith? . . . my hope? . . . my love? Quietly reflect on these questions.*

*The fear of the LORD is the beginning of
   knowledge,
But fools despise wisdom and instruction.*
                                    —PROV. 1:7

Solomon, one of the wisest men who ever lived, stated that the beginning of wisdom and knowledge comes from fearing the Lord.

What does it mean to fear the Lord?

The fear described here is not cowering, intimidation, or paralysis. Instead, it means to respect, reverence and worship the Lord.

If you want to gain wisdom, Solomon says, "Begin with God." Make Him your focus. Center on Him. Make Him the number one priority in your life. See God for who He is.

You might begin each day by looking in the Bible for one characteristic that describes God, and think on that quality. Consider how that truth could impact your life that day. Consider what you might do differently in light of that fact.

For example, Jesus is called the "Light of the World." Do you ever feel during the day that you are fumbling in the dark, and that you can't clearly see your way? Stop and pray. Ask God to bring clarity to your darkness and direction to your sense of being lost.

Wisdom comes from lifting our eyes from the problem to our powerful God, from the difficulty to the divine.

*For the word of God is living and powerful, and
sharper than any two-edged sword, piercing even to
the division of soul and spirit, and of joints and
marrow, and is a discerner of the thoughts and
intents of the heart. And there is no creature hidden
from His sight, but all things are naked and open
to the eyes of Him to whom we must give account.*
—HEB. 4:12–13

One of the invaluable advances in the medical field
has been the development of the X-ray machine. Because it allows the surgeon to get a clearer picture and
understanding of what is below the skin, it can give
direction to the appropriate treatment.

In much the same way, in a spiritual or emotional
sense, God sees deep inside us to our core, to our inner
motives. The Old Testament says man looks on the outward appearance, but God looks at the heart. The
Bible functions like an X-ray machine. It pierces to the
core of who we are and discerns the thoughts and intents of our heart.

The Word of God exposes us in order that we can get
a clearer picture of ourselves and what we need to
change. The Word of God is not something to be afraid
of because of what it reveals. Just like the X-ray machine, it reveals the truth about us that needs to be
acted on and can give us specific direction in the area
of change. And the truth sets us free from bad habits
and addictive tendencies, as well as from anxiety and
depression.

*Dear Lord, thank you for the gift of your Word, which sets me free
daily from the power of self-deception.*

The righteous cry out, and the LORD
  hears,
And delivers them out of all their troubles.
The LORD is near to those who have a
  broken heart,
And saves such as have a contrite spirit.
                    —PS. 34:17–19

The psalmist David models for us that it is OK to ask God for our personal needs.

First of all, he mentions the troubles of life, the daily frustrations. They can get to a person, right? You know what I mean . . . the car that won't start, a long line at the supermarket, the baby who fills his diaper just as you are ready to leave the house, or your spouse who forgets to pick you up at the right time. Frustration is like the little stone in your shoe. It is so insignificant, but it brings much discomfort.

Secondly, he says the issues that lead to a broken heart can be shared with God. Typically someone with a broken heart has experienced a traumatic event. He or she may be grieving following a separation, divorce, or death of a loved one. God is near in those times.

Thirdly, God says He saves those who have a *contrite spirit,* which means those who have a "crushed" spirit. This is someone who has faced repeated trauma, who has been beaten down by life. God is there for the one who has lost hope.

He promises deliverance to His children. There is hope beyond the pain of my current affliction.

God demonstrates His love for me by carrying my daily afflictions and granting me daily deliverance.

> *For God has not given us a spirit of fear, but of*
> *power and of love and of a sound mind.*
>
> —2 TIM. 1:7

Fear is usually a root issue and core emotion for adult children of alcoholics. Adult children fear many things, including rejection, humiliation, weakness, vulnerability, failure, loss, and fear itself. The transcending fear is often the fear of abandonment. It can immobilize. It promotes timidity, withdrawal from close relationships, and distorted thinking.

However, the apostle Paul says God wants to give us three gifts: power to the timid, love to the abandoned, and clear thinking to the distorted thinker.

First of all, He wants to give power to those feeling confused, unsure, and timid. He wants them to experience a spirit of confidence and strength.

Secondly, He offers genuine, lasting, unconditional love for the ACA or any of us who are trying to cope with feelings of abandonment.

Finally, God promises to give us a sound mind. He wants us to be able to see things clearly and not distort reality. Most often the confused thinking centers on how the ACA views himself. Guilt over some wrongdoing quickly shifts to shame. Guilt says, "I have done something bad," but shame is more destructive. It says, "I *am* something bad."

God promises us power, love, and a sound mind. He will help us overcome these destructive patterns.

May God grant me the serenity to accept His gift of power, love, and clear thinking. Greater serenity will be the result.

I know, O LORD, that Your judgments are right,
And that in faithfulness You have afflicted me.
—PS. 119:75

When we take advantage of other people, we use so much rationalization and denial that the guilt may be suppressed. Consciously, most of us don't want to hurt anybody, and I'm sure David didn't either.

But David had watched Bathsheba take a bath in her fenced-in backyard from the roof of his house. He rationalized an affair, and Bathsheba became pregnant. Her husband, a loyal soldier, was killed by David, so he could marry her quickly and cover up the truth about the pregnancy. But David's guilt was suppressed.

Nathan the prophet was sent by God to confront the King. Nathan's knees must have been knocking. Nathan was indirective. He told David about a rich man who had many sheep, but took his servant's pet lamb to serve for his own dinner. David said angrily, "Kill him!"

Nathan then said, "David, you are that man!" David was afflicted by his loving, faithful God.

After all this, God still called David a man after His own heart. He had disciplined His child, had forgiven him, and it was done with.

God afflicts us with necessary pain when He needs to because He loves us. His discipline is designed to bring us back into a right relationship with Him.

> *See, I have set before you an open door, and no*
> *one can shut it; for you have a little strength, have*
> *kept My word, and have not denied My name.*
> —REV. 3:8

Philadelphia was an agricultural city in Asia Minor that was named after a king of Pergamum, Attabus Philadelphus, who built it. The Greek word *philadelphia* means "brotherly love."

Christ reassured the Philadelphian church members that He holds the key of David, referring back to Isaiah 22:22. It is a key to spiritual treasures God offers you, and no one can reopen the doors of opportunity He has decided to shut. Christ praised the members of the Philadelphia church for having "a little" strength (courage). It doesn't take much, you know. Faith as a grain of mustard seed can move a mountain.

It was enough courage to enable them to keep obeying God's Word and to not deny the faith in spite of persecution.

Like the members of the church at Philadelphia, God doesn't expect great courage—just a little. A little strength and courage is enough to permit God to accomplish His will in our lives. He wants us to bond, to set boundaries of self-protection, to assume responsibility for our own well-being, and to be our own best friend. He uses circumstances, people, the Bible, and the Holy Spirit to bring about these changes. May God grant us a little courage—enough to listen to His messages of truth and enough to persevere.

Behold, how good and how pleasant it is
For brethren to dwell together in unity! . . .
It is like the dew of Hermon,
Descending upon the mountains of Zion;
For there the LORD commanded the
*   blessing—*
Life forevermore.   —PS. 133:1, 3

One of the characteristics of a sociopath is that he or she gets a charge out of pitting one person against another. The sociopath tends to thrive on disunity, which brings adventure to break the boredom of his or her life. He or she receives an adrenalin rush from the interpersonal fireworks he or she creates. However, for the majority of individuals, disunity and unresolved interpersonal conflict can be a physical and emotional drain.

Unity, on the other hand, is wonderful. David compared it to the dew coming down from Mount Hermon, which was usually a heavy dew that refreshed and invigorated the trees and shrubbery on Mount Zion in Israel. The implication is clear.

As a loving and caring individual, I can leave behind the promotion of disunity and instead work toward unity in my home, my marriage, my work, and my community. If I strive to be this kind of person, I can bring a freshness and invigorating life to my relationships.

———————

Is there an unresolved conflict that is draining my energy? Is there a relationship in which I could work toward unity?

> *"If you abide in My word, you are My disciples indeed. And you shall know the truth, and the truth shall make you free."*
> —JOHN 8:31–32

Many people today would rather live in denial than look at the truth about their world, their relationships, and themselves. Jeff was no exception. He entered therapy anxious, suspicious, and angry at his employer. He blamed his supervisor for many things, yet lived in denial about his own behavior. It soon surfaced that although his job description called for forty-two hours per week, many weeks he had been only putting in about thirty hours. He began to look at himself in the mirror and honestly see the truth.

Yes, the truth will set you free, but first it will make you miserable. This happened for Jeff. However, he faced the truth, straightened things out with his employer, and changed his pattern.

Often the truth is hard to face, but the results are worth it. After facing the truth, Jeff experienced release from his anxiety. The suspiciousness disappeared and he found a new zest for life.

The Scripture is full of truth about our world, about making and maintaining relationships, and about our value and significance as individuals.

Do you want to experience new freedom? Try focusing more and more on the truth of the Bible. Allow the truth to make you free.

The truth, even if it hurts, leads to a new freedom!

*And the LORD spoke to Moses, saying: "Speak
to Aaron and his sons, saying, 'This is the
way you shall bless the children of Israel.
Say to them: "The LORD bless you and
keep you;*
*The LORD make His face shine upon you, and
be gracious to you;*
*The LORD lift up His countenance upon you,
And give you peace."' So they shall put My
name on the children of Israel, and I will
bless them."* —NUM. 6:22–27

We often wish we could talk to the Lord in person, but that will not happen until "life after life." In the meantime, He uses each of us to minister to each other, just as He used Moses and Aaron in the lives of the Israelites.

We can also learn a few things about what He is like from the words of blessing He gave Moses for the children of Israel.

The Lord obviously wishes to bless our lives and take care of us. He pays loving attention to every moment of our lives. He gives us continual favors we do not deserve and peace (serenity). He puts His name on those who trust Him, giving them the divine significance of becoming sons and daughters of the almighty Creator-God.

If you are a believer in the one true God, you belong to Him. He watches you with love and uses angelic and human instruments to give you blessings, grace, serenity, and significance.

Who may ascend into the hill of the LORD?
Or who may stand in His holy place?
He who has clean hands and a pure heart,
Who has not lifted up his soul to an idol,
Nor sworn deceitfully.
He shall receive blessing from the LORD,
And righteousness from the God of his
*   salvation.*
                                    —PS. 24:3–5

The twenty-fourth psalm is known as the "Psalm of the King of Glory." The "hill of the LORD" refers to the tabernacle on the hill in Israel, which was built there by Solomon after David's death. Those who were right with God, who were not worshiping idols or living a lie, could come to God's tabernacle to worship.

If we continue in habitual, willful sin, sin becomes our idol, and our prayers will not be heard. If we pray with selfish motives or with a prideful attitude, God will not answer our requests.

But those who seek a right relationship with God and are willing to learn how to experience and return His love will be blessed. They will be welcomed into fellowship with God and will be given personal righteousness, the ability to see things as they are and handle each situation as Christ would.

Close fellowship with God requires that we have right attitudes, choose to turn away from deliberate sin, and avoid deceit.

*And those who are Christ's have crucified the flesh
with its passions and desires. If we live in the Spirit,
let us also walk in the Spirit.* —GAL. 5:24–25

An alcoholic woman, about thirty-five years of age,
called me recently. She has been an alcoholic for many
years and decided two weeks ago to quit drinking for
the first time. She had been to outpatient therapy twice
a week since then and was angry that her therapist
hadn't "cured" her already. I didn't know her therapist,
but told her that getting stronger emotionally would be
hard work and would take a long time in therapy plus
the help of an AA Group in her area. She wanted to see
a psychiatrist for free. I told her we would not see her
for free so she angrily hung up on me. She expects
growth to be easy and expects something for nothing.
Her expectations may very well kill her.

The apostle Paul contrasts what will happen in our
lives if we yield to the Holy Spirit with what will happen if we resist Him. God does His part, but the rest
depends on our cooperation and hard work.

If we "crucify the flesh" by trusting Christ as Savior,
identifying with His death and resurrection, then we
need to begin the hard work of "walking in the Spirit."
Walking implies dependence on the Holy Spirit. God
won't walk for us; we must do our part. If we try to do it
all in our own power, we will "become conceited, pro-
voking one another, envying one another." It is not
easy, but it is the only way.

---

*Overcoming our negative addictions, is hard work and takes time
and often sacrifice. God won't do it for us and we can't do it alone.*

I will cry out to God Most High,
To God who performs all things for me.
He shall send from heaven and save me;
He reproaches the one who would swallow
*   me up.*
                                          —PS. 57:2

It's hard to find something nice to say about King Saul. He didn't even seriously consider fighting Goliath himself, but sent a teenager named David into the battle instead. David grew into a mighty warrior, loyal to King Saul. But Saul's citizens were singing, "Saul has killed his thousands and David his *ten thousands*." Saul was so enraged he wanted to kill David. He wanted all the attention, but didn't want to do the work.

David fled from Saul, hid in a cave, and wrote this psalm there. He accepted the reality that King Saul was a wicked man, yet David respected authority so much that he didn't lay a hand on King Saul when he had the opportunity to kill him. David prayed for God's mercy and protection. He felt certain God would save him in this situation because God had already shown him through Samuel that he would be the next king.

David turned vengeance over to God and patiently waited for God's timing. He knew that God's mercy and truth would win out in the long run. David's job in the meantime was to hide, to grow, to forgive, to learn, and to wait patiently for God to slay Saul and anoint him as King. He trusted that God was in control.

Sometimes, when we are hiding in our own "caves" of life, it becomes very difficult to accept the Lord's timing. We need to depend on God's justice and protection when we cry out to Him.

> *Therefore we also, since we are surrounded by so great a cloud of witnesses, let us lay aside every weight, and the sin which so easily ensnares us, and let us run with endurance the race that is set before us.*
> —HEB. 12:1

One genuine source of courage to me is the example of men and women of courage, both living and deceased. When I study my Bible, I love to study the Bible characters.

Paul tells us that we are surrounded by a "Hall of Fame" of men and women of faith. They have gone before us in this same "race." We can be encouraged by these men and women of faith. Then we should set aside the weights and sins that keep us from courageously enduring the race called life. Weights are hindrances in our lives that keep us from serenity, keep us from winning emotional battles, or keep us from maturing as rapidly as we reasonably could.

They are often "emotional wounds" such as false guilt or fear of intimacy, left in us from mistakes our parents or others have made in our past.

These "weights" are not our fault. But they are our responsibility to overcome. They frequently require insight-oriented psychotherapy by a trained, biblically-oriented, professional therapist.

_____

The men and women in God's Hall of Fame include a repentant prostitute, several liars, and a few murderers. But God used them because of their faith. Let their examples and the examples of living men and women of faith encourage you.

> *Blessed is he whose transgression is forgiven,*
> *Whose sin is covered.*
> *Blessed is the man to whom the LORD does*
> *not impute iniquity.*　　　　—PS. 32:1

When we refuse to forgive ourselves for past sins or mistakes, we are playing God—and God does not want or need us to do so. We are God's children if we have trusted Christ, and we have no right to punish ourselves for our sins. Doing so leaves us chronically tired, depressed, and useless for God's service.

Christ paid for all our past, present and future sins. When we reject His forgiveness, we reject what He did for us on the cross. He may need to discipline us in love to prevent the same sin in the future, and there may be natural consequences to our disobedience, but God does not vindictively punish His children.

When David "kept silent" and stuffed his guilt feelings, he "groaned all day long" with clinical depression until he finally accepted God's forgiveness and forgave himself. Then he could write our passage for today: "Blessed is he whose transgression is forgiven." Blessed is the person whose sin is covered by the blood of the Lamb of God who takes away the sins of the world, allowing the righteous Heavenly Father to "impute" our iniquity to Christ rather than hold it against us.

Forgive me, Lord, for my unwillingness to forgive myself. I know the price you paid for my sin, and that I am precious and clean in Your eyes. Thank you for forgiving me.

And He said to them, "Is a lamp brought to be put under a basket or under a bed? Is it not to be set on a lampstand? For there is nothing hidden which will not be revealed, nor has anything been kept secret but that it should come to light."

—MARK 4:21–23

A lamp in Jesus' day was a shallow day bowl which held oil and a lighted wick. In order to illuminate everything in the room, the lamp was placed on a lampstand.

When I do insight-oriented therapy, I see my role as being a "light." I listen to what my patients say, but I study their emotional responses, their body language, their family of origin patterns, their current behavior patterns, and their apparent motives. I choose to love them no matter what I see or hear. I attempt to flood them with the truth as I uncover it. But, as they become aware of the truth, my patients choose whether or not to make appropriate changes in their behavior or thinking processes. Recovery or continued misery is their choice.

I sometimes miss some important insights that become apparent later. But God doesn't miss a thing. We have no secrets from God. He sees every behavior, every thought, and even our unconscious motives. He brings our personal truths to light in His own divine timing to help us grow. Then we must choose what to do with the truth God reveals.

May God grant us wisdom to see the light, make responsible choices, then lovingly share His light with those around us.

> *The LORD looks from heaven;*
> *He sees all the sons of men. . . .*
> *He fashions their hearts individually;*
> *He considers all their works.*
> —PS. 33:13–15

Today's passage is almost an Old Testament version of the "Parable of the Lamp" in Mark 4:21–23. Let's take a close look at what God inspired David to teach us.

God the Father sits in heaven studying every single human on the earth. It is difficult to fathom, but He knows each one of us intimately, and He thinks about us individually more times each day than we could possibly count.

The Father sees our every thought, feeling, motive, and deed. He knows about every one of our sins, and somehow, He loves us anyway. The Father considers all of our works and "fashions" our hearts individually. He rewards the humble and opposes the proud. He causes those who love and obey Him to grow in maturity and Christlikeness.

We know from the Scriptures that if anyone sincerely wants a God-fashioned heart, he will somehow be given righteousness. Are we willing to learn the truth about ourselves from the Bible, from devotional books, from divine circumstances, and from loving confrontation? If so, our humble willingness will be richly rewarded with "righteousness," which means right behavior.

Thank you, Lord, for personally considering all my motives and behaviors, and lovingly fashioning my heart.

*He said to His disciples, "Beware of the scribes,
who desire to walk in long robes, love greetings in
the marketplaces, the best seats in the synagogues,
and the best places at feasts, who devour widows'
houses, and for a pretense make long prayers.
These will receive greater condemnation."*
—LUKE 20:45–47

It's worth noting that Jesus often used self-righteous religious leaders as negative illustrations. Those in positions of authority can easily fall into sinful pride.

The scribes in this passage loved to wear long, attention-getting robes and to get special treatment in the marketplaces. They demanded the best seats at feasts or in the synagogue, and encouraged poor widows to donate all their money to the synagogue.

They also prayed long prayers, and were full of arrogance. There is nothing wrong with praying for hours, as long as it is in private, between you and God. There is nothing wrong with public prayers either, as long as they are sincere and designed to bring glory to God rather than to yourself.

In fact, Jesus told us that where two or three of us gather together to worship Him or to pray, He is there with us.

What He doesn't want us to do is pray long, verbose, pious, attention-seeking, dramatic prayers with the conscious or subconscious intent to make others think we are something we are not. We call that super-spirituality or phoney spirituality.

During private or public prayers, pray first for the Holy Spirit to grant you sincerity and sensitivity to others.

> *In the multitude of my anxieties*
> *within me,*
> *Your comforts delight my soul.*
> —PS. 94:17–19

There are four major developmental areas in child-hood that require a lot of parental guidance. We all need to learn *bonding*—how to love and be loved. We all need to develop *boundaries*. We need to learn how to be the *boss* of our own lives, while learning dependence on God for power and guidance.

Today's passage is about the fourth developmental "B": *badness*. We all need to look at and accept our "badness", and cooperate with God to change it.

Without the LORD's help, David would have given up and simply settled on silence—perhaps as an alcoholic, perhaps as a chronically depressed person.

Anxiety comes primarily from a fear of looking at the truth about our badness. God's Word, His Holy Spirit and His people all help us to look at the truth about ourselves. Our brothers and sisters in Christ love us anyway, helping us to accept ourselves as we really are and love ourselves as God loves us.

When we look at the truth in our inner selves, we see rage, bitterness, true and false guilt, false feelings of insignificance, vengeful motives, jealousy, greed, and many other things. But if we realize these things are present to variable degrees in all of us and present our badness to the Lord, asking Him to sanctify that badness, then it becomes bearable.

May God grant us the serenity to accept our badness and the courage to change it.

Beloved, do not avenge yourselves, but rather give place to wrath; for it is written, "Vengeance is Mine, I will repay," says the Lord.
—ROM. 12:17–19

Sally slumped into the chair in the therapy office. She was depressed and it showed in her body language, her speech, and her facial expression. She began to share her story. Three months ago, she discovered that her husband had been having an affair for over a year. After the initial shock, she became furious and would lie awake at night thinking up ways she could get revenge. One night she punctured all four of his tires. On another occasion she got into his apartment, took scissors and ruined a pair of his good slacks. Several months had passed and now the anger had turned to depression.

The apostle Paul talked about anger in his writings. He challenged us to "be angry and sin not." It's important to notice that Paul did not say "Don't be angry." It was normal and natural for Sally to be angry over what took place. However for Sally, the anger turned into vengeful motives and actions. She took revenge into her own hands, and allowed her anger to control her.

The apostle Paul challenged us to not let the anger grow to the point that we are acting out of revenge. Instead we must turn it over to God and leave the situation in His hands. Taking vengeance is not our responsibility.

May God help me to be aware of my anger, to verbalize it, and to forgive, leaving the vengeance issue up to Him.

> *"For the eyes of the LORD run to and fro*
> *throughout the whole earth, to show Himself strong*
> *on behalf of those whose heart is loyal to Him."*
> —2 CHRON. 16:9a

This would be a great verse to write down on a 3 x 5 card and carry with you wherever you go. You could memorize it, meditate on it, and pull it up from your memory the rest of your life when you need courage.

God is sitting on His throne in heaven, examining the heart of every human moment by moment. He is watching those whose hearts are loyal to Him so He can encourage and help them. He loves you and loves to help you.

People who grew up without a father are sometimes atheists as a result. They think there is no God. Others who had workaholic dads tend to be agnostic. They think there is a God out there somewhere, but He doesn't really pay much attention to us and doesn't really care. But God is not like our earthly fathers. By meditating on passages like this one, we can see our Heavenly Father as He really is.

Only God can possibly love us so much that He observes every moment, gives us the freedom to live our own lives by grace, and is always there in strength.

*Dare any of you, having a matter against another,
go to law before the unrighteous, and not before
the saints? Do you not know that the saints will
judge the world?*   —1 COR. 6:1

The Corinthian church was very immature. Paul had
to correct them because they were pressuring fellow
church members to do business with them, then rip-
ping each other off and repeatedly taking each other
to court. It was a very sad situation not only because it
caused splitting in the church, but also because the
non-Christians in Corinth would not see the power of
God unless the believers grew up.

Paul told them to change their behavior and settle
their disputes among themselves, reminding them that
they would be judges on earth someday. The settling of
disputes is discussed in numerous other passages as
well. If we feel anger toward someone, or if we suspect
he or she feels anger toward us, we are encouraged to
go talk to the person and settle the dispute one on one,
whenever possible.

If a businessperson or investor tells you that you
should do business with him or her merely because he
or she is a Christian, watch out! Don't be foolish like
the Corinthians were. Take time to check out his or her
credentials. Avoid getting into situations which may
end up in court. If a conflict does arise, apply God's
principles to the situation.

*Settle your disputes within local church settings whenever possible.
Begin by going to your brother or sister in love, and trying to resolve
the situation.*

> *It is better to trust in the LORD*
> *Than to put confidence in*
> *man.* —PS. 118:8

Many years ago, someone counted how many verses there were in the Bible. It is interesting that he found the verse in the very middle of the Bible to be Psalm 118:8, which tells us not to put our trust in people.

Now, this verse is not telling us to become so paranoid that we assume everyone is out to get us or use us or take advantage of us financially. But it does remind us to be wise.

Over the years, hundreds of believers have lost much or all of their savings by trusting fellow believers in business. Christians feel somehow unchristian if they feel healthy suspicion toward another believer. There are some con artists who go to churches and pretend to be Christians, to find gullible investors. There is nothing wrong with being cautious in deciding to trust someone, particularly with our finances.

If we depend on people, or human institutions, to meet our needs or provide our security, we will eventually be disappointed. That is why it is far better to put our trust in the Lord, who will never let us down.

Thank you, Lord, that although even the people I love will sometimes fail me, I can always trust in You.

Neither death nor life, nor angels nor principalities
nor powers, nor things present nor things to come,
nor height nor depth, nor any other created thing,
shall be able to separate us from the love of God
which is in Christ Jesus our Lord.

—ROM. 8:38–39

What can separate you, if you have trusted Christ, from His love for you? What can keep you from spending eternity with the Messiah on whom you have chosen to depend? When I was growing up, my pastor often asked in his sermons, "If you aren't as close to God as you once were, who moved?"

We can do *many* things that separate us from our love for Christ, but nothing, absolutely nothing can separate us from His love for us. Nothing we do in life can make Christ reject us. None of the necessary and unnecessary pains we experience in life, pressure or distress, abuse, or poverty *can* separate us from eternal salvation and the eternal love of Christ. Neither can danger, war, crime, or even *death* cut us off from God's love.

In all these things, Christ's love for us continually empowers us to be more than conquerors. The Greek word for "conquerors" here is *hypernikōmen*, meaning that His love enables us to "keep on winning a glorious victory."

We have a Messiah whose love and salvation are eternal. They won't quit because He won't quit.

> All the paths of the LORD are mercy and
>   truth,
> To such as keep His covenant and His
>   testimonies.
> For Your name's sake, O LORD,
> Pardon my iniquity, for it is great.
> —PS. 25:10–11

God the Father is good and upright. He guides and teaches His wise principles to those who are humble enough to listen. He is merciful to the repentant and is always truthful, keeping every promise He makes to us. He lives up to every statement the Bible makes about Him.

We can have confidence to come before the throne of Almighty God to ask Him a very great favor. We can ask Him to grant us forgiveness for everything we have ever done wrong. Because of God's unchanging character, because of everything His name represents, He will respond to our plea.

God has promised to never cast anyone out who comes to Him in sincerity. There has never been, nor will there ever be, a repentant sinner the Father has rejected.

The Father promised it. He wants us to respect Him, to reverentially trust Him. He longs for eternal fellowship with us, and He loves to remind us of His great and tender mercy, love, and forgiveness.

If you ask the Father to forgive you, based on Christ's shed blood in payment for your sins, He will—for His own name's sake.

> *Therefore if there is any consolation in Christ, if*
> *any comfort of love, if any fellowship of the Spirit,*
> *if any affection and mercy, fulfill my joy by being*
> *like-minded, having the same love, being of one*
> *accord, of one mind. Let nothing be done through*
> *selfish ambition or conceit, but in lowliness of mind*
> *let each esteem others better than himself.*
> —PHIL. 2:1–3

We could easily call this beautiful passage, "Serenity through Unity by Humility." Serenity and humility always go hand in hand, just as frustration and arrogant pride go hand in hand.

In the original Greek, the "if" clauses are first-class conditions, so they are virtual certainties. In modern English, we would use the word *since*.

Since we have encouragement from being united in Christ; comfort from being loved by Him; continual fellowship with the Holy Spirit; tenderness and compassion with each other—since we have these things, we should be like-minded. This doesn't mean we must agree with everybody about everything. It means to share the same love for Christ and for each other, to be in one accord in wanting to serve Christ and each other, and to be single-minded in building the kingdom. We must treat our fellow believers as though they were more important than we are.

May God grant us serenity to accept the dignity and rights of others, especially of our fellow believers.

> *As a father pities his children,*
> *So the LORD pities those who fear Him.*
> —PS. 103:13

In Romans 3:10, the apostle Paul tells us that not one solitary human being has ever been righteous in God's eyes. One murder makes a murderer. One affair, even in the mind, makes an adulterer. One lie makes a liar. There is no perfect person anywhere, and God the Father only allows perfect people into heaven.

Imagine that you owe a million dollars to the IRS and they are going to throw you in prison. Suddenly, someone comes along and tells the IRS he wants to pay your debt. The IRS asks if you will accept the billionaire's gift. If you say yes, you are forgiven. If you say no, the IRS cannot legally accept the payment for your debt. What would you say?

No one is righteous enough to pay the debt of their own sin. But since Christ was perfect and paid the death penalty in our place, the Father who demands perfection is satisfied.

The Father pities us in the same way that a loving earthly father would pity his own children if they were suffering. He understands our failures, our mixed motives, our subconscious drives, our addictions, and our weaknesses and scars. He remembers that He made us out of dust and so gave us a Savior.

We can accept our imperfection while working hard to grow in grace, because the same Father who demands perfection sent His perfect Son to die in our place.

*His divine power has given to us all things that
pertain to life and godliness, through the
knowledge of Him who called us by glory and
virtue.* —2 PETER 1:3

At first glance, this passage might seem to be saying
we can accomplish anything in life by using the Bible
as our only resource. But as we examine the Word of
God, it's clear God intended us to use the many resources He has given us. Jesus said sick people need
doctors, and people in tough situations need counselors.

Actually, a clearer translation of the original Greek
words might be, "Christ's divine power is all we need
to develop *spiritual vitality*." Spiritual power, courage,
and growth are enhanced in our lives through an intimate knowledge of Christ.

The Bible does contain many practical things to help
us live in our world, but if your car breaks down, you
will need to consult the owner's manual or a mechanic.
You will need a scientist to find a cure for diabetes or
anorexia nervosa or schizophrenia. We should thank
God for these helps.

Jesus has bestowed "exceedingly great and precious
promises" on us so we could be sanctified. We can gain
courage and power to avoid the corruption in the
world, and we will gradually take on aspects of Christlikeness.

*Through God's power, developing an intimate knowledge of Christ
will enhance the courage we need to live a life of spiritual vitality.*

> *Trust in the LORD, and do good;*
> *Dwell in the land, and feed on His faithfulness.*
> *Delight yourself also in the LORD,*
> *And He shall give you the desires of your heart.*
> *Commit your way to the LORD,*
> *Trust also in Him.*
>
> —PS. 37:3–5

God knows what we need to do to eliminate the needless suffering in our lives. He also knows how we can find comfort and meaning in necessary pain. In today's passage, we discover some essential guidelines for living the Christian life.

Trust in the Lord. Depend on the Messiah to save you. Depend on the Father to help you through life, with the Holy Spirit's guidance.

Do good. Learn to live by biblical values.

Dwell in the land. Live *in* the world as an ambassador for Christ.

Feed on His faithfulness. Enjoy God's promise to be always with you.

Delight yourself in the Lord. Study passages about what He is like. Talk to Him. Dedicate yourself to Him. Get excited about His plans for you.

Commit your way to the Lord. Every morning, think about how you can please Him while taking good care of your needs and the needs of your family.

Trust Him to show you what changes you need to make in your life to fit in with His plans for you.

Lord, teach me to trust in You and to feed on Your faithfulness.

> *But Simon answered and said to Him, "Master, we have toiled all night and caught nothing; nevertheless at Your word I will let down the net."*
> —LUKE 5:5

When I was twelve years old, my father used to pay me fifty cents of his hard-earned money for reading each of Charles Haddon Spurgeon's sermons. One sermon, "Nevertheless at Thy Word," stood out to me more than any other.

Jesus stood by a lake to preach. As the crowds pressed Him into the water, Jesus saw two empty fishing boats. So He stepped into one of them and sat down and preached. The boat belonged to Simon Peter.

When Jesus finished preaching, he looked at Simon and said, "Launch out into the deep and let down your nets for a catch." Simon was frustrated by this command. He had been out fishing all night long and had caught *no* fish. He was certain going back out would be a total waste of time. But he had enough respect for Jesus to say, "Nevertheless at Your word I will let down the net." You know the rest of the story. They caught so many fish both boats began to sink.

It finally dawned on Peter that he had been fishing with the One who *created* the fish. He fell on his knees before Jesus and said, "Depart from me, for I am a sinful man, O Lord!" With his words of humility and repentance, Simon the fisherman became Peter the disciple of Christ.

Like Peter, I often get frustrated when I don't understand God's purposes. I am humbled when I tell God, "Nevertheless at Your word."

> *As the deer pants for the water brooks,*
> *So pants my soul for You, O God.*
> —PS. 42:1

Dr. Frank Minirth is a Christian psychiatrist, my business partner since 1976, and one of my closest friends since we were "cadaver-mates" in medical school. Neither of us knew the other was a believer, and both of us were looking and praying for an opportunity to share our excitement about Christ with the other.

One day we put our cadaver back in the formaldehyde and walked down the stairs together. We both blurted out something about Christ at the same second. We had a good laugh about it, and have been close friends ever since.

Today's verse is one of his favorites. He has often quoted me this verse to express his joy in the Lord.

Just as the deer needs water to sustain her physical life, we need an intimate bonding with Christ to sustain our spiritual life and mental health.

That's what King David felt when he thought about Jesus. It was a sparkle, a delight, an excitement, a longing, a thirsting, and even a "panting." I have seen that sparkle in the eyes of my good friend, Frank, and in many other believers who are committed to His kingdom now and who long for His Messianic Kingdom in the near future.

––––––––––––

We have a God worth getting excited about—one who can fill a thirsty soul with living water.

*And coming out, He went to the Mount of Olives, as
He was accustomed, and His disciples also followed
Him. When He came to the place, He said to them,
"Pray that you may not enter into temptation."*
—LUKE 22:39–40

I love the mountains. I live in California now where I
can always see the mountains out my window. It's so
peaceful, and the rest of the world looks somehow
smaller and less overwhelming.

Jesus liked to take his disciples up on the Mount of
Olives to get away from the crowds, to fellowship with
each other, and to pray. In today's passage, Jesus told
His disciples to pray specifically "that you may not enter into temptation."

Since all sins hurt people, why in the world are we
tempted to do things that hurt people?

All of us have inferiority feelings. Deep down on the
inside, we all feel like a nobody to some extent or another, and we tend to go through life trying to prove
that we are *not* a nobody. In a sinful and unhealthy
way, using or controlling somebody else eases the pain
of feeling like a nobody.

We can decrease our temptation levels by filling the
deep needs that drive us toward sinful addictions and
habits. We can work at loving and being loved. We can
also meditate on Scripture and begin to think as Jesus
thinks. We can experience true significance as we find
ways to serve people instead of using them.

*May God grant us the courage not only to resist temptations, but to
fill the holes in our souls that cause sinful behavior patterns.*

I will sing to the LORD as long as I live;
I will sing praise to my God while I
have my being.
May my meditation be sweet to Him;
I will be glad in the LORD.
                                    —PS. 104:33–34

Life gets pretty frustrating in so many ways that it is a real relief to think about the day that Jesus will take control. He will put an end to discrimination, abuse, famine, and war. His glory will endure forever.

When God created everything, He rejoiced in all His works, including man and woman. But it didn't take too many generations before God Himself was discouraged by the way men and women were treating each other, and He regretted that He had made them.

Fortunately, He decided to salvage mankind and sent Jesus to save us eternally. In heaven we will be perfect, as He created us to be. God will again be able to rejoice in all His works.

He is powerful enough to make the earth tremble and quake, and to make the hills produce volcanic steam. Someday He will burn up this polluted world of ours and create a new pollution-free version of it.

We can sing praises to the Lord our God all our lives, despite our limited perspective of what He is really like. We can meditate on what the Bible says about Him. But someday we will be able to sing praises to Him knowing Him intimately, face-to-face. Then we will truly "be glad in the Lord."

———————

"I will sing to the LORD as long as I live. . . . May my meditation be sweet to Him; I will be glad in the LORD."

For as the sufferings of Christ abound in us, so our consolation also abounds through Christ. And our hope for you is steadfast, because we know that as you are partakers of the sufferings, so also you will partake of the consolation. —2 COR. 1:5, 7

Some suffering in life is unavoidable. To maintain sanity and serenity, we must somehow learn to accept it. Serving God and dedicating our lives to helping others should decrease our suffering significantly—or so we think. And it does, to some extent. We like ourselves more. We enjoy seeing improvements in the lives we touch. We love more, and receive more love. But our passage for today shows us that service to God is also associated with some necessary suffering.

Paul suffered a great deal at the hands of people who felt threatened by him. He also suffered when he saw the Corinthian believers behaving so immaturely and not loving as they were capable of loving. So Paul wrote 1st Corinthians, a strong letter of loving rebuke. The Corinthian church took it to heart after taking a deep look at their own areas of immaturity, irresponsibility, and selfishness.

Second Corinthians was a kinder, gentler letter. It was a letter of love, acceptance, and consolation. Paul told them how God had consoled him when he suffered. He reassured them that God would bring consolation to them as well in their sufferings.

A shared burden is half a burden. In the same way, grieving in empathy with fellow sufferers brings consolation and comfort to both.

> *And he said, "Listen, all you of Judah and you*
> *inhabitants of Jerusalem, and you, King*
> *Jehoshaphat! Thus says the LORD to you: 'Do not*
> *be afraid nor dismayed because of this great*
> *multitude, for the battle is not yours, but God's.'"*
> —2 CHRON. 20:15

Jehoshaphat was a great king. He delighted in God's wise principles. He brought revival to Judah. He overthrew idol-worship and taught God's Word to the people.

Jehoshaphat demonstrated great courage during a battle against the Moabites, Ammonites, and Meunites who came from across the Jordan to attack Judah. Jehoshaphat found out this great combined army was heading toward Jerusalem, so he proclaimed a national fast to pray for courage and strength from the Lord. The Holy Spirit came upon Jahaziel, who gave words of courage to the people.

The next day, Jehoshaphat took his singers and soldiers to the battlefield. The singers sang words of encouragement to the troops as they prepared for battle.

But then God caused all the enemies to become confused and attack each other, until there were no survivors. The soldiers of Judah never lifted a sword. There was so much plunder that the men of Judah couldn't even carry it all away. They gathered in the Valley of Berach, which means "the valley of praise" to thank God for His victory.

The next time you feel overwhelmed and outnumbered, review this historical passage to remind yourself that you and God are a majority. Courage comes from trusting Him to deliver you.

*Let the husband render to his wife the affection due
her, and likewise also the wife to her husband. The
wife does not have authority over her own body,
but the husband does. And likewise the husband
does not have authority over his own body, but the
wife does. Do not deprive one another.*

—1 COR. 7:3–5

Our world seems to abound with people who view
extramarital affairs as exciting and romantic, but
whose marriages are the exact opposite. Their lives
are sadly lacking in romance and creativity.

What has gone wrong? And more importantly, what
can be done to change it?

If we are open to following God's instructions for a
successful marriage, we can experience the security,
love, and trust of a committed relationship, while at
the same time delighting one another sexually.

The foundation of a healthy physical relationship is
mutual affection and respect. Affection can be shared
in words, attitudes and actions. But equality and reci-
procity is needed. Both husband and wife can initiate.

If sex has been used as a means of control, or if it has
been experienced in abusive ways, couples may need
counseling to work through these special problems.
God designed us to enjoy each other. He gives us freedom within marriage to have fun with our mate.

*Plan a romantic rendezvous with your spouse. Let your spouse know
how much he or she is valued and appreciated.*

Search me, O God, and know my heart;
Try me, and know my anxieties;
And see if there is any wicked way in me,
And lead me in the way everlasting.
—PS. 139:23–24

One of the goals for any kind of therapy is to assist clients in developing greater insight into themselves, their behavior, their motivations, their past, and their personality.

Is there a difference between wisdom and insight? I believe there is. Probably the simplest way to describe it would be to say that insight is personalized wisdom. It means gaining a clearer understanding of ourselves, of how and why we function in the way we do.

In this psalm, David focuses on insight. He asks God to search him, to look deep inside him, to see his very core and help him identify wrongdoing, wrong motives and sources of anxiety. He asks the Lord to reveal or bring out those secret or hidden dimensions of his heart.

God wants us to have a personalized wisdom, or true insight. With it we are able to follow more clearly what He says to us, and obey Him more freely.

May God grant me the courage to pursue insight—personalized wisdom.

Oh, the depth of the riches both of the wisdom and knowledge of God! How unsearchable are His judgments and His ways past finding out!
—ROM. 11:33–34

I am reminded of a college acquaintance who prided himself that he was all he needed. He didn't need or want a higher power, our God. However, his life was restricted by the smallness of his greatness!

Our God is unsearchable and His ways beyond our understanding. That reality should encourage us to feel secure, supported, and safe. If we are seeking a God who can help us change and conquer life's disappointments, then that God must be more than we are and know more than we know. Only what transcends can transform.

We will not always understand all He does. However, we can depend on God. Our belief in Him can provide us with emotional security.

A child had just accomplished the major feat of learning to ride his bike. His dad applauded him from the sidewalk. The little guy slammed on his brakes and skidded to a halt in front of his Dad. "You know how I did it, Dad?" he squealed excitedly. "I pretended you were holding my bike." We often feel God has abandoned us. We cry out in despair. "Where are you God?" "Why has this happened to me?" "Why are you silent?" The truth is God is there. Not only is He offering us His presence, He offers us His perspective and His peace.

Our path to healing and wholeness can come as we live our lives in harmony with God Himself. Lean on this Higher Power—the real God—so you will be able to stand on your own two feet.

> *Likewise the Spirit also helps in our weaknesses.*
> *For we do not know what we should pray for as*
> *we ought, but the Spirit Himself makes intercession*
> *for us with groanings which cannot be uttered.*
> —ROM. 8:26

Have you ever felt so confused by your circumstances that you did not even know what to pray?

Just a month ago, a friend was taken to the hospital because of blackouts. She was only thirty-five years old and had three young children at home. Extensive tests were run, and the results came back: she had a tumor on the brain.

She underwent a delicate surgery to remove the tumor, but then lapsed into a coma. Several days passed, then a week, then two weeks. No change.

The children didn't understand what had happened to their loving, enthusiastic mother. Her husband was trying his best to cope.

We struggled with what we should pray for. What would be best? Should we ask God to bring her out of the coma? If she did regain consciousness, would she be so restricted that she would be like another child for her husband to care for?

If we prayed that the Lord take her home to heaven, how would her family respond? We didn't know what to pray, but we prayed. Today she is alive and well.

In such times the Holy Spirit prays with and for us. The Holy Spirit knows the mind and will of Christ, and He understands our intent, so He prays on our behalf.

Trust that the Holy Spirit is praying for your need, even if you are intensely confused.

Faithful are the wounds of a friend,
But the kisses of an enemy are deceitful.
—PROV. 27:6

All my life I have been taught that when we get angry over something, we should forgive the person and not harbor anger and resentment. But I'm afraid that we as Christians are often too quick to say, "It was no big deal: I forgive you." And in many cases we are not honest; what was done or not done truly caused some deep hurt. A quick "I forgive you" is not truthful or healthy when the wound is severe.

We have a choice to either pretend and gloss over a deep hurt or to face the incident and communicate directly the intensity of the pain; to let the other person see and feel the result of their action. Sometimes we are afraid our loving but honest confrontation will wound the friend who wounded us, so we keep silent. But Solomon says these loving, confrontational wounds are faithful and beneficial in the long run. These kinds of faithful wounds help us sharpen each other and mature us toward Christlikeness.

Lord, help me to control my anger by being loving, honest and direct in sharing my feelings. Help my confrontational wounds promote growth, healing, and true emotional healing.

> *Then Ananias answered, "Lord, I have heard from*
> *many about this man, how much harm he has*
> *done to Your saints in Jerusalem. . . ." But the Lord*
> *said to him, "Go for he is a chosen vessel of Mine*
> *to bear My name before Gentiles, kings, and the*
> *children of Israel. For I will show him how many*
> *things he must suffer for My name's sake."*
> —ACTS 9:13–16

Saul was the number one enemy of Christianity. He had killed many believers and put others in prison with great zealousness.

But as Saul traveled to Damascus, he had a face-to-face encounter with the Lord. Saul's eyes were blinded, but his heart was made to see the truth. He arrived in Damascus a changed man. Meanwhile, the Lord revealed His plans for Saul to Ananias, a faithful Christian in Damascus. Ananias was to go to Saul and accept him as a new brother in Christ.

Saul became the apostle Paul, who wrote a majority of the New Testament books and evangelized the world for Christ. But he also suffered greatly for the cause of Christ.

Paul may have suffered more than any of the Christians he persecuted. He was nearly stoned to death, beaten, shipwrecked, imprisoned, and persecuted. On top of that, God gave Paul some unknown "thorn in the flesh" to keep him humble. Paul had a choice. But once he had met Jesus face to face, the choice to accept this suffering in order to serve Christ became easy.

Our natural response to suffering is to run. But sometimes we must accept it and praise God for His grace in it.

> *Therefore be very courageous to keep and to do all that is written in the Book of the Law of Moses, lest you turn aside from it to the right hand or to the left. . . . One man of you shall chase a thousand, for the LORD your God is He who fights for you, as He has promised you. Therefore take diligent heed to yourselves, that you love the LORD your God."*
> —JOSH. 23:6, 10–11

Joshua, who led Israel after the death of Moses, died himself at the age of one hundred and ten, in 1390 B.C.

The passage for today records some of Joshua's last words to the people he loved, the nation of Israel. He told them how important it was to remain courageous. Being courageous does not just happen. Like most good things in life, it takes hard work. Being courageous is a choice! It requires the self-discipline to obey God's principles even when we don't feel like it. One courageous believer, depending on God for power, can do the impossible.

Joshua also told the people of Israel to work diligently at loving the Lord their God. Our culture defines love as an emotion that just happens. People "fall" in love. Couples divorce because they "just don't love each other anymore." In reality, true love is a choice.

Choose self-discipline. Choose to work diligently at loving God by removing, brick by brick, the psychological barriers from your past that hinder your relationship with Him. Choose to be courageous!

> So when they continued asking Him, He raised
> Himself up and said to them, "He who is without
> sin among you, let him throw a stone at her first."
> —JOHN 8:7–9

Jesus had spent the night on the Mount of Olives. Early in the morning, He went down to the temple to teach. The scribes and Pharisees, who were evil, self-righteous hypocrites, had caught a couple committing adultery. Unjust as it was, the law specified only that the woman be stoned to death. The Pharisees must have known Jesus would have compassion on the woman, and they brought her to Him, trying to trap Him into contradicting their law.

Jesus, of course, could see through their false piety to the truth. He stooped down and began writing things on the ground as though He didn't hear them.

When they persisted, Jesus indirectly told all those around Him about their own depravity by saying, "He who is without sin among you, let him throw a stone at her first." He wanted to arouse true guilt, and it worked.

When no one but the adulterous woman was left, He did *not* tell her it was OK to commit adultery, but He did forgive her because she repented.

Then He told her, "Go and sin no more." What she had done was sin, and she needed to make a choice to give up that addictive behavior. Jesus asked her to give up the willful sin of adultery, to make a conscious choice to leave it out of her options.

Are you choosing to continue in a sin that is harmful to you and to others? Repent of your sin. "Go, and sin no more."

So the king and Haman went to dine with Queen Esther. And on the second day, at the banquet of wine, the king again said to Esther, "What is your petition, Queen Esther?" . . . Then Queen Esther answered and said, "If I have found favor in your sight, O king, and if it pleases the king, let my life be given to me at my petition, and my people at my request."

EST. 7:1–4

Whenever we feel like a nobody, we devote enormous time and energy trying to prove otherwise. We may devalue people of other races, colors, religions, or genders to look better ourselves. It doesn't work. This form of rivalry has been an evil throughout human history. Cain killed Abel because Abel's sacrifice pleased God and Cain's didn't. He couldn't stand being compared unfavorably to someone else. Gold held him accountable for his rash behavior.

Esther was a beautiful Jewish girl who married King Ahasuerus, the ruler of Persia. After Esther was crowned, the king's right-hand man, Haman, plotted to have the Jews in Persia wiped out. He was especially jealous of the success of one Jew, Mordecai, who "just happened" to be Esther's cousin. Haman didn't realize that Queen Esther was Jewish. Unfortunately for Haman, Esther heard about his plan, and at the right time, persuaded Ahasuerus to save the Jews. Ironically, Haman was hanged on the very gallows he had built to hang Mordecai, and the Jewish people survived.

When we find ourselves threatened by any form of rivalry, we can learn wisdom from Esther by being our own best friend, being assertive, and protecting ourselves with God's help.

> *For God so loved the world that He gave His only begotten Son, that whoever believes in Him should not perish but have everlasting life.*
>
> —JOHN 3:16

This is perhaps the most frequently quoted verse in the Bible, and rightfully so. In a nutshell, it tells the gospel story for the first coming of the Messiah.

Unlimited by time and space as we are, God the Father looked down on all humans of all time, and He loved each one, no matter how sinful. Although He always hated sin, He has always loved the sinner.

The Father saw you even before He created the world. If you were the only person who lived, He still would have sent His only Son, Jesus Christ, to pay for your sins. He loves you more than you can possibly understand.

God the Father cannot tolerate any evil at all. But when Jesus died for you, the Father accepted that substitution. Jesus rose from the dead to give you power over death. If you accept His gift of taking *your* punishment, the Father can look you in the eye, see you as perfect, and accept you into heaven. If you refuse to accept Christ as your Savior, the Father cannot accept you into heaven. He cannot accept anyone who rejects the Holy Spirit's call to salvation. But He accepts with open arms those who depend on what Christ did for them. That is what He wants for every single person on the earth. That is the only way we can know Him in an intimate way.

Be thankful He died for you. You don't have to suffer in eternity! God has offered you the free gift of salvation. The choice is yours.

*When I consider Your heavens, the work of Your
fingers, the moon and the stars, which You have
ordained, What is man that You are mindful of
him, and the son of man that You visit him? For
You have made him a little lower than the angels.
And You have crowned him with glory and honor.*
—PS. 8:3–5

Jennifer's father was verbally abusive. He called her
names and talked down to her constantly. He also had
few long-term plans and very little self-control.

As an adult, Jennifer couldn't trust God to love her,
to value her, or to have good long-term plans for her
until she got therapy to work through her feelings
about her earthly father and studied passages like
Psalm 8 to understand what the real Father-God is like.

David, who wrote Psalm 8, couldn't understand why
the Creator would esteem His creatures so highly. God
made us a little lower in power than the angels, but
higher in position. The angels are our servants and will
be for eternity. God has certainly crowned us with
glory and honor. Someday we will rule on earth with
Christ.

God will recreate heaven and earth and the stars
and planets. Then we believers will enjoy royal privileges as we spend eternity together with Him with the
whole universe at our disposal. We are important to
Him!

---

*Our God is infinitely creative and powerful, and yet we are individu-
ally important to Him.*

> *"I am the door. If anyone enters by Me, he will be saved, and will go in and out and find pasture. The thief does not come except to steal, and to kill, and to destroy. I have come that they may have life, and that they may have it more abundantly."*
>
> —JOHN 10:9–10

There is a great contrast between unhealthy codependency and healthy dependency. Someone who subconsciously or consciously wants to control us, manipulate us, or even destroy us could well be called a *thief*. He or she wants to take something from us that is rightfully ours. Maintaining a relationship with such a person requires that we give up a large part of who we are. The codependent pattern actually steals, kills, and destroys.

Jesus, on the other hand, came to *give* us life. We are dependent on Him as our Good Shepherd, to care for us and provide meaning and purpose to our lives. Unlike a thief, whose selfish goal is to take from others, the Good Shepherd has good motives. Jesus loves us and came to earth to die for us so He could give us *abundant* life—a life of serenity and significance as adopted sons and daughters of God. There is freedom in our relationship with Him. We live by grace, and we are loved for who we are, and for who we are becoming.

Thank you, Lord, for the abundant life you offer. Give me wisdom to see the difference between healthy interdependence and unhealthy codependence. Protect me from thieves who would steal life from me, and help me, by Your grace, never to be a "thief" in my relationships.

> *"For I know that my Redeemer lives,*
> *And He shall stand at last on the earth;*
> *And after my skin is destroyed, this I know,*
> *That in my flesh I shall see God,*
> *Whom I shall see for myself,*
> *And my eyes shall behold, and not another.*
> *How my heart yearns within me!"*
>
> —JOB 19:25–27

After losing his children, his wealth, and his health, Job still saw his life from God's perspective. He knew that after his body was destroyed, he would immediately be present with God in a new body.

Having gone through this degree of suffering, many people would be intensely bitter toward God. I have seen such people denounce God and even pretend He didn't exist. They were so angry at God they became "functional atheists."

Job's response was just the opposite. He never doubted that God loved him, even though God allowed him to suffer. Job knew some human suffering was to be expected. He accepted what he could not change.

Job also had an eternal perspective, an attitude sadly absent from many people's lives. If there is life after death, then we would be fools not to trust Christ and spend that eternity with Him. And if we know we will be with God in perfect new bodies, then our suffering here becomes more bearable.

Lord, help me to see my suffering with Your perspective. When my life is painful, remind me of Your great love for me.

> *For the message of the cross is foolishness to those*
> *who are perishing, but to us who are being saved*
> *it is the power of God.* —1 COR. 1:18

It takes courage to be a Bible-believing Christian in this era. I guess it always has. The Bible says some very unpopular things! For fear of appearing narrow-minded and intolerant, many people will avoid taking a stand. They may say the Bible is a good book and Jesus was a good man. But Jesus not only said He was God, but that not a single mark of punctuation was wrong in all of His Word.

If we believe there are no errors in the original text of the Scriptures, then we may appear foolish to those who disagree. And if we trust in the Lord, we will definitely appear foolish to those who don't believe He exists.

The Bible certainly contains more true wisdom for daily life than any other book ever written. But the wisdom of the Bible contradicts much of the "people are basically good" philosophies of humanism, and confronts depravity head-on. God's Word is true. We can courageously depend on it.

———————

If you believe what Jesus said about Himself and about His Word, be prepared to face ridicule from those who see you as a fool and see themselves as wise. Take courage from God's love for you and the support of other committed believers.

"With the merciful You will show Yourself merciful;
With a blameless man You will show Yourself blameless;
With the pure You will show Yourself pure;
And with the devious You will show Yourself shrewd.
You will save the humble people;
But Your eyes are on the haughty,
that You may bring them down." —2 SAM. 22:26–28

If we want God to be merciful to us, we must develop a humble, merciful attitude of forgiveness toward those who offend us. God doesn't expect perfection, but if we honestly strive to pursue what is right and stay away from what we know is wrong, God will honor our obedience.

If we are pure of *heart* (notice the greater emphasis on inward than outward behavior), then God will show us His purity. He wants us to be vulnerable. Real. Not phony. If we are devious, God will show Himself to be shrewd with us. He will do whatever it takes to bring us to repentance, even if that means He must take us home to heaven.

God loves to answer the cries of the humble. He promises to save them. David and his son Solomon wrote openly and brokenheartedly about their own moral failures, and we have a lasting record of God's gracious forgiveness.

God sees what no one else may ever see; He sees the attitudes and motives in my heart. As I become aware of deceitfulness and pride in myself, I will confess them to the Lord and work at replacing them with mercy, blamelessness, and purity.

Then Jesus said to His disciples, "If anyone desires to come after Me, let him deny himself, and take up his cross, and follow Me. For whoever desires to save his life will lose it, and whoever loses his life for My sake will find it. —MATT. 16:24–25

The best decision a person can make is to follow Jesus Christ as a committed believer. But a wise person will also count the cost. Jesus encouraged His disciples to do just that.

To make that lifelong commitment, you must deny yourself. What does that mean? It means giving up trying to prove your significance through possessions, work, power, prestige, illicit sex, and popularity. If these are what you have lived your life for, it may seem like a lot to give up. But since those things ultimately won't work, you're not really giving up anything of value.

To take up our cross means to expect some pain as we identify with His sufferings and purposes. Jesus said, "Follow me." Develop His values. Love as He loves. Forgive as He forgives.

Whoever loses his or her life for Christ's sake will find it. What a paradox! We must lose our worldly ambitions and sinful desires, in other words, to find a life of meaning and save that life for God's use and eternal rewards.

Living to protect myself and serve my own desires is an attempt to "save" my life. But Jesus said that if I truly want to save my life, I must give my life away in love and service to the Lord and others.

My God, My God, why have You forsaken Me? Why are You so far from helping Me, And from the words of My groaning? . . . They pierced My hands and My feet.
—PS. 22:1, 16b

Four-year-old Thomas was afraid of the dark. He would often call out for his daddy when he saw imaginary animals in the shadows. Even though Thomas couldn't see his daddy in the dark, his daddy was there in the next room. Every time Thomas cried out, his daddy was there for him. As Thomas grew, he learned that he could trust his daddy. His daddy also taught him to face real threats in life. He helped Thomas overcome the paralyzing fear of the unknown.

As adults, our fears of real and imagined foes drive us to addictive behaviors. We can't handle our fears alone. Twelve Step recovery programs require us to depend on our "heavenly Daddy" whom we can't see or touch.

Even Jesus, the God-Man, experienced some of these painful emotions when He was crucified. He knew His Father could resurrect Him, but He groaned in His agony. He called out to His Daddy for help.

King David, was inspired by the same Father to write these words a thousand years before the Romans devised the method of punishment we call crucifixion. God the Father knew ahead of time what His Son, and you, would experience. He has promised to walk through those painful times with us, holding our hand and soothing our fears.

We can't see or touch our "heavenly Daddy," and yet He can deliver us from both real and imagined foes.

> *"Bless those who curse you, and pray for those*
> *who spitefully use you."*
> —LUKE 6:28

During the course of our lives, all of us have been treated badly by someone. An abused child tends to blame him- or herself for the abuse. But deep inside, he or she is filled with rage. That anger may be completely repressed, and it may follow the child into adulthood.

This verse tells us to bless those who verbally abuse us, and *pray* for those who have spitefully used us. What an incredible command! Let us first understand what this does *not* mean. It is not God's intent that victims of any form of abuse should simply forgive, and allow the abuse to continue. Neither does this suggest that those who harm others should not have to face the consequences of their behavior.

God *does* want us to see things as He sees them. He hates the sin . . . but He loves the sinner. The person who abused you was very likely a victim of abuse. Pity him or her. Pray for his or her salvation. No one is beyond hope of being changed into a Christlike person through the power of God.

The primary damage from being abused comes from lowered self-esteem and holding repressed vengeful motives. Praying for the one who has hurt you will help you respect yourself more and make it a little easier to forgive him or her.

We bless and pray for those who have mistreated us, not because they deserve it, but because it is part of the path to our wholeness.

The LORD sat enthroned at the Flood,
And the LORD sits as King forever.
The LORD will give strength to His people;
The LORD will bless His people with peace.
—PS. 29:10–11

About 5000 years ago, there were no committed believers on the earth except for Noah and his family. So God told Noah and his family to build a three-story, 450-foot-long boat and seal it with pitch, so they would be spared. Then God destroyed everyone on the earth with a worldwide flood.

It is something of a paradox that the God who sat enthroned during the Flood, destroying the then-known world, is the same God who gives us peace. But it is true. God sits as our King and the King of the Universe forever. He is all-powerful. If anyone could give us serenity, wouldn't it be a loving, all-powerful, just, all-knowing God?

He exchanges His strength for our weaknesses, making us stronger through the years. And He blesses His people with serenity. That was true even in the days of Noah. Noah's family was ridiculed. They endured months at sea with a boat full of animals. They witnessed the greatest environmental catastrophe the world has known. But Noah's family found serenity in the midst of it all.

The God we serve is both powerful and gentle. He gives those who love and fear Him strength and serenity.

> *"We must through many tribulations enter the kingdom of God."*
> —ACTS 14:22

God allowed His chosen apostle Paul to be stoned so badly that he was presumed dead. They even dragged his body out of the city for disposal.

When the crowd left him, his disciples snuck up to check on his body. Paul surprised them by getting up, brushing himself off, and going right back into the same city. Talk about courage!

Paul had a purpose in putting his life on the line. He returned to this hostile city in order to strengthen the souls of the disciples and exhort them to continue in the faith. Paul had seen some disciples serve Christ enthusiastically for a while and then fall back into the rat race. His friend Demas, for example, assisted him for a while, only to go back to his old lifestyle because he loved too much what the world had to offer. Paul also wanted to warn them they would suffer many tribulations, and to encourage them that it would be worth it someday when they entered the kingdom of God.

We, too, can expect some trials in this life. We also need encouragement from other believers to continue faithfully in our Christian walk. It is easy to get distracted by the treasures of this world and lose our focus on what's really important. God does bless financially at times. That is biblical. But He blesses most committed Christians in better ways, such as with rich relationships.

Only three things last forever: God, God's Word, and people. Invest wisely in what will last.

Moreover David said, "The Lord, who delivered me from the paw of the lion and from the paw of the bear, He will deliver me from the hand of this Philistine."
—1 SAM. 17:34–37

This passage demonstrates one of the reasons why God called David "a man after my own heart." From his youth, David had so much love for God and faith in God that his courage was unbelievably great.

He was probably about sixteen years old or so at this time. He had already killed a lion and a bear when they were stealing his sheep. One 9-foot warrior like Goliath would be no big deal because Goliath defied the armies of the living God.

David killed Goliath with one stone. Then he took Goliath's huge sword and beheaded him. The Philistines fled in terror because their hero was dead.

David depended on God, but he still followed his plan to kill the giant the only way he knew how. The human odds were stacked against him, but he stood up for what he knew was right. His courage came from knowing Who was in charge.

In any situation where you lack courage, remind yourself that you and God are the majority. Life has many giants, including our own addictive tendencies. We must trust God's wisdom and power, then diligently carry out the steps to recovery.

May the Lord give us courage to fight our own inner "Goliaths."

> *A new commandment I give to you, that you love*
> *one another; as I have loved you, that you also love*
> *one another. By this all will know that you are My*
> *disciples, if you have love for one another."*
> —JOHN 13:34–35

The Pharisees had a long list of rules by which they measured someone's spirituality. Jesus had a better way to tell who His true disciples were: if they loved each other. Like most worthwhile things, love is easy to talk about but hard to work at.

Bonding with God and with other believers is vital for our mental health. But most of us love selfishly. "I love you" tends to mean *I love what you do for me, or how you make me feel*. Christian love wants to do something to benefit the other person even if there is no profit for us.

Christian love also involves the freedom to share our deep feelings with each other, confess faults and failures to each other without being rejected, confront each other, and encourage each other.

When we put our trust in Christ and depend on what He did for us on the cross because of His immense love for us, we immediately become filled with the Holy Spirit. The Holy Spirit is then in us, enabling us to love as God loves. We can never have more or less of the Holy Spirit, but we can *yield* more or less to the Holy Spirit's convictions in our lives. The more we yield, the more we love.

Can others tell you are a believer by how healthy and sincere your love is?

For day and night Your hand was heavy upon me;
My vitality was turned into the drought of
  summer. . . .
I acknowledged my sin to You, . . .
And You forgave the iniquity of my sin.
                              —PS. 32:4–5

David had just experienced a full-blown clinical depression. Although he had been a godly man since his youth, David committed adultery and then murder to cover it up. When confronted with the truth, David's denial systems and defense mechanisms broke down, and he recognized the terrible evil he had rationalized away.

David could have avoided a great deal of pain by taking time to grieve deeply over his sins and forgive himself right at that moment. But David refused. As a result, he experienced many of the symptoms of clinical depression.

He had physical aches and pains. He groaned all day long and was very unhappy. His thoughts and emotions were painful. His heart was heavy and guilt-ridden. He experienced a loss of vitality and decreased motivation and concentration.

David began to recover from depression when he finally decided to forgive himself. He found forgiveness in the Lord, who surrounded him with unconditional love and a song of deliverance. God offers that to you too!

Accepting His forgiveness, then forgiving yourself, is a kind and courageous act on behalf of a child God really loves—you.

> *"Let not your heart be troubled; you believe in God, believe also in Me. In My Father's house are many mansions; if it were not so, I would have told you. I go to prepare a place for you. And if I go and prepare a place for you, I will come again and receive you to Myself; that where I am, there you may be also."*
>
> —JOHN 14:1-3

In this passage, Jesus tells us a lot about the nature of God the Father and about Himself.

He expresses concern for our anxiety level and fears. The "heart" represents your mind, emotions, and will.

He tells us *how* to relieve much of our anxiety and fears, too, by trusting God the Father and Jesus the Son. God knows each of us intimately. He knows what is best for us and has good plans for us. He is even now preparing our future. Do we trust Him?

Anxiety is the fear of the unknown. It is a fear of finding out the truth about ourselves. The Holy Spirit helps us grow emotionally and spiritually by gently pushing the truth up from our unconscious and subconscious minds to our conscious awareness. Our depraved and untrusting minds frantically shove the truth back down. That tension between the Spirit pushing up and our human minds shoving down is *anxiety*. When we trust God, we can look at whatever is inside us without fear of rejection.

We have a God who loves us in spite of our buried thoughts. He can help us recognize the truth and work through our fears.

You have made him to have dominion
over the works of Your hands;
You have put all things under his feet,
All sheep and oxen—
Even the beasts of the field,
The birds of the air,
And the fish of the sea
That pass through the paths of the seas.
—PS. 8:6–9

When God created man in His likeness, He was talking about likeness of character—emotional, spiritual, and intellectual. Jesus didn't have a body yet. The Father, Son, and Holy Spirit were three personalities without bodies who have fellowshipped with each other since eternity past. It is impossible for us, as finite humans, to fully comprehend, but I am relieved by the fact that the opposite alternative—no God at all—would be a much greater leap of faith.

God loves, so He teaches us the value of bonding. He teaches us also to develop boundaries to protect ourselves from codependency.

God also has authority over the Universe. Because we become His sons and daughters when we put our faith in His Son, He delegates a lot of authority to us. He wants us to have authority and responsibility.

Begin working on a plan to assume responsibility for your own spiritual growth, healing emotional wounds, your body's health, your marriage, your children, your gifts and talents.

> *My sheep hear My voice, and I know them, and*
> *they follow Me. And I give them eternal life,*
> *and they shall never perish; neither shall anyone*
> *snatch them out of My hand. My Father, who has*
> *given them to Me, is greater than all; and no one is*
> *able to snatch them out of My Father's hand. I and*
> *My Father are one."* —JOHN 10:27–30

During times of personal anxiety, this passage has helped restore my own serenity more than any other passage in scripture. I like to visualize Jesus about fifty feet tall because of His great power. He reaches out His open hand to me, and like a little child, I climb into His palm, lie down comfortably, and relax. Then Jesus wraps His hand lovingly around me and reminds me of His promise.

When we hear His voice and respond to His call, we can climb into the shelter of God's hand. He knows and recognizes us. We follow and obey Him, and He promises us eternal life. He promises that even though our temporary bodies will die, our souls, personalities, minds, and emotions will never perish. Jesus holds us firmly in His hand. We cannot lose our salvation or our relationship with Him. No one can snatch us out of His hand.

The Father, in His mercy, has adopted us into His family. He loves us and will keep us forever. We are eternally secure.

─────────────

Visualize the reality of this passage in your own life. If you have trusted Christ, He will never, ever let you go.

But He knows the way that I take;
When He has tested me, I shall come forth as gold.
My foot has held fast to His steps;
I have kept His way and not turned aside.
I have not departed from the commandment of His
      lips;
                              —JOB 23:10–11

When Job spoke these words, he was in a great deal of pain. He had lost his children, his wealth and his health. His friends were pious and unsupportive. Job's response is a great example of how we can accept the things we cannot change.

Job had so much faith in God that he actually thought positive thoughts, even though no one encouraged him. In fact, Job's friends blamed him for his own trouble. Even his wife told him to curse God and die.

But Job thought to himself, "God knows all about me. He is allowing me to suffer right now for my own good, and when this suffering is over, I will come out of it refined like precious gold. I will be an even better person—a wiser person—with more appreciation for every good thing God gives me both in this life and in eternity. I have stayed in fellowship with God in spite of my suffering. I have obeyed His command, and I have meditated daily on the treasured words of His mouth.

What an outstanding attitude!

Acceptance of the things we cannot change comes from faith, and faith comes from meditating on God's Word.

> *Behold, I tell you a mystery: We shall not all sleep,*
> *but we shall all be changed in a moment, in the*
> *twinkling of an eye, at the last trumpet.*
> —1 COR. 15:51

When your courage is on a momentary decline, think about this passage. Christ has given us something to look forward to: the rapture of all believers. He has promised to come back to earth to end our suffering. Do you ever try to imagine how exciting the new heaven and earth will be? No crime, no pain—and the Lord's comforting presence always with us.

The word *sleep* is used when a believer dies. Paul is saying that not all believers will experience death. Some will be raptured, instantly, as fast as an eye can blink.

In one instant, we will receive new bodies. They will be new and incorruptible, better than any "superman" body we can imagine. But an even greater joy will be to have a new incorruptible *mind,* leaving behind all our contaminated, depraved motives and urges. We will be free from the physical and psychological "prisons" we have made for ourselves: chemical and food addictions, unhealthy relationships, destructive thought patterns, everything we do to make our own lives miserable.

We will instantly become immortal. We will be able to stand beside the apostle Paul and joyfully shout, "Death is swallowed up in victory."

Though I am sometimes discouraged about my body and often discouraged about the mixed motives of my mind, I will one day be transformed into a new creation.

I have made a covenant with my eyes;
Why then should I look upon a young woman?
—JOB 31:1

The Serenity Prayer asks God to help us change the things we can. Have you ever stopped to think of all the physical, psychological, spiritual, and financial damage sexual sins do in the world each year? Sexually transmitted diseases, AIDS, infertility, abortions. . . . Then there are affairs, divorces, and the effects of these on children. The physical damages of violating God's sexual standards are devastating.

Thousands of patients come in and out of our Minirth-Meier Clinics who have to work through the psychological damage from sexual sins committed by them or against them. The wounds are curable, but take a lot of time, a lot of work, a lot of grieving, and a lot of forgiving.

The spiritual damages are also great. The guilt. The rage. The grudges. The unconscious vengeful motives. The strong addiction to sexual sins to fill holes in our souls is both a spiritual and psychological problem. Lust leads to sin, which leads to addictions, which leads in many cases to the refusal to trust Christ.

Job recognized that lust was sin, and that the ultimate result of allowing that sin in his life would be destruction and disaster. He chose to say no to lust. He made a promise to himself to remain pure before the God who sees every step we take.

Sex was invented by a creative God for us to enjoy with our mate. His boundaries are the best for us.

> *"Is it not lawful for me to do what I wish with my own things? Or is your eye evil because I am good?"*
> —MATT. 20:15

When we were young, we wasted a great deal of time trying to decide what is fair. When we got a little older, we discovered that it doesn't really matter because life on earth isn't totally fair anyway.

Jesus told a story about a landowner who went out to hire laborers to work in his vineyard. He told them they would get one denarius for working a twelve-hour day. The workers accepted. Three hours later the owner promised more workers the same wage for working the remaining nine hours. Three hours later, he offered a denarius to a few more people for six hours' work, and finally he offered more workers a whole denarius for only three hours of labor.

At the end of the day, those who worked only three hours were paid first. The twelve-hour laborers saw what the others received and assumed the owner had changed his mind and would pay them more for working longer. They were astonished when they received the same pay as those who worked less time, even though they had agreed to work for the wage.

Jesus says, "I own the vineyard. I make the rules. In the Kingdom, the last will be first, and the first last." When your peers end up with better "things", will you be happy for them or envious? Inner tranquility is of far greater value than one's possessions.

Thank You, God, for the gifts You have lavished on me.

When my father and my mother forsake me,
Then the LORD will take care of me.
—PS. 27:10

Many millions of children have felt forsaken by their fathers and mothers, who either abuse them or are too caught up in their own pursuits.

We each have a God-shaped hole in our soul that nothing else can adequately fill. But adult children of abuse need God's loving care even more, though they tend to find it much more difficult to feel loved by Him despite constant reassurance that He does.

When a three-year-old girl prays, "Dear Heavenly Father," she is thinking, *Dear Heavenly version of my earthly Father*. If her father is an alcoholic, or a workaholic, or abusive in any way, then she will have difficulty throughout life trusting authority figures, whether at school, at work, or at church.

The solution for such a person comes through looking at the truth about the parental abuse, verbalizing the anger to an understanding therapist, and then *forgiving* the abuser, which requires God's supernatural help. The adult child of abuse needs to examine what Scripture says about the nature of God to separate their image of God from the real God. They are then better able to both accept and experience God's love.

You can live a satisfying life without the love and acceptance of your parents. But you can't do it without God's love. Learn who He is, then learn to trust Him.

Then He spoke a parable to them, that men always ought to pray and not lose heart. . . .

—LUKE 18:1

Your prayer life is very important. It can dramatically enhance your life. But the vast majority of people do not know how to pray, or they do not take advantage of it.

We have a very real God who has the power to grant our requests in ways that are always in our long-term best interests.

Sometimes we think we know better than He does what is best for us: the best job, the best mate, the best health, the best house, the best car. When God says no to a request, we may get angry at Him for not doing things our way.

God wants prayer to be a part of our daily lifestyle. He wants us to discuss all aspects of our lives with Him and to ask for His guidance. As we spend time with Him in prayer, we can begin to accept necessary pain maturely. We can ask Him to help change our bad habits. He knows best what we really need in the long run. And He loves to meet our needs.

So pray when you wake up. Pray when you work. Pray on your coffee break. Pray when you drive (with your eyes open, preferably). Pray before you go to sleep. Pray privately as well as with other believers.

Pray often each day, without vain repetitions. You will receive blessings and personal growth as you depend more on God for moment by moment help and guidance.

You laid affliction on our back. . . . But You
brought us out to rich fulfillment.
—PS. 66:11–12

One day I was driving home from visiting hospital patients and listening to Bible tapes. The tape "happened" to be playing the Psalms. And as I listened, the passage above particularly stood out to me.

Barely a minute later, these verses took on new meaning. Another car ran into mine and flipped me and my car over on the roof. The other car was totaled and mine looked like a squashed accordion. God literally laid me on my back.

Difficult as it may be to believe, as I flipped in the air, my honest thoughts were very serene: *Oh, is this what You have in store for me today, Lord?* I didn't feel scared at all . . . until I unfastened my seat belt, crawled out a window, and saw what had happened. Car fluids were steaming, and I moved quickly away for fear the car would explode. But no one in either car was even scratched. God spared me that day and "brought me out to rich fulfillment."

God does not exempt me or anyone else from death or suffering. But on that day, God taught me that meditating on Scripture really does produce serenity, especially in a crisis. He also reminded me to number my days and use them wisely for Him.

Meditation on Scripture changes your way of looking at everything in life. I wouldn't want to live (or die) without it.

> *For I consider that the sufferings of this present*
> *time are not worthy to be compared with the glory*
> *which shall be revealed in us.* —ROM. 8:18

God is my Father and I am His child. If we are children of God, we will share in Christ's suffering, and someday, in His glory.

There is no doubt in my mind that Christians will suffer for the sake of Christ. Christ was rejected by His own people, was whipped and beaten, and suffered intensely on the cross, yet He kept an eternal perspective. He was not a masochist, but He was able to accept His suffering because He understood it was part of God's plan, and that glory lay ahead. Christ's suffering was necessary to make us children of God.

If we can realize that the suffering we experience on earth is temporary and the glory to come will be eternal, our perspective will change dramatically. The sufferings of this present time are not even worthy to be compared with the glory that we will experience.

That is not to say we no longer hurt. We do, and we still have to grieve those hurts and losses. We are not required to like our suffering, but we will experience more peace if we accept it. When we experience suffering because of living out our faith in Christ, we start to understand some of what Christ suffered for us. We "fellowship" in His sufferings, and we can remind ourselves of the glory ahead that we will also share with Him.

Suffering is painful, yes, but it is a small part of the picture. An eternity of joy awaits us.

Be of good courage, and let us be strong for our people and for the cities of our God. And may the LORD do what seems good to Him."
—2 SAM. 10:11–12

David had brought many nations under his subjection including Ammon and its ruler, Nahash.

Nahash had been kind to David, so when King Nahash died and was succeeded by his son Hanun, David sent ambassadors to Hanun to express sympathy for his father's death and to wish him peace. But Hanun's advisors told him David's ambassadors were probably spies. They convinced Hanun to shave off half the beards and remove half of the garments of David's ambassadors, sending them home in absolute shame and disgrace. It was not a very bright move.

Then Hanun hired Syrian mercenaries to help him conquer David. David sent Joab and Abishai to fight the Ammonites and the Syrians at Medeba. God used Joab, Abishai, and the Israelite warriors to accomplish His purposes and won an enormous victory. More than 40,000 of the hired Syrian soldiers in the battle were killed. Hanun fled for his life.

All the surrounding kingdoms immediately sent diplomats and gifts to make peace with David. They saw his God could deliver him, and didn't want to suffer the same fate as Hanun.

We must remember never to fight our personal battles alone. To build our courage for fighting our battles in life, we need the support of our "brothers" in Christ.

Healthy dependence on God and our peers is necessary to our sanity.

> *And do not be conformed to this world, but be transformed by the renewing of your mind, that you may prove what is that good and acceptable and perfect will of God.*
> —ROM.12:1–2

God wants more than our hearts—He wants all of us. Every aspect of our lives is important to Him, and our bodies are no exception. He formed us and breathed life into us. He created us, and we belong to Him.

It is also obvious that God does not want us to have terrible lives. He knows that what we do with our bodies will have a lasting impact on our minds, emotions, and souls. If we conform to the standards of this world, which do not acknowledge our bodies as the temple of God, we fall into Satan's trap. We will dishonor God, and we will be miserable. How do we present our bodies as holy and acceptable offerings to God? By *renewing our minds*. As we begin to think as God thinks, we will love what He loves and behave as He would want us to. In short, we will be transformed! Our minds control our actions and attitudes. If we are transformed by renewing our minds, we prove that God's will is good for believers. It is as if God has given us a map and directions for a joyful life on earth, and we have the option to follow and apply it or to stumble our way along without it. I think our Heavenly Father knows best.

God's Word has the power to transform my life. As I meditate on Scripture and conform to its principles, every part of me can be honoring to God.

*Therefore you are inexcusable, O man, whoever
you are who judge, for in whatever you judge
another you condemn yourself; for you who judge
practice the same things. But we know that the
judgment of God is according to truth against those
who practice such things. And do you think this, O
man, you who judge those practicing such things,
and doing the same, that you will escape the
judgment of God?*
                                                        —ROM. 2:1-3

One of the most common defense mechanisms that
we consciously and unconsciously use in our daily lives
is that of projection. You've heard the phrase, "It takes
one to know one." I have found that often the thing that
bothers me the most in someone else is something that
I am presently subconsciously struggling with. It is so
easy to take on a judging, critical attitude and focus on
the other person's failure rather than addressing my
own issue and struggle.

Real wisdom comes from breaking free of the defense mechanism of projection and stopping the condemning and judging. Before I judge I need to look in
the mirror and ask myself, "How am I doing in this
area?"

A wise person lets God be the judge.

> *Bless the LORD, O my soul, . . .*
> *Who forgives all your iniquities,*
> *Who heals all your diseases.*
> —PS. 103:1–3

There are many ways in which God reaches out to us. He gives us many benefits. He forgives our failures and sins. He heals our diseases.

What are the benefits God has given to you? Stop and list some right now. Stay with that list and focus with a grateful heart on what God has done for you.

God also forgives us for all our failures and sins. If He forgives us, we can forgive ourselves. If we don't, we can become paralyzed and tied up in knots emotionally. We become as prisoners. God wants to set us free.

God also heals our diseases. He can heal instantaneously, but most often He lets the natural healing capacities of the body go to work. The real problem is that often because of stress there is a decrease of the antibodies in our systems that fight disease. As we focus on God, rather than being so consumed with stress, the natural antibodies can go to work to fight the disease.

It is interesting to see from these verses that God wants to have an active part in our physical and emotional wholeness.

Your choice of attitude can make you sick or well, imprison or free you, and make you bitter or better! We have a God who wants to help.

Then He said to them, "Why do you sleep? Rise and pray, lest you enter into temptation."
—LUKE 22:46

Shakespeare said, "To be or not to be, that is the question." Jesus challenged us: to pray or not to pray in times of trouble, that is our choice.

On the night He died, He warned His disciples, whom He loved deeply and with whom He invested three years of His life, to pray in times of need lest they be tempted. The temptation for them came in trying to avoid and deny the problem at hand, or trying to escape the difficulty by sleeping.

What is your tendency? Do you want to escape the problems of your life by eating, drinking, drugs, busyness, or sleeping? Why not try praying? Personalize this prayer and make it your own.

"Dear God, thank You that you are always there for me. Your arms of love surround me. Your heart desires to assure and comfort me. Lord, You know about (my problem). You know about my hopeless feelings. Help me not to escape from facing problems by (my tendency). Help me to follow Your example of praying about (my deepest hurt) . . . and (my deepest fear). Draw me closer to You. Thank You that You not only hear but will answer me."

God knows my greatest temptations. He also knows that prayer can help me overcome them. The next time I feel pressure or panic, I will pray.

> *Deceit is in the heart of those who devise evil,*
> *But counselors of peace have joy.*
> —PROV. 12:20

There are two kinds of people in the world: those who build walls, and those who build bridges. Solomon briefly describes both of these kinds of people in this verse. It seems there are those who get a charge out of creating a rift or division. They thrive on devising clever ways to bring dissension. They expect the worst of people and thereby promote a paranoid, hostile, and defensive stance in others.

Then there are those who are committed to building bridges. These are the individuals who desire and work toward peace. They focus on resolving conflict that is creating dissension and distance in relationships. Solomon uses the phrase, "counselors of peace." This kind of person looks for the good and positive in others, expects the best from others, and is slow to condemn. Solomon says the result of being a bridge builder is that we will experience joy.

To pursue joy itself will lead to discouragement. However, joy is a by-product of being a bridge builder or peacemaker.

Do I foster hostility or harmony in relationships? Am I a wall builder or a bridge builder?

For to you it has been granted on behalf of Christ,
not only to believe in Him, but also to suffer for His
sake. —PHIL. 1:29

Some people today are open to anything, but stand for nothing. However, to become a Christian means we have someone and something worthwhile to stand for. When we make this decision to follow Christ and His way, we become a light in this dark world.

I am reminded of the lighthouse standing on the rocky coastline we saw on our last vacation. Each evening as it got dark, the light would begin to flash on and off, and would continue until daylight. The light stood out in the darkness and warned the boats passing by of the danger. The lighthouse may cause a sailor or captain to change direction.

If you let your light shine as a Christian, some people may see the need to change their direction but not want to. As a result, they may attack you for your stand on some issue. You may, as Paul discusses in this passage, have to "suffer for Christ's sake."

I have to admit there are those who stand out and suffer because they are intolerant, closeminded, and arrogant. Paul is not talking about suffering because of that, but because of our stand for Christ. To take such a stand is a loving act. Just as the lighthouse beaming out the warning, so our stand for Christ should be: an expression of our true concern for the people around us.

Christ suffered because of His love for the world. As His follower, I can expect to suffer as I love the people in my world.

> *If you faint in the day of adversity,*
> *Your strength is small.*
> —PROV. 24:10

One way to strengthen yourself for the days of adversity which come to all of us is to have realistic expectations. Evaluate yourself on the following expectations:

Yes	No	
____	____	I expect to be liked by everyone.
____	____	I should have everyone's approval.
____	____	I should be accepted by everyone.
____	____	I should have all my desires met.
____	____	I can't accept it if someone disagrees with me.
____	____	I should please everyone.
____	____	I should be able to handle my problems on my own.
____	____	I should not make mistakes.
____	____	I should never say no.
____	____	I should always feel competent.
____	____	I should excel at everything.
____	____	I should not get tired.

If you answered yes to any of these questions, you are setting yourself up for a let down and subsequent discouragement and depression. These expectations are unrealistic. You will be bombarded externally by life's reality and internally by your unrealistic expectations. That will often be overwhelming in adversity.

Am I undermining my strength with unrealistic expectations?

Now concerning the collection for the saints, as I have given orders to the churches of Galatia, so you must do also: on the first day of the week let each one of you lay something aside, storing up as he may prosper, that there be no collections when I come. —1 COR. 16:1–2

An attitude of gratitude can have profound effects on both the person living that way and those close to him or her.

Jesus told a story about ten lepers who came to Him. He lovingly touched and healed each one of them. All left with excitement, probably going to tell their family and friends what had happened. The Gospel records that just one of the ten lepers returned to say "thanks." In summary, Luke said, "All ten were healed, but only one was made *whole!*" The mark of wholeness is a thankful, grateful spirit. Do you want to be a whole person? Then practice an attitude of gratitude.

A concrete way we demonstrate our gratitude to God is by our financial giving to the needy through a church. The apostle Paul challenged Christians to get into the habit of giving on the first day of every week. This really moves us from a grateful attitude to practicing a grateful action; from feeling grateful to being grateful. Grateful behavior can become our normal, regular and systematic response to God's blessings on our lives.

Giving warms the heart of the giver as well as the recipient of the gift. Lord, help me to cultivate daily an attitude of gratitude.

> *And He said, "Do not lay your hand on the lad, or do anything to him; for now I know that you fear God, since you have not withheld your son, your only son, from Me."* —GEN. 22:9–12

What could be more foolish than slaying one's own son as a sacrifice? And yet this is exactly what God commanded Abraham to do. Abraham didn't argue with God. He obeyed because he knew that God had proven Himself worthy of obedience.

God did not intend for Abraham to go through with the sacrifice. Instead, God wanted His servant to learn to trust Him even more. Abraham trusted, and God did not disappoint him. God provided the sacrifice to take Isaac's place, and the father and son rejoiced in the goodness of God.

This story is a vivid reminder that the wisdom of God often seems absurd to man. It reminds us that we cannot rely on our own sense of right and wrong if we want to truly follow and obey God. We cannot rely on our own opinions; we must rely on God's. We cannot use our own wisdom; we must use God's. His paths may seem winding and steep, but that is only because they lead to the mountaintop. And as we choose those paths that the Lord leads us to, our legs grow stronger and the paths become easier to follow.

The next time you think, "In my opinion. . . ," think about what God's opinion would be. God's wisdom may seem foolish to you in forethought, but it will never seem foolish in afterthought. Choose God's path.

By faith we understand that the worlds were framed by the word of God, so that the things which are seen were not made of things which are visible. —HEB. 11:3

God is the God of creation. By His word our world was made. The world about us is a picture of His creative artwork. The majestic rugged mountains, the calm and quiet lake, the raging rapids of a mountain stream, the diverse color of the alpine flowers, and the waves breaking on the seacoast all point to the diversity of God, the Creator.

God is not only the Creator of the universe, He is our maker. We are His workmanship. He made us.

Just as God has the power to create, He has the power to re-create. What is it in your life that needs to be recreated? Is it your mindset? Is it your way of thinking?

Instead of viewing yourself as a failure, do you need to say to yourself, "I made a mistake, but *I'm* not a mistake." Instead of letting others define you, say "I know who I am in Christ." Instead of letting others direct your life, choose to make decisions for your life with God's help. Instead of violating your personal values to please others, tell yourself "I am not willing to do anything just to maintain a relationship. I have my own personal values."

We all have thinking patterns that need to be changed. God wants to be active within us, re-creating us in that area.

May the God of creation re-create me.

> *"Hear my prayer, O LORD,*
> *And give ear to my cry;*
> *Do not be silent at my tears;*
> *For I am a stranger with You,*
> *A sojourner, as all my fathers were.*
> —PS. 39:12

More and more people today seem to struggle with feelings of isolation and alienation. The "me" generation has fostered a group of people who are more aware of their own needs, but in the process has also led them to feel disconnected and cut off from others. The closeness of extended families is not typically a priority in our culture. Neighbors hardly know each other's names in the fast-paced life of the cities. Many families are fragmented, and the result is loneliness.

David addresses this problem in this psalm. He realizes that he feels like a stranger to others and to God. So what does he suggest? This is the time to go to God in prayer and lay it on the line. Our lonely time is a good time to pray. Prayer is being intimate with God, and intimacy and relationship are what we need. Begin by connecting with God. Move out then to connect with God's people. We are not meant to be islands. We are not meant to be lone rangers. We are made for relationships. If you are alone, re-connect!

With two-way prayers, we are never alone. Let God speak to you. Talk to Him today.

*Remind them to be subject to rulers and
authorities, to obey, to be ready for every good
work, to speak evil of no one, to be peaceable,
gentle, showing all humility to all men.*
—TITUS 3:1–2

God calls us to be peacemakers, not peacekeepers. What is the difference? One of the tendencies of someone who grows up in a dysfunctional home is to try to avoid conflict, argument, and disagreement. Often fear wells up in times of disagreement and conflict. Therefore the bottom line is a strong desire to keep peace at any cost, to keep the waters calm, not to heighten the conflict by bringing up his or her own thoughts and needs. The result is that he or she ends up "stuffing" feelings and thoughts, and then feeling stifled and controlled.

In contrast, God calls us to be peacemakers. A peacemaker seeks to be honest about his or her perspective and speaks up, but is not bull-headed, opinionated or dogmatic. A peacemaker is gentle and humble, willing to hear the other person's perspective. There is a realization that there may be more than one perspective on the issue, and he or she is open to listen and discuss. The peacemaker can be real and can appreciate differences in opinion and perspective. He or she looks for ways to allow the other person an opportunity to express his or her true feelings.

May God help me learn to recognize situations in which I need to move from being a peacekeeper to being a peacemaker.

> *Those who sow in tears*
> *Shall reap in joy.*
> *He who continually goes forth weeping,*
> *Bearing seed for sowing,*
> *Shall doubtless come again with rejoicing,*
> *Bringing his sheaves with him.*
>
> —PS. 126:5–6

Often in therapy someone will, through the years, make a statement like, "I don't know if this is worth the pain," or "Will it ever change? I keep trying, but therapy is hard. It would be easier to go back to drinking, or drugs, or sexual affairs."

The psalmist writes to encourage those who are agonizing and tearful over what they are trying to accomplish.

He uses the analogy from agriculture. If we plant the seeds, even if we come to tears in the process, there will be a positive result. The psalmist says there will doubtless be a celebration as we see the results of our effort.

Can you allow the tears to come in therapy? Are you willing to plant the seeds and work hard? Accept the tears and expect results; the harvest will come eventually. It will take time. You can't force the seed to grow. To expect an instantaneous cure in therapy is unrealistic. Accept the tears and keep working. The results will come.

If we block our tears, then we also blur our joys, and we are no more than half alive.

*But You, O L*ORD*, are a shield for me,*
My glory and the One who lifts up my head.
*I cried to the L*ORD *with my voice,*
And He heard me from His holy hill. . . .
I lay down and slept;
*I awoke, for the L*ORD *sustained me.*
I will not be afraid of ten thousands of people
Who have set themselves against me all
    around.
                —PS. 3:3–6

I have had people come into my office desperate and discouraged, with their heads down. They appear to be afraid to even make eye contact. They feel that everyone is against them, and that all of life has gone wrong. Many times the severity of their problems has left them with a sleep disturbance. They feel vulnerable, like an exposed victim waiting to be taken advantage of once again.

There is a promise of hope for this kind of person. The Lord is a shield to protect. The Lord is the one that lifts up his or her head. As he or she comes to the Lord and cries out in prayer, the Lord is there. The Lord enables the overwhelmed person to be able to lie down, sleep, and awake sustained.

Take courage and see the Lord work in your circumstances and your problems.

God is alive and active. Take heart. Have courage today.

> *Behold. You desire truth in the inward parts,*
> *And in the hidden part You will make me to*
> *   know wisdom.*
> *Purge me with hyssop, and I shall be clean;*
> *Wash me, and I shall be whiter than snow.*
> *Make me to hear joy and gladness,*
> *That the bones which You have broken may*
> *   rejoice.*
> *Hide Your face from my sins,*
> *And blot out all my iniquities.*
> *Create in me a clean heart, O God.*
> *And renew a steadfast spirit within me.*
> *   —PS. 51:6–10*

When the topic of change comes to the foreground, most of us feel, "If only my spouse, children, friend, employers, or employees would change, life could be much better." We overlook areas we need to change, point to others, and expect them to change. The truth is, the only time you can change other people is when they are babies in diapers.

It is so easy to try to force factors outside ourselves to change. However, lasting significant change begins inside rather than outside ourselves. The change needs to begin within us. As we ask God to help us see the truth about ourselves, we must realize we have some blind spots. We must not be afraid to see where we have fallen short, because we also know God will forgive, wash away, and blot out our failures and sins.

Lord, help me see the truth about myself.

*For what I am doing, I do not understand. For
what I will to do, that I do not practice; but what I
hate, that I do.* —ROM. 7:15

The Eskimos, who love and rely on their huskies, have an intriguing story. It is a story of a little boy. When he was asked why he did something wrong, he quickly replied "I don't know." However, his father wasn't satisfied and continued to probe.

The little boy responded: "It is as if I have two dogs inside me and they are fighting each other. One is a good dog, and one is a bad dog. Each one wants to be able to influence, direct, and control me." The little boy went on to describe the intensity of the fights. The dad interrupted and asked, "Son, which dog usually wins out?" The son answered, "The one I feed the most!"

The Scripture teaches us that we are both good and bad. Paul was struggling with that fact in today's passage. He expressed his frustration that he often did what he didn't want to do and vice versa.

Real wisdom comes in acknowledging that we are human. We do fail. We don't need to panic, because God still loves and accepts us. As we accept Christ He comes to live within us. He represents the "good dog" of our story. However, the reality is that there is the "bad dog" too, which Paul calls our "flesh" or our humanness. The wonderful hope of the Bible is that God embraces both the good and the bad in us.

No matter which force is winning out in your life today, accept God's love. He'll help the "good dog" in you grow.

> *. . . Who forgives all your iniquities,*
> *Who heals all your diseases, . . .*
> —PS. 103:3

Have you ever gone on a "thank you" walk? Here is how it works. It can take place in the woods, on a mountain trail, beside the roaring waves of the ocean, or along the edge of a quiet lake or stream. The location is up to you. It can be done by yourself or with a friend or family member. The "thank you" walk involves saying "thank you" to God for something or someone with each step you take. It enables you to focus on what the Lord has done and is doing in your life.

Psalm 103 lists some things God specifically does for us.

The first is that He forgives our failure and sin. All of us can think back over those times we have failed, and thank God that He forgives them.

God also heals, both emotionally and physically. God protects us from destruction. He gives us special blessings and benefits. He feeds us. He renews our depleted strength. He acts fairly and brings justice to those who are oppressed. "He made known His acts to the children of Israel." God continues to make visible His acts to us. Do we see what He is doing on our behalf?

Why not stop in the midst of your busy schedule this week and reflect on what God has done and is doing for you. Take a "thank you" walk.

*Then the multitude rose up together against them;
and the magistrates tore off their clothes and
commanded them to be beaten with rods. And
when they had laid many stripes on them, they
threw them into prison, commanding the jailer to
keep them securely. Having received such a charge,
he put them into the inner prison and fastened their
feet in the stocks. But at midnight Paul and Silas
were praying and singing hymns to God, and the
prisoners were listening to them.*

—ACTS 16:22–25

What do you do when you find yourself in a state of
crisis? When you feel that you are imprisoned?

When we are in crisis, we usually do not all of a sud-
den learn a new set of behaviors. We usually continue
what is familiar. Paul and Silas were happy men who
sang and prayed in daily life. When the tragedy hit and
they were beaten and thrown in jail, they didn't just
give up but continued to carry on their practice of
praying and singing to God.

As you can imagine, this was unusual for prisoners
to do. They caught the ears and the eyes of their fellow
prisoners. Paul and Silas were not controlled by their
external circumstances, by the people around them or
by the other prisoners' opinion of them. Paul and Silas
were controlled by the Lord within them.

*Are you controlled by your environment, or do you make an impact
on those around you? Are you externally or internally controlled?*

> *When a man's ways please the LORD,*
> *He makes even his enemies to be at*
> *peace with him.* —PROV. 16:7

To a large extent, the serenity we experience is our own responsibility. We have to take into consideration that many people have been the victims of abuse. They were innocent victims. Their serenity was stolen from them. With lots of love and therapy, their serenity can be restored.

But often our lack of serenity is not the result of victimization, but rather the result of our own pride and irresponsibility. God hates pride. Unless we confess and forsake our pride, every incident of pride will result in some form of discipline.

God's mercy caused Him to provide a way for our sins to be forgiven. Salvation is a gift, not something we can earn. But reverentially trusting God will help us to depart from habitual evil and do good works because we want to please Him.

When we please God with good works, He will make our enemies be at peace with us. He will give us the gift of serenity. When we rebel against Him, we rob ourselves of serenity, because sin always hurts someone.

God grant us the wisdom to obtain and maintain serenity by forsaking pride, fearing You, departing from evil, and doing good works.

*I have learned in whatever state I am, to be
content: I know how to be abased, and I know how
to abound.* —PHIL. 4:11–12

The Serenity Prayer uses the phrase, "to accept what I cannot change." That involves contentment. The Serenity Prayer also talks about changing what we can. This is referring to what needs to be conquered in our lives. It takes discernment to know what it is that requires contentment and what needs to be conquered.

My sister was born with cerebral palsy. She was never able to walk or talk, and was restricted to a reclining wheel chair or to bed. When she was a small child, my parents did not just accept this with contentment. They took her to specialists in New York and Toronto, Canada. They read books and journals and had people pray for her. However, nothing could be done to significantly alter her condition. They had to come to the place of accepting the reality, and make the best of this difficult and disappointing reality. At age 32, my sister passed away, but not without leaving us a rich family legacy of patience and courage.

In contrast to this situation, I know there have been times I gave up and became content when I really needed to push ahead and conquer. The apostle Paul shared in these verses that he had learned that we need both to be content and to be courageous and conquering. Christ can give us the wisdom to decide which path we need to choose.

Lord, help me to stay with and conquer what I can change and be content with what I can't change.

> *. . . For a righteous man may fall seven times*
> *And rise again. . . .*
> —PROV. 24:16a

Real success depends on what we do after we fail. In fact most often there is never success without failure.

When I was in the third grade, our family relocated to Alberta, Canada. It seemed that everyone there knew how to ice skate, and I decided I wanted to learn. I got a secondhand pair of skates, laced them on and proceeded onto the smooth sheet of ice at a nearby pond. I almost immediately lost my balance and fell. There I sat, watching a number of my new friends gliding artistically and effortlessly around the pond. I somehow managed to get to an upright position, only to fall again a few seconds later. It seemed so easy for everyone else. Why was it so hard for me? I wanted to learn to skate, but I wanted to say "forget it" at the same time.

In the next several months I kept trying and kept falling. However, the falls came less often. I started to feel more and more confident and secure. I didn't give up and I learned to skate. In fact, I took up ice hockey and played college hockey at the University of Toronto years later. I still love to skate. And I still fall from time to time, but I will always be glad I didn't quit.

Solomon makes it clear that none of us are perfect. The righteous man fails over and over . . . but he rises again. He doesn't quit and throw in the towel. He gets up and gives it another shot.

After you fall, are you willing to get up and try again?

Therefore, if anyone is in Christ, he is a new creation; old things have passed away; behold, all things have become new. —2 COR. 5:17

Growth and change take time. The old ways, habits and patterns of life do not disappear in an instant just because a person has chosen to become a Christian. In therapy, there is so often the expectation of instantaneous results. Unfortunately, the quick-fix approach to therapy usually does not get to the root of the problem.

This passage offers the encouragement that all things are in the process of becoming new. It refers to a present growth, rather than a completed project.

If I take a beautiful rose bud and try to pull it open prematurely, I will damage the flower; but if I nurture it with water and sunlight, it will naturally open into an exquisite masterpiece.

During my schooling days, I used to do room additions to provide income. After we would pour a cement slab for a new bedroom or recreation room, we did not try to rush things and begin to do the framing of the walls and place them on the wet, sloppy cement. The cement needed to set, harden, and cure before that was possible. Time was needed.

Effective, lasting change also requires time. Allow the Lord and your therapist time to help you experience the change you desire.

———————

When I became a Christian, my sanctification process began and my attitudes and behaviors started becoming new. Sometimes I remind my loved ones to be patient, because God isn't finished with me yet.

> *Trust in the LORD with all your heart,*
> *And lean not on your own understanding;*
> —PROV. 3:5

Following the San Francisco earthquake, a mysterious crack appeared in the wall on the forty-second floor of a gigantic skyscraper. The managing director of the building immediately sent for an architect. Informed of his arrival, the manager went up to the forty-second floor to meet him, but he wasn't there.

Eventually he was located in the sixth basement of the skyscraper.

"What are you doing down here?" he demanded. "We have a serious crack on the forty-second floor."

"Sir, you may have a crack on the forty-second floor, but your problem is here in the basement."

It seems a security guard had chiseled a brick out of the wall every night for six years in order to build a garage onto his home. The earthquake had revealed the weak spot on the 42nd floor.

Our lives can withstand some tremors even if what we are putting our trust in is untrustworthy. It's when the earthquakes of life hit that our foundation is exposed for what it really is. If you've been fired from a job you love, undergone a devastating divorce, or had a child die, you have gone through an earthquake experience. Did your foundation hold?

If you have committed yourself heart, mind and soul to the Lord Jesus Christ; if you have built your life on the foundation of God's Word; then then your foundation will stand firm in the storms of life.

Every good gift and every perfect gift is from above,
and comes down from the Father of lights.
                                        —JAMES 1:17

Love means different things to each individual. The Bible tells us that God is love. It seems that one way God displays love is in the area of gift giving. He loves to give gifts to His children.

For many, Christmas is the time of year when the majority of gifts are given. Children experience the excitement and joy of gifts and family and cultural traditions. One of the common practices is to say to them, "I hope you have been good and not naughty so that Santa Claus can bring you some gifts." Although this is often done in jest, it implies to the child that gifts are given conditionally.

James reinforced the fact that every good and perfect gift comes from God, and there is no variation on His part based on our actions. God loves and God gives, period! God's gifts are many and varied. He gives us good health, a restful night's sleep, a deep inner peace in the midst of a stressful situation, or the gift of a new friend. He gives spiritual gifts, such as the gift of salvation and freedom from guilt and condemnation. He gives the gift of emotional healing. His gifts take many forms. The special thing about His gifts is that they reveal something about Him. He is a giver. He is love. He gives according to our need.

Thank You, Lord, for the many gifts You give me. Open my eyes to see how good You have been to me.

> *Cast your burden on the LORD,*
> *And He shall sustain you;*
> *He shall never permit the righteous to be moved.*
> —PS. 55:22

Most of us carry burdens God never meant for us to carry. As we try to lovingly and empathetically listen to another's problems, it is easy to feel weighted down. When I first started counseling, there were times when I took on responsibility that was really not meant to be mine. I would become responsible for a client and feel an incredible weight or burden. It would make it hard to go home at night and be able to be with my family.

I have learned to be responsible not *for* but *to* my clients. I have learned to help them look at their options, but then allow them to make their own decisions.

There are some days, I admit, that I feel the burden. On those days as I drive home I try to practice this verse.

I cast my burden on the Lord. Sometimes I envision myself in a relay race. All day as I have worked with clients it is as if I have been carrying the baton. Now I have run my laps. In my time of prayer I take the baton and pass it on to the Lord Jesus. I say, "Lord you know I have done my best. I have tried to fully listen and understand. Now you take the baton, Lord, and work in each person's life until I have the opportunity to see them again and take back the baton."

My load could be a lot lighter if I would cast my burdens on the Lord.

*For if Joshua had given them rest, then He would
not afterward have spoken of another day. There
remains therefore a rest for the people of God. For
he who has entered His rest has himself also ceased
from his works as God did from His.*
—HEB. 4:8–10

It is wise for each of us to enter into a Sabbath rest or
time of peace and serenity following concerted con-
quests or intense projects.

When Joshua led the people of Israel into the Promised Land, they had to fight a number of battles in order to get possession of the land. Joshua challenged
the people of Israel to continue to do battle until the job
was done, until they had conquered all of Israel. However, they stopped and settled down and tried to have
the rest prematurely. The implication for us is clear.
Persevere; don't give up; keep going; see the challenge
through until it is complete.

In contrast to the people of Israel, God did not stop to
rest until His work of creation was complete.

Genesis 1 says after six days, God finished His work
of creation. On the seventh day He rested. God was
modeling a natural pattern for us. It is not wrong to
rest. It is essential, and can be thoroughly enjoyed as
we complete what God has called us to accomplish.

*Our lives are often filled with more than we can reasonably accom-
plish in one day, but God's design is that after a day or a week of
effort, we are to rest. We need to take care of our mental and spiritual
health.*

> *I will praise You, for I am fearfully and*
> *wonderfully made.* —PS. 139:14

Children love to read fairy tales. Fantasy is exhilarating. Have you ever noticed that in fairy tales the good characters are beautiful or handsome, and the wicked ones are ugly?

As teens and adults the exhilarating fantasy of childhood becomes an excruciating nightmare. We often feel like the ugly characters. And we compare others' best, which is all we see, to our worst, which is all we ever feel.

Our appearance is not a surprise to the creator God. God made us. Our responsibility lies in what we do with what God has fashioned. Our appearance is a sign to God, to ourselves, and to others of the value we place on God's creation.

So often victims of sexual abuse choose to dress either impeccably or in a sloppy, slovenly manner; their outward appearance betrays their inward feelings of shame. What a wondrous change would take place if we chose to look at ourselves with God's perspective. We would see ourselves through loving eyes rather than eyes of disdain. We would be grateful for what we had been given rather than ungratefully comparing ourselves with everyone around us.

A positive self-image must take place in your imagination before it will ever be useful in the skirmishes of your life.

The LORD also will be a refuge
for the oppressed,
A refuge in times of trouble.
And those who know Your name
will put their trust in You;
For You, LORD, have not forsaken
those who seek You.
—PS. 9:9–10

Sylvia sat in my office curled in a defensive pose. She had never been to see a psychologist before and was extremely fearful. She had grown up in a home where her father constantly put her down and judged her. No matter how hard she tried to do something, it was never enough. In therapy, she projected fear of her dad onto me as another male authority figure in her life. She would come into a session and for no apparent reason feel as if I was judging her. Later, it became clear that she also saw God as a judging Father.

The Lord is a refuge for the oppressed, a stronghold in times of trouble. The Hebrew word translated *refuge* means "a safe and secure place." David reminds us that we can have courage and feel safe because "the Lord has never forsaken those who seek Him."

What a promise! God is our refuge and He will never abandon us. God speaks hope to two of our strongest fears: fear of being hurt, and fear of abandonment.

Do you need to return to God's place of refuge and realize He has not abandoned you?

Thank You, Lord, for protecting and not abandoning me.

My son, if you become surety for your friend,
If you have shaken hands in pledge for a stranger,
You are snared by the words of your own mouth;
You are taken by the words of your mouth.
—PROV. 6:1–2

The Serenity Prayer challenges us to change the things we can. The Scripture passage today challenges us to make changes in the area of finances, and particularly in the area of co-signing for someone else. Co-signing is a form of financial codependency.

This proverb addressed people who co-signed without having a clear understanding of the situation and, by so doing, lost control. Apparently they had also co-signed on some loans that had unfairly high interest rates.

Unfortunately, this kind of situation can lead to broken relationships and friendships if the person taking out the loan defaults on it. The person who co-signed is left in a lurch, and it can affect him personally and emotionally.

I experienced this and had to make a payment of $12,000 over a two-year period because of my friend's defaulting. I have to admit, each month as I would make out the check, I would find myself getting upset and angry. Our friendship was negatively affected, but the experience taught me to obey every aspect of God's Word, even in financial matters.

Lord help me to be giving and caring, but also help me not to carelessly encourage someone else's immaturity by taking financial responsibility for him.

*I find then a law, that evil is present with me, the
one who wills to do good. . . . O wretched man
that I am! Who will deliver me from this body of
death? I thank God—through Jesus Christ our Lord!*
                                                    —ROM. 7:21–24

Unless we can embrace both the goodness and badness in ourselves, we can never be fully at peace. If we
pretend that we are all goodness, we live in denial.
Rather than seeing our journey through life as a process, we race through life consumed with and controlled by the quest for perfection. If, on the other
hand, we see only badness in ourselves, we make ourselves and those around us miserable.

When God accepts us because of what Christ has
done, He accepts all of us. He embraces both our goodness and our badness, and covers it all with the blood
of Jesus Christ.

When we think that God only accepts the good part
of us, we are deceived and we become pretenders. We
go through life feigning innocence and perfection and
deny our need to grow.

Only as a result of facing God's unconditional acceptance of us can we embrace the deep insecurity and
doubt underlying our constant need to impress by pretending and then be free in His love to know that He
isn't finished with us yet. Each new day is an opportunity to embrace this reality at a new level.

*I am God's child. I am in process. Today instead of pretending inno-
cence, projecting blame and protecting my insecurities I am going to
admit my powerlessness, and ask Christ to be my power.*

> *The LORD is merciful and gracious,*
> *Slow to anger, and abounding in mercy.*
> *He will not always strive with us,*
> *Nor will He keep His anger forever.*
> —PS. 103:8–9

How we handle anger reflects on our character. There are many different ways to react.

Some explode.

Some deny they are angry.

Some push the anger down.

Some become physically sick.

Some get depressed.

Some pout.

Some punish themselves.

Some express it directly and honestly, and then forgive.

Whatever your pattern, it is essential to be aware of it and to consider the consequences of your approach. Your anger has the potential to literally hurt or kill you.

The Scripture, which emphasizes the fact that God is love, states that anger is OK. God gets angry, but He is slow to anger. He doesn't have a quick fuse. His anger is linked to His mercy. In other words, at times He gets upset with us out of His love. He wants the best for us and desires that we get back on track.

The psalmist also says that this God of mercy does not keep His anger if we repent. He deals with us directly, and then lets go of His anger.

Lord, help me not to run from my anger, but to look for what my anger means; then have the courage to confront it and to change.

Turn Yourself to me, and have mercy on me,
For I am desolate and afflicted.
The troubles of my heart have enlarged;
Oh, bring me out of my distresses!
Look on my affliction and my pain,
And forgive all my sins. —PS. 25:16–18

What do you do when the bottom falls out of your world? Some people get busier, others get depressed and sleep to escape. Others try to gain relief from the pain by using drugs or alcohol. Still others pray.

You will often hear people making fun of someone who prays saying he or she must be weak to pray. However, David did not fit into this category. He had confidence and charisma. He was a leader. He had served as king of the nation Israel, and he was well liked and appreciated.

However, David did experience psychological difficulty. He felt he was alone and desolate. He was aware of his failures and sins, and felt distant from God. He pleaded with God.

David was in psychological, physical and spiritual pain. His negative thoughts grew out of proportion.

In all of his pain and self-pity, David cried out to God. It is no disgrace to be hurting and to call on God for help.

If King David could ask God to grant him relief from pain, so can we.

Lord, grant me the courage to face whatever life holds, and grant me the wisdom and humility to call on You for help.

> *Finally, brethren, whatever things are true,*
> *whatever things are noble, whatever things are just,*
> *whatever things are pure, whatever things are*
> *lovely, whatever things are of good report, if there*
> *is any virtue and if there is anything*
> *praiseworthy—meditate on these things.*
> —PHIL. 4:7–8

Do you spend more time on positive thoughts or negative thinking? Do you wallow in worry or find peace as a result of prayer?

A woman was overheard speaking about a mutual friend. She said, "Jane has a wide circle of friends. It is too bad it doesn't include herself."

If you are like Jane, you feel slightly uneasy affirming yourself. If this has not been your habit pattern, a part of your mind may even suggest that this isn't in line with Scripture and is a sign of arrogance. However, the Bible challenges us to think on what is noble, just, pure, lovely, and positive.

We need to align our lives with the positive affirmations and promises of Scripture. Never is God glorified, nor are His people helped, as a result of negativity. God wants us to be positive rather than negative. When I am positive, I look at myself, situations, and other people through the eyes of faith and hope rather than doubt and despair.

Choose today to focus on what God has done in your life rather than on the part not yet finished.

*"Blessed are those who are persecuted for
  righteousness' sake,
For theirs is the kingdom of heaven.
Blessed are you when they revile and persecute
  you, and say all kinds of evil against you
  falsely for My sake.
Rejoice and be exceedingly glad, for great is
  your reward in heaven, for so they
  persecuted the prophets who were before
  you."*
—MATT. 5:10–12

Christians who believe in the ultimate authority of scriptures have suffered persecution down through the ages. During the Inquisition of the Dark Ages alone, over 50 million were tortured and killed.

In the current era, the persecution is more subtle. A college student mentioned on his medical school application that he wanted to serve God and help humanity, and was told by a professor on the admissions committee, "You'd better take that 'God' stuff out of your application, or most medical schools will automatically reject you."

Across our nation and around the world people who love the Lord are facing opposition. Speaking up for what is right may make you unpopular. It could even land you in jail. How good to know that when we are persecuted for righteousness' sake, God is always on our side.

Christians are being subtly and openly persecuted today in America, as well as in other countries. Pray for them. If you are being persecuted, read today's scripture again and take heart. God's blessing is upon you!

> *"He is the Rock, His work is perfect;*
> *For all His ways are justice,*
> *A God of truth and without injustice;*
> *Righteous and upright is He."*
> —DEUT. 32:4

During medical school, Dr. Minirth and I memorized many outstanding passages of scripture, and this was one of our favorites. It gave us courage countless times when we felt persecuted, tired, or defeated, or that God wasn't being fair.

God is as emotionally and spiritually solid as a rock. He may not always do things the way we'd like Him to, but someday we will discover that all His works and plans were perfect!

And not only that, we will discover answers to all the questions we now can only guess about. Why does God allow the innocent to suffer? Someday we will understand.

In the meantime, we can praise God courageously and with all sincerity. Our God is honest, without sin and without any injustice whatsoever. He is righteous and straightforward. How fortunate we are that the all-powerful Creator-God also happens to be fair, loving, holy, and compassionate.

When you lack courage, meditate on this passage and on who God is. He is the Rock.

But their scribes and the Pharisees murmured against His disciples, saying, "Why do You eat and drink with tax collectors and sinners?" And Jesus answered and said to them, "Those who are well do not need a physician, but those who are sick. I have not come to call the righteous, but sinners, to repentance."
—LUKE 5:30–32

Luke was a medical doctor, and he was a wise and godly man. Jesus was called the Great Physician, but unlike Luke, He never attended medical school. He didn't need to. He created all the scientific, medical and physiological rules of the universe we are still discovering today.

Luke was probably delighted when the Holy Spirit inspired him to record Jesus' words in this passage.

His message, simply put, was this: those who are physically sick need a physician, and those who are spiritually sick need to repent, change the direction of their lives, and trust Jesus Christ as Lord and Savior.

If you have a brain tumor, request prayer, but go see the most qualified neurosurgeon you can find. If you have an emotional disorder, request prayer, but find the best Christian psychiatrist you can. If you have a spiritual problem, request prayer, then seek wise counsel from your pastor, a godly friend, a Christian therapist, or whoever can assist you in applying the truth of God's Word to your life.

There are extremists who say we don't need medical doctors or psychiatrists, and those at the other extreme who say there is no such thing as a spiritual problem—The Bible has a balanced answer.

> "... Now, O LORD my God, You have made Your
> servant king instead of my father David, but I am a
> little child; I do not know how to go out or come
> in. ... Therefore give to Your servant an
> understanding heart to judge Your people, that I
> may discern between good and evil. For who is
> able to judge this great people of Yours?" And the
> speech pleased the LORD, that Solomon had asked
> this thing.
> —1 KINGS 3:7, 9–10

Solomon was given the opportunity of a lifetime. "Ask!" God said to him. "What shall I give you?"

Such a proposition could be a dangerous thing in the hands of a greedy or selfish person. But God knew what He was doing. Solomon could have requested great power or riches, but he asked instead for the gift of wisdom. He knew he would need it to rule God's people well.

Solomon's request pleased the Lord and He made Solomon wiser than any human being who ever lived. We can benefit from his great wisdom when we read his writings in Proverbs and Ecclesiastes. He wrote about some of his own mistakes and about the meaninglessness of life apart from God. Solomon discovered the richness of godly wisdom. It teaches us to love and be loved, enables us to help others, and relieves much of life's pain. How meaningful life can be if we live to serve God.

We need wisdom to guide our lives, our families and our careers. We can please God as Solomon did, by praying for wisdom. God will be delighted to give it to us.

"O Jerusalem, Jerusalem, the one who kills the prophets and stones those who are sent to her! How often I wanted to gather your children together, as a hen gathers her chicks under her wings, but you were not willing!"
                                              —MATT. 23:37

We've all known someone we might jokingly describe as being "protective as a mother hen." It's not often a compliment, and yet Jesus used this image in reference to Himself with good reason. As any farmer can tell you, mother hens are devoted to caring for their chicks. During a hailstorm, a mother hen will call her babies until they scramble to hide under her wings. Covering the chicks with her wings, she will stay put, even if she dies in the fury of the storm.

Jesus knew what He was doing when He compared Himself to a mother hen. He loves us. He created us in His own psychological and spiritual image, to be sons and daughters of the Heavenly Father. And for some unknown reason, Jesus has always had a special place in His heart for Jews. He chose to be born to a young Jewish girl, and He calls the Jews His chosen people.

Jesus suffered tremendous grief when the people so close to His heart refused to believe He was the Messiah. He still longs for unbelieving hearts to believe.

Like a mother hen, Jesus calls His beloved "chicks" to hide under His Almighty wings by trusting Him. Will we come when He calls?

We have a humble, loving, compassionate Lord who feels our pain even more deeply than we do. Listen for His voice in the storms of your life. Let Him cover you with His wings.

> *"If My people who are called by My name will humble themselves, and pray and seek My face, and turn from their wicked ways, then I will hear from heaven, and will forgive their sin and heal their land."*
>
> —2 CHRON. 7:14

God's love for you is unconditional—you cannot do a thing that would make Him quit loving you. But God's peace and blessings may seem at times to elude you. Have you wondered why?

God loves to bless His children, but He also wants us to grow, and to obey Him. Sometimes He waits for us to ask, because He knows we need to be dependent on Him. Sometimes He gives us blessings we haven't asked for, to demonstrate His grace.

Sometimes He deliberately withholds His blessing. If we aren't treating our mate with respect, if we are involved in willful sin, if we ask with selfish rather than loving motives, He will not bless us. In that sense, God's peace and blessings are conditional.

In order for God to answer our requests we must first be true believers. Secondly, we must have a degree of humility. We must ask what *He* wants for our lives and not ask out of selfish motives. Finally, we must repent and turn from any behavior patterns that hurt ourselves or others. If we do these things, God will answer our prayers, forgive our sins, and ultimately heal our nation.

Choose to trust Christ right now. Humble yourself before Him and pray for His will to be done in your life. God hears you, and He will answer.

> *"Whoever humbles himself as this little child is the greatest in the kingdom of heaven."*
> —MATT. 18:4

Imagine an arrogant person driving down a busy highway. What do you see? An impatient driver with unrealistic expectations? An aggressive driver who thinks he or she owns the road? Is this a picture of serenity? Absolutely not. Serenity requires humility, which is the opposite of arrogance.

A prideful heart can damage others. Arrogant parents do not enjoy fellowship with their children. They are too busy pursuing significance with other adults. They get angry at normal, childish mistakes, and are so concerned about appearances that they demand perfection from their kids. Rarely do they weep with their children when they are sad, or rejoice when they are happy. Often they ignore them, and frequently they abuse them, verbally, physically, or sexually.

Unfortunately, many adult children of abuse are not serene, even though they are humble. They have repressed their anger, and have turned it toward themselves. They believe the lie that they were not good enough to deserve their parents' approval, and it continues to haunt them. In reality the rejection they experienced had nothing to do with them and everything to do with the sinful pride of their parents.

Jesus valued children. Jesus stopped, hugged the children, and put them on His lap. He wants us to humble ourselves like little children, so He can place us on His lap and give us love and serenity.

So she said to them, "Do not call me Naomi; call me Mara, for the Almighty has dealt very bitterly with me.
—RUTH 1:20–21

About 1200 B.C., when the judges ruled Israel, there was a famine in the land. Elimelech and his wife Naomi traveled to Moab to find food, but Elimelech died there, and Naomi remained in Moab with her two sons, who married Ruth and Orpah, women of Moab. They lived near each other for a decade, then both sons died and Naomi was left alone with her daughters-in-law.

Naomi encouraged both daughters-in-law to re-marry in Moab while she returned to her hometown of Bethlehem. Orpah accepted the freedom, but Ruth begged Naomi to allow her to travel with her to Bethle-hem because she loved Naomi and wanted to worship her God.

Naomi was bitter against God for taking away her husband and her children. Perhaps she thought God had made a mistake and her own usefulness was over. She had lost a lot, and she must have been depressed. Yet in the midst of her grief, God gave Naomi a loyal and loving daughter. God had not forgotten Naomi, and He had not made a mistake. He lovingly provided for her needs when her life seemed hopeless, and Ruth became the progenitor of both King David and Jesus Christ.

Are you bitter toward God because you don't understand His plan for your life? Don't stay there. God has better plans for you!

> *And the witnesses laid down their clothes at the feet*
> *of a young man named Saul. And they stoned*
> *Stephen as he was calling on God and saying,*
> *"Lord Jesus, receive my spirit." Then he knelt down*
> *and cried out with a loud voice, "Lord, do not*
> *charge them with this sin."* —ACTS 7:58–60

Stephen was elected to be a deacon in the early post-resurrection church. His job was to take care of widows. But the Holy Spirit led Stephen the deacon to preach one of the most courageous (and shortest) sermons you will ever read or hear. Read it all in Acts 7.

When he concluded the sermon, the listeners were "cut to the heart" and gnashed their teeth with guilt and rage (verse 54). They stoned him to death as Stephen continued to pray for God to forgive and save them. He must have been confident of Christ's resurrection, to give up his life like that!

What is interesting also is that the leader of those who stoned Stephen to death was a Jewish intellectual named Saul, who was later miraculously converted, and wrote a majority of the New Testament books. Stephen's dying prayer request was answered when Saul became the Apostle Paul.

Don't dedicate your life totally to Christ unless and until you are ready to count the cost. And if you had untrustworthy parents, it will be especially difficult to make that kind of commitment. But with God's grace you can do it.

Jesus promises to bless us if we will courageously have love and faith like Stephen.

> *"You shall not hate your brother in your heart. You shall surely rebuke your neighbor, and not bear sin because of him. You shall not take vengeance, nor bear any grudge against the children of your people, but you shall love your neighbor as yourself: I am the Lord."*
>
> —LEV. 19:17–18

We could eliminate the vast majority of clinical depressions and much of the unnecessary pain we suffer if we followed God's simple rules found in these two verses. When your parent, mate, child, boss, employee, pastor, friend, sweetheart, or neighbor offends you:

- Decide, as hard as it may be, not to hate the person who caused your anger.

- Be sure to confront him or her. Do this tactfully, respectfully and lovingly—but do it! This will make it easier for you to forgive the offender, regardless of whether he or she apologizes.

- Don't get vengeance. That's God's job.

- Don't hold grudges. You must forgive to have freedom from being codependent on whoever hurt or abused you. Give up all grudges to the Lord.

- The offender should face the consequences of his or her behavior, but when all is said and done, love the person who hurt or abused you.

Lord, make me aware of hatred I hold in my heart. Help me to truly love and forgive the people who have hurt or angered me.

*"And why do you look at the speck in your
brother's eye, but do not consider the plank in your
own eye? Or how can you say to your brother, "Let
me remove the speck out of your eye"; and look, a
plank is in your own eye?*   —MATT. 7:3–4

Defense mechanisms are the ways we lie to ourselves
without even knowing that we are doing so. They can
cause great emotional pain, and it is important that we
understand them. There are examples and explana-
tions of all forty defense mechanisms in the Scriptures.

One of the most commonly used defense mechanisms is *projection*. When you put your hand on an
overhead projector, you see a huge hand on the
screen, but of course the hand is really on the projector. In the same way, if you have lots of rage (from being abused, for example) in your unconscious, then you
will *project* it. You will see rage in someone else, but it
will be blocked from your self-awareness if it is too
painful for you to face the truth.

The unconscious anger you have toward yourself for
your "badness" will be projected to someone who reminds you of yourself, and it will be very difficult for
you to accept and love that person. A father tends to
project on his oldest son and a mother on her oldest
daughter. Most teenagers project their own faults onto
their parents. Is it any wonder unconditional love and
acceptance take so much work in families?

*Is there someone who greatly irritates me? Someone I find almost
impossible to love? Maybe it's time to take a hard look at myself. Am I
projecting painful or ugly things inside me onto him or her?*

> *Therefore David blessed the LORD before all*
> *the congregation; and David said:*
> *"Blessed are You, LORD God of Israel,*
> *our Father, forever and ever.*
> *Yours, O LORD, is the greatness,*
> *The power and the glory,*
> *The victory and the majesty; for all that is*
> *in heaven and in earth is Yours; Yours is*
> *the kingdom, O LORD, and You are*
> *exalted as head over all.*
> *Both riches and honor come from You,*
> *And You reign over all.*
> —1 CHRON. 29:10–12

David died at a ripe old age, full of riches and honor. He was able to joyfully oversee his son Solomon's coronation. Today's passage is part of David's final public prayer of thanksgiving before his death. What can we learn about the nature of God from this prayer?

God enjoys it when we bless Him, just as He enjoys blessing us. He will be the Father of true believers forever in heaven. He is awesome, powerful, glorious, and majestic. He is and will always be victorious. Everything in heaven and earth are His. Riches and honor come from God the Father to true believers. This is no guarantee that all devout believers will be financially successful, or that the wicked will not prosper.

God is in ultimate authority, even though He allows a lot of things to happen that He hates. Someday He will eliminate all evil.

At the end of a long and eventful life, David knew his God well. May we be able to say the same!

*Immediately Jesus made His disciples get into the
boat and go before Him to the other side, while He
sent the multitudes away. And when He had sent
the multitudes away, He went up on a mountain by
Himself to pray.* —MATT. 14:22–23

The life of Jesus is interesting to study. Not only are
His teachings of vital importance, but also His lifestyle
and His emotions. It is interesting to observe His attitudes toward children (especially orphans), widows,
evil people, religious leaders, the physically handicapped, the humble, the proud, the rich, and the poor.

Jesus lived a balanced lifestyle. He was not a workaholic. Even though He was God and man, His body
required sleep every night. He worked with His
earthly father, Joseph, as a carpenter and studied until
He was nearly thirty years old, then began His ministry.

Out of His love and compassion, He healed thousands of blind, handicapped, diseased, and demon-
possessed people, and yet a small percentage of His
typical ministry day was spent ministering to the
masses. He invested a larger portion of time with His
twelve disciples and in prayer to His Father.

On this occasion, Jesus sent His disciples on a trip in
a boat, sent the crowds away, and got alone on a mountaintop to pray.

*Like Jesus, we need to spend time each day listening to the Father by
meditating on God's Word and talking with Him. We need our own
quiet mountaintop or closet to get alone daily to share our feelings
with the Father and seek His will.*

> *The LORD is my shepherd;*
> *I shall not want.*
> *He makes me to lie down in green pastures;*
> *He leads me beside the still waters.*
> *He restores my soul;*
> *He leads me in the paths of righteousness*
> *For His name's sake.*   —PS. 23:1–3

The twenty-third psalm could easily be called "The Serenity Psalm." Let's look at the first three verses.

The Lord is my shepherd. King David wrote this psalm, and after years of tending sheep as a boy, he observed that the Father's relationship to us is much like a loving, caring shepherd.

I shall not want. The Hebrew word translated *want* really means "lack." We will not lack anything physically, emotionally, or spiritually that we truly need. God will provide.

He makes me to lie down in green pastures; He leads me beside the still waters. God nourishes us with His Word, the Bible. Without it, we starve spiritually and our behavior and emotions show it.

He restores my soul. Sanctification, restoration is a slow, steady process.

He leads me in the paths of righteousness for His name's sake. We hardly ever notice when He does it. But He is intimately involved in every second of our lives, making us like Christ.

If we are God's sheep, we follow our Shepherd. He provides serenity and renewal to us if we will drink of the peaceful waters.

"These things I have spoken to you, that in Me you may have peace. In the world you will have tribulation; but be of good cheer, I have overcome the world."
                                                    —JOHN 16:33

If someone tells you that spending all your money on his ministry will bring you certain financial prosperity, assume that he is either a con-man or extremely ignorant of Scripture. If someone promises you freedom from diseases, death or taxes, don't believe him. If someone promises you a mate and children who will never suffer any major failures, please do not believe him. Lots of people never trust Christ as Savior because they hear so many foolish con-men in the media making ridiculous claims for Christianity that Jesus never made, so the unsaved assume all of Christianity is that foolish and mythological.

Jesus, in John 16:33, promises His followers two things: *peace* and *tribulation*. These seem like contradictory terms, but they are not. He promises *peace during tribulation*. He *promises* us we *will* have *tribulation* in this world. But since Jesus has overcome the world, He offers us peace and help during our tribulations and an eventual future, in eternity, free of tribulation.

Thwarted expectations arouse bitterness that leads to depression, so don't expect heaven on earth in this life. For now, be thankful for God's peace during our current problems.

Keep your heart with all diligence,
For out of it spring the issues of life.
—PROV. 4:23

How much unnecessary effort and worry do we put into trying to change things that are out of our control? We cannot change other people. We can only change ourselves. As you read this you may be feeling as if your life is out of control. Solomon clearly states that we have to exercise self-control in four ways.

We are to control our heart with all diligence. The heart is more than our mind or emotions; it encompasses our values. We are in control of our character.

We are also to be in control of our communication. Not only are we in charge of what we say, we are in control of how we say it. Each of us would be healthier if we would contemplate before we communicate.

We are also in control of what we concentrate on. Do we see the good in people, the opportunity in challenges, and the possibilities, even in pain? Do we look at our world with eyes of faith, or do we view ourselves as victims of fate? Do we focus on things that are true, noble, wise, pure, lovely, of good report and praiseworthy, or are we critical, condemning, and cranky? The choice is ours.

The last thing we can control, according to this passage, is our conduct. We must be responsible for how we act.

If we focus on the four areas over which we do have control, we will be so busy there won't be any time or energy left to try to change anyone else.

"But take heed to yourselves, lest your hearts be weighed down with carousing, drunkenness, and cares of this life, and that Day come on you unexpectedly. "For it will come as a snare on all those who dwell on the face of the whole earth. "Watch therefore, and pray always that you may be counted worthy to escape all these things that will come to pass, and to stand before the Son of Man."
—LUKE 21:34–36

Jesus had just explained to His disciples that Solomon's temple would soon be destroyed (which Titus and the Roman legions accomplished in 70 A.D.). Jesus then told about the great earthquakes, famines, and catastrophes that will take place during the Great Tribulation (the 3½ year period prior to the Lord's return to set up the 1000 year Kingdom). We won't be here during the Great Tribulation, because the Lord will rapture us out of here some time before the beginning of the 7 year Tribulation period (see 1 Thessalonians 4:16–18), the last half of which is called the *Great* Tribulation.

Verses 34–36 could refer to non-believers who are living wild lives at the time of the rapture and are left to face the tribulation, or they could also apply to worldly people *during* the Tribulation period here on earth. Many passages have dual meanings. Regardless, Christ's future predictions should motivate us to live sober, meaningful lives while we wait for His return.

Lord, please help me to change my cravings for worldly pleasures and status into a desire to be found loving and serving when Your great day comes.

And he prayed that he might die, and said, "It is enough! Now, LORD, take my life, for I am no better than my fathers!"
—1 KINGS 19:4

Around 900 B.C. there lived a very powerful and courageous prophet named Elijah. God brought about many miracles through Elijah, including raising a boy from the dead. In a showdown with the false prophets of Baal, Elijah called down fire on the sacrifice to God in front of wicked King Ahab. Then he killed the prophets of Baal.

Amazingly, when King Ahab's wife, the notorious Jezebel, became furious at Elijah and threatened his life, he ran from her and became suicidal with fear.

God had a great treatment plan for Elijah's depression. He made him get plenty of sleep and fed him nourishing food. He corrected Elijah's distorted perspective, confronted his self-pity, and reassured him. What wisdom can we gain from this true story?

God can use us powerfully, despite our human frailties, doubts, fears, and misconceptions. God can lift us out of depression. We aren't alone. There are many others who faithfully serve God and also suffer discouragement.

Sometimes we have great victories over enormous obstacles, then fail miserably at a small temptation. When we do fail, we need to eat right, get some sleep, tell it to Jesus, forgive ourselves, and go on.

Remind me of Your constant love for me, and get me back on my feet, just as You did for Elijah.

*"Surely you are one of them; for you are a
Galilean, and your speech shows it." But [Peter]
began to curse and swear, "I do not know this Man
of whom you speak!"* —MARK 14:70–71

Peter was extroverted, emotional, enthusiastic, impulsive, courageous, and very dedicated to Christ. As Judas betrayed Jesus, Peter courageously drew his sword and impulsively slashed at the men who had come to arrest his Lord.

It's hard to imagine what Peter must have been feeling that night. Embarrassment for his rash action? Confusion at Christ's refusal to defend Himself? Frustration and anger at his own inability to stop the men from arresting Jesus?

As the possibility grew that he might be exposed as a disciple of this outlaw, Peter gave in to his fear and denied the man he loved so dearly. And then perhaps the worst emotion of all overcame him: shame. He, too, had betrayed Jesus.

Fortunately for Peter and for us, the story did not end there. God not only forgave Peter, He healed his shame. God had chosen Peter to be one of His greatest leaders of all time. We have a Messiah who knows all of our frailties and yet shed His blood to make those of us who trust Him His eternal friends.

Are you carrying the shame of something you have done, convinced that it is too "bad" to be forgiven? Accept Christ's forgiveness, and allow Him to free you from the burden of shame.

> *Give ear to my words, O Lord, consider*
> *my meditation.*
> *Give heed to the voice of my cry.*
> —PS. 5:1

This psalm was written by our good friend King David at a time when he was being threatened by his enemies. We can safely assume his days were full and his mind was occupied by many thoughts, and yet he began his mornings in prayer. He may have been king of the most powerful nation of his time, but he kneeled to worship the King of kings.

How do you begin *your* day? How easy it is to go all day without even thinking about God, then hastily mumble a prayer before falling asleep at night. If this sounds familiar to you, we offer this challenge: pray as soon as you wake up. Dedicate that day to three purposes: 1. to become more Christlike in your gradual sanctification process; 2. to serve God in your own way that day by being a good mate, a good parent, a good friend, a good worker, a good example all day long (even in your driving habits); 3. to stay out of trouble that day. We are sinful by nature, but by God's grace we can avoid deliberate, willful sins. Our motives will always be mixed, but that cannot stop us from trying to do good, and serving Him as best we can.

Like David, may each of us make a lifelong personal commitment to pray a dedication prayer every day, first thing in the morning, perhaps even before getting out of bed.

"And you, child, will be called the prophet of the
Highest;
For you will go before the face of the Lord to
prepare His ways, . . .
To give light to those who sit in darkness and the
shadow of death,
To guide our feet into the way of peace."
—LUKE 1:76, 79

John was a little eccentric. He spent quite a bit of time alone in the desert. He wore a camel skin robe and ate locusts and wild honey. But his God-given purpose included restoring the hearts of fathers to their children and children to their fathers. It included bluntly confronting the amazed crowds with the truth about their sins. It included calling for repentance, with baptism by immersion in water to signify the coming Messiah's burial and resurrection. Those being baptized so signified that they were dying to their old way of life and being resurrected to living a new life of godliness.

John's purpose also included giving "light" or *insight into the truth* to "those who sit in darkness and the shadow of death." What does this mean? Most of our thoughts are not in our conscious awareness. Instead, as the prophet Jeremiah said, our minds, emotions and wills (our "hearts") are amazingly deceitful and desperately wicked. We truly "sit in darkness and the shadow of death."

The good news is that the light of God's truth can "guide our feet into the way of peace."

Lord, please shine Your light into my life and expose the darkness in my heart. Help me to walk in Your peace.

> *"Shall we indeed accept good from God, and shall
> we not accept adversity?"* In all this Job did not sin
> with his lips.
>
> —JOB 2:10b

Job was a godly man. He helped the poor and needy. He was a good husband and father. He was good to his friends. He knew God's Word backwards and forwards. He lived as he said he believed, and he willingly taught others.

Satan approached God with a vengeful scheme. Job, he claimed, was only grateful to God because he was being blessed. If God allowed him to suffer, the truth would come out. Job would turn away from God.

God decided to allow Job, whom He loved, to suffer for a time. He knew that Satan would be proven wrong, and that Job would not curse Him because of the suffering. Job's children were all killed, his entire fortune was lost, and Satan gave him a very painful skin disease.

By God's grace, Job was able to hold on to his faith during all these catastrophes. He knew his Lord, and was able to sincerely say, "Shall we indeed accept good from God, and shall we not accept adversity?"

God gives and God takes away, and He has loving reasons we don't always understand for doing so. In the painful times God gives us the grace to hold on. We don't have to turn away from Him. We can cling to the Father we know and trust.

And so we went toward Rome. And from there, when the brethren heard about us, they came to meet us as far as Appii Forum and Three Inns. When Paul saw them, he thanked God and took courage. —ACTS 28:14–15

Paul was on his way to Rome as a prisoner. It was a long voyage and the seas had been rough, and Paul knew that more persecution was waiting at his destination. But when the wind blew them to Puteoli, Paul found some fellow believers at this Italian seaport 152 miles south of Rome. They excitedly invited him to stay with them for seven days.

When the believers in Rome heard that Paul and his companions were on their way to Rome, they eagerly traveled to the nearest ports to greet them. The noun *apantesin* used here for "to meet" is used in Greek literature to describe the greeting of an important visiting official.

When Paul saw these pockets of believers he had never before met, "he thanked God and took courage." I can identify with Paul in that regard. In order to complete my training as a psychiatrist, my family and I had to move to various states. Everywhere we moved, we would look for a church that upheld the things we believed in, such as the inerrancy of Scripture. In each place we found a loving, committed group of evangelical believers who welcomed us to worship with them. How exciting to be part of an immense family!

What fun it is to find a pocket of believers and share the excitement of a common cause.

> *If you walk in My statutes and keep My*
> *commandments, and perform them,*
> *then I will give you rain in its season, the land*
> *shall yield its produce, and the trees of the*
> *field shall yield their fruit.* —LEV. 26:3–4

Our God is a God of love, but He is also a God of justice. He has established a simple code of right and wrong by which He deals with us spiritually, emotionally, mentally, and physically. When we follow His word, and live in obedience, we will flourish. Our labor will be worthwhile and our needs will be met.

But in order to keep God's commandments, we must know what they are. We must study God's Word and begin applying it to our everyday lives.

If we continue to live in willful sin, however, we cause pain to ourselves and to others, and we forfeit God's blessing and protection. How good it is to know that God's offer still stands. Regardless of our past or present disobedience, He is willing to meet us where we are, and repeat His promise: "If you walk in My statutes. . . ."

If we read on in Chapter 26, we find another promise from God. Those who live by God's principles will have peace, and God will walk among them.

As our Creator, God is the ultimate authority on our spirits, minds, emotions, and bodies. As our Father, He lovingly desires the very best for us. And as our Lord, He deserves our obedience and worship.

*"Therefore whoever hears these sayings of Mine,
and does them, I will liken him to a wise man who
built his house on the rock: and the rain descended,
the floods came, and the winds blew and beat on
that house; and it did not fall, for it was founded
on the rock.*
                                        —MATT. 7:24–25

Children attending Sunday school learn a song about the wise man building his house upon a rock, the foolish man building his house on the sand, and the rains coming tumbling down. The song is based on this passage, and has some very important principles for our lives.

Most people build their houses on sand. In other words, they build their whole lives and futures on things that in time will collapse. Some trust their bank accounts. Their entire futures are based on their accumulated fortunes. But even banks can go bankrupt.

Some base their happiness on an exciting new romance. They are swept off their feet and hastily give up their mates and children and self-respect. When the excitement fades they are left with nothing.

Some try to control everyone and everything they possibly can. Control is everything until life reminds them of how little control they really have over things, including their own lives and health. *God* is in control, and should be.

Building our house on a rock means building our plans and hopes on the person Jesus Christ, our Rock and our Redeemer.

If your life is built on the Rock, you will not be destroyed.

For He performs what is appointed for me,
And many such things are with Him.
Therefore I am terrified at His presence;
When I consider this, I am afraid of Him.
　　　　　　　　　　　—JOB 23:14–15

After losing his children, his fortune, and developing a wasting, painful skin disease, Job was still able to say, "Shall we indeed accept good from God, and shall we not accept adversity?"

And yet Job was not without emotion. He grieved the losses and was gravely disappointed. Although he trusted God, he didn't understand the reason for his suffering. He knew he was not being punished by God, and at the same time, he felt God had turned against him, and it filled his heart with fear. Job knew God would choose to do as He wished. No one dictates God's actions. We cannot change God. He is the way He is—the same yesterday, today and forever.

We also have limited control, because God carries out whatever He appoints for our lives, and there are many things that He does appoint for our lives. Job admitted that he was terrified at God's presence. He felt weak of heart. And yet, through it all, Job trusted God. We too can trust God. He is all-powerful, and yet He loves us.

_____

There are times, Lord, that I fear You because of what I am afraid You will do. Teach me the difference between a healthy fear and fear that says I'm not trusting You.

*"Watch and pray, lest you enter into temptation.
The spirit indeed is willing, but the flesh is weak."*
—MATT. 26:41

Jesus had mixed feelings just prior to His crucifixion. As God, He wanted to die for us to pay for our sins. Before we even existed, He loved us and wanted to fellowship with us forever. But He was also fully human, and He feared and dreaded separation from the Father even though He knew it would only be temporary. Jesus was full of anguish and fear as He prayed in the garden that night.

This is why Jesus understands our struggles so well. He realizes we want to obey God and do right. But at the same time, we want the pleasures of sin and can easily fall into sin. God knows that our spirit is willing to live a life of obedience but the "flesh" is weak.

For proper mental health we must accept our "badness." But this does not mean that we condone willful sin. It is difficult to find the balance. It's not right to excuse our sins and keep on sinning, but neither is it right to beat our heads against the wall in self-condemnation for not being perfect. We need to accept our "badness" but watch out for it and pray for God's help in the gradual sanctification of our lives.

Lord, I confess my sin to You and know I am forgiven. Help me to leave the past behind.

> *Yea, though I walk through the valley of*
>   *the shadow of death,*
> *I will fear no evil;*
> *For You are with me;*
> *Your rod and Your staff, they comfort me.*
> *You prepare a table before me in the*
>   *presence of my enemies;*
> *You anoint my head with oil;*
> *My cup runs over.*
> *Surely goodness and mercy shall follow me*
> *All the days of my life;*
> *And I will dwell in the house of the LORD*
> *Forever.*
>   —PS. 23:4–6

This psalm shows the basis of serenity for the believer: trust in God.

Even on the verge of death, David was not afraid that God would abandon him. In fact, David trusted God to remain with him.

Anointing someone's head with oil was an ancient tradition to signify honor and blessing. Our cups run over with abundant, undeserved blessings.

The Hebrew word for "goodness" in verse 6 is *hesed*, implying "good loyal love." God's good loyal love for us results in blessings and continued mercy and forgiveness throughout all the days of our lives.

―――――――――――――

I do not need to fear the shadowing trials in my life, or even death, because the Lord is with me.

*. . . that no one should be shaken by these
afflictions; for you yourselves know that we are
appointed to this.*　　　　—1 THESS. 3:3

Life isn't fair, but God is good! Too many of us still hang on to the notion that life should be rosy and we shouldn't have to face any difficulties. God never promised you a rose garden. The rose garden, if it is there, certainly has many thorns. Difficulties and afflictions are part of life.

Paul's message in these verses is a reminder that we should expect and accept troubles and tribulation.

Tina and Paul came into therapy six months after their wedding. It was apparent that they were disillusioned and depressed. They had entered marriage walking on cloud nine. Everything seemed to be going their way. Both of them had good jobs, and they had big dreams for their lives. They had excitedly purchased a new home and two new cars. Three months later, Paul was laid off because of cutbacks in the aerospace industry. A month after that, Tina discovered a small lump in her breast.

They were on the brink of losing their house and cars. They said, "Life isn't fair!"

Life will have its ups and downs. We need to expect there will be trials. Life will not always be rosy. For Paul and Tina, working through the tough times together built greater loyalty and intimacy in their marriage. It was worth the growing pains.

*God promises to be with me through my afflictions and tribulations.
Facing them will deepen my faith and develop my character.*

> *Whoever has no rule over his own spirit*
> *Is like a city broken down, without walls.*
> —PROV. 25:28

One of the tasks of healthy maturing involves setting appropriate boundaries. The codependent typically experiences a serious lack in the ability to set appropriate boundaries. Boundaries allow a person to set limits so that they do not feel walked on. Boundaries allow an individual to choose what to do or not do.

Barb struggled with boundaries. She could not choose what she wanted to do apart from what others wanted her to do. She couldn't say no. She felt powerless and resented the control others had over her.

If someone is manipulating or controlling you and you do not take control of yourself and your decisions, then you are like a city with broken-down walls. Such a city would be easy prey for another nation to besiege and control. Similarly, if you do not set boundaries, you can be easily taken over by others. When that begins to happen, there is the tendency to lose control of your emotions and develop irrational thinking. Often there is the likelihood of distorting reality. Proverbs 28:1 speaks of one who flees "when no one pursues." Fleeing or running away can happen by escaping with all kinds of addictive behaviors such as alcohol, drugs, sex, or workaholism. But we do not need to run away. The righteous can be courageous and bold as a lion.

God gives us the courage to set boundaries in order to help us see our limits, and to help us protect ourselves from others.

For the weapons of our warfare are not carnal but mighty in God for pulling down strongholds, casting down arguments and every high thing that exalts itself against the knowledge of God, bringing every thought into captivity to the obedience of Christ.
—2 COR. 10:4–5

Research into human behavior has revealed that it usually takes about 21 days to establish a habit. Beyond that point, the habit or thinking process becomes even more entrenched as it is further practiced and repeated. Often these behaviors seem unchangeable. They feel permanent.

This passage refers to them as "strongholds." Historically, a stronghold was a well established city that could withstand any outside forces that might attempt to enter and overtake it.

In God, we have weapons that can be used to help us break the strongholds in our lives.

What behavior or thought has put down a root in your life? What habit has taken up permanent residence in you? What habit has become part of you?

Since a new habit can be set in 21 days of practice, you can choose to behave differently. Yes, it will take effort, but you can change. God's weapons to assist you in change are His Word, His people and prayer. The old pattern can be broken. The stronghold can be torn down. You can establish a new habit.

What habit has become a stronghold in my life? Will I invest 21 days of concentrated effort with God's help to make the change?

Happy is the man who finds wisdom,
And the man who gains understanding;
For her proceeds are better than the
  profits of silver,
And her gain than fine gold.
—PROV. 3:13–14

If someone offered you wisdom or wealth, which would you choose? The billionaire, John D. Rockefeller, was once asked by a reporter how much money it would take to make him happy. Rockefeller scratched his chin, thought for a moment, and then replied, "Just a little bit more." John D. eventually committed his life to God and donated great fortunes to charity.

Is your search for significance resulting in an insatiable appetite for sexual affairs, power, money or prestige? Do you constantly desire "just a little bit more?"

Wisdom alone satisfies, and the fear of the Lord is the beginning of wisdom. As we comprehend the depth of God's love for us, we are filled with awe. As we grasp the incredible truth of grace we are filled with wonder; and as we come to understand God's majesty and power, we are filled with humility.

Our ultimate sense of well-being can come only from a personal relationship with God through Jesus Christ. The wisdom that comes as a result of building our life on this foundation brings genuine happiness. The personal application of that wisdom is the best way to obtain joy, peace, and emotional maturity.

Which would you rather have: wisdom or wealth?

The wisdom that is a result of a personal relationship with Jesus Christ leaves me with a quality of life that money can't buy.

All Scripture is given by inspiration of God, and is profitable for doctrine, for reproof, for correction, for instruction in righteousness. . . .

—2 TIM. 3:16

One vital characteristic of a leader is that he or she be an effective communicator. All kinds of problems can develop in a company, a community, a family, or a marriage when communication breaks down. The effective leader is concerned about what is communicated and how it is communicated. He or she wants the communication to be clear and accurate so that it can achieve its intended purpose.

God, as our leader, did not let the writing of His Word just happen. He was deeply involved in the process, guiding the prophets and apostles as they delivered a permanent, written account.

God did not want there to be a misunderstanding or distortion of the truth. He did not want us to get off track.

The fact that God was so involved in influencing the writers and directing their writing can help us have confidence in what was recorded. The result is that God's Word can make a greater impact in our lives. It can have a more influencing power. We can confidently rely on it for direction, instruction and for correction of our life and lifestyle.

Thank You, Lord, that I can trust the accuracy, reliability and truth of Your written Word. I may not always understand it completely, but since I know You are true and You inspired its writing, I can follow it with a new confidence.

Hear my cry, O God;
Attend to my prayer.
—PS. 61:1–2

Several months ago we were enjoying a cookout on the beach in California. This particular section of beach had a number of tidepools surrounded by kelp beds. Because of this, it is a favorite spot for fishing. During the low tide, we noticed a man had proceeded out to a rock a great distance from shore from which he could fish. Several hours later the tide had risen and the wave swells picked up. We saw the man swept from his fishing perch into the surrounding waters. We tried to yell to him to swim to his left, to a large rock that is never submerged. The man was not a good swimmer and couldn't hear us above the roar of the waves. He bobbed and went under. We sensed that he was feeling overwhelmed. Then he spotted the huge rock and dog-paddled to it. We breathed a sigh of relief as he clutched the rock and climbed up out of danger.

The psalmist gives us a similar picture as he describes feeling overwhelmed by the storms of life. In his panic, he cries out to God and asks Him to lead him to a place of safety.

Visualize God providing a way out of the overwhelming, stormy waters of your life. Our prayer to God is not that He do it all, but that He lift us out of our overwhelming problems.

Sometimes the storm doesn't subside, but God directs us to look to Him. He is the rock that lifts us above our stormy, turbulent circumstances.

Do not let your beauty be that outward adorning of arranging the hair, of wearing gold, or of putting on fine apparel; but let it be the hidden person of the heart, with the incorruptible ornament of a gentle and quiet spirit, which is very precious in the sight of God. —1 PETER 3:3-4

I know an incredible elderly woman. Her hands are gnarled because of arthritis. She doesn't stand as tall and straight as she once did. A walker makes it possible for her to shuffle from place to place. Not very attractive, right? Wrong! When she smiles, the entire room lights up. She laughs easily, her eyes sparkle, and gentleness seems to emanate from her.

Our society prizes costly clothes and fine jewelry as necessary ingredients of beauty. Peter challenged women to work just as hard at developing their inner beauty: the beauty found in a gentle and quiet spirit. Not only does God prize these beautiful attributes, so do husbands and children.

A woman with a gentle and quiet spirit is not passive and boring. She is gentle because she feels loved and respected by God Himself. This woman has felt God's unconditional acceptance. She is at peace with herself. This is the source of genuine beauty.

When a woman with this core of inner beauty, inner peace and inner strength puts on a lovely dress or nice jewelry, watch out! She will radiate beauty. But you will notice *her* before you notice what she is wearing.

Today, Lord, help me to be more concerned with my inner beauty than with how I look. Help me to grow more and more like You.

For whom the LORD loves He corrects,
Just as a father the son in whom he delights.
—PROV. 3:12

One of the common defense mechanisms used by the person struggling with addictions is denial. It is difficult to even admit there is a problem that needs attention. The initial treatment for such a person often involves an intervention by family members.

The family members are asked to keep a specific account of how the person's dependency has impacted their lives. Practical results of the behavior are then shared with the offender. A child may say, "Daddy, you promised to come to my baseball game, but instead you went to the bar. That hurt me." A wife may say, "You were drinking last Wednesday and forgot it was my birthday."

Confrontation and correction is needed to break through the denial. Loving action on the part of family members is not to pretend that everything is fine, but to honestly communicate the truth.

As our loving father, God is not going to sit idly by and let us continue on in denial. Out of His love, He is going to confront and correct us.

Can we accept His desire to break through our denial system? Solomon challenges us not to despise or detest God's correction. His blasting of our denial system is His display of family love.

Loving is not denying problems, but facing problems of denial.

LORD, You have heard the desire of the humble;
You will prepare their heart;
You will cause Your ear to hear,
To do justice to the fatherless and the
     oppressed.
                               —PS. 10:17–18

Our close friend and neighbor is president of an organization known as Child Help. Child Help is committed to working with children who are orphans or come from broken homes, and have experienced physical or sexual abuse.

These children carry deep emotional wounds. A number of our adult friends have shared with us the pain of growing up without a father. Some of them lost their dad because of death. Other friends we knew lost contact with their dad following a divorce.

These situations undoubtedly leave their mark on the child. In most cases, the child will feel it is unfair and unjust. He or she feels oppressed.

The psalmist reminds us that God has a special place in His heart for the hurting child or the adult who grew up without a father. God says He will be fair to the fatherless. He does not want the fatherless to live under the shadow of a dark cloud. He promises to bring deliverance to those who are oppressed because of what happened to them as a child. Take courage if you happen to be a fatherless child. God is working specially on your behalf.

Thank You, Lord, that You have a heart for the fatherless.

Do not say, "I will recompense evil";
Wait for the LORD, and He will save you.
—PROV. 20:22

We have all heard the slogan, "Don't get mad, get even." Brad was feeling this way when he came into therapy. He had just found out that a close friend had been attempting to break up his relationship with Pam. He and Pam had been friends for over a year, and their friendship was moving toward engagement. Brad muttered, "I can't believe Doug tried to take Pam out! How could he do that?" Brad and I discussed how natural it was for him to be upset and explored his options. Brad finally decided to share the hurt with Doug, but agreed not to let the confrontation get out of control. He decided not to get revenge.

After he talked with Doug, Brad was able to move toward forgiveness. An unforgiving spirit has a way of hurting the person holding the grudge. Corrie Ten Boom put it this way. "To forgive is to set a prisoner free and realize that prisoner is me!" That is so true. If I will not forgive, I become tied up in knots internally. I become paralyzed. I am immobilized. As I come to forgive, I am set free.

God eventually will even the score. I need to let God take care of the situation. He will do it perfectly and fairly.

Do you have a resentment or feeling of revenge that is paralyzing you? Release it and experience new freedom today.

But why do you judge your brother? Or why do you show contempt for your brother? For we shall all stand before the judgment seat of Christ.

—ROM. 14:10

I grew up in a German family with lots of love, but also strict discipline. I didn't look forward to facing my father when I had disobeyed. In school, I certainly didn't like to go to the principal's office.

It's difficult to stand before someone else and admit we have done wrong. We may fear punishment or rejection. We may believe we will never be trusted again, or that what we have done is too awful to be forgiven.

Today's passage tells about the *Judgment Seat of Christ* for believers. We know for sure we will get a variety of rewards. We know there won't be any punishment. But we may very well see all our sins, one last time, in front of everyone.

As a psychiatrist, I have seen the cleansing and healing that comes from confession. In a group therapy session, members often confess painful secrets they have never told, and are loved and accepted by their fellow group members in spite of it all. It is wonderful to see, and it is even more wonderful to experience.

It is comforting to know that the judgment seat of Christ will set the stage for an eternity of humility toward each other and an appreciation of God's grace.

Lord, You see my every action and thought. Help me to focus on my own growth and recovery rather than judging others.

For as the heavens are high above the earth,
So great is His mercy toward those who fear
Him;
As far as the east is from the west,
So far has He removed our transgressions
from us.
—PS. 103:11

God's way of dealing with failure and sin is the same for all people. His Word teaches us that all of us commit sin. This does not surprise God or catch Him off guard.

God wants to remove our sin as far from us as the east is from the west. He does not want us to deny our sin or live in denial. He sees our sin and wants to set us free from its hold on us.

It seems many times we have a hard time letting go of our sin and feelings of worthlessness, even after God has forgiven us.

Many people have come into my office overwhelmed with guilt. These people often shared sins from their past which they had never told anyone else. I don't know how many times I have heard the question, "How can God forgive me for . . . ?"

They have been relieved when we studied and applied this passage together. God loves, pities, and forgives the sinner. He delights in removing your worst sins as far as the east is from the west.

From what sin do you need God to set you free? Remember, God specializes in sin-removal.

*And my God shall supply all your need according
to His riches in glory by Christ Jesus.*
—PHIL. 4:19

During my doctoral training, my wife and I came to claim this verse on almost a daily basis. We had planned to support ourselves during my graduate training. Janet had a teaching job lined up at a Christian university, but at the last minute, her work permit was denied.

Our first feeling was panic, then anger and hurt. But over the next several years we experienced unexpected surprises. It seemed each month we did not know how we would pay our bills and buy food, but God supplied our need. During the last year, we received an anonymous note each month, along with a scripture verse and a crisp $100 bill. We still do not know who sent it.

One time while we had guests staying with us, we awoke to find the carpet covered by water an inch deep. A water pipe in the wall had broken and flooded our house while we slept. I repaired the damage to the pipe and wall myself, and paid our bills that month with the settlement from the insurance.

God will supply our need. Not our wish or our want, but our need. We found this verse to be a practical reality. God has infinite resources, and as we come and ask Him in prayer, He desires to meet our need.

*God's resources are more extensive than our need. Don't be afraid to
ask Him to meet your need today.*

> *By humility and the fear of the Lord*
> *Are riches and honor and life.*
> —PROV. 22:4

We human beings have the tendency to live at extremes. We adopt an "all or nothing" mentality. We feel like an all-capable hot shot or a failure. We fluctuate between being too dependent and too independent.

Unfortunately, humility is thought to be the extreme of feeling like a nobody or a nothing. Being humble does not mean that we are nothing or no good.

Phillip Brooks put it this way: "The way to be humble is not to stoop until you are smaller than yourself, but to stand at your real height against some higher nature; that will show you what the real smallness of your greatness is."

Being humble then is a balanced position. Being humble is standing tall with our shoulders back; but as we do that, having a clear picture of the greatness of our God. Being humble is living as an interdependent person, in contrast to the extremes of dependence or independence.

It is possible to live in this balanced place as we fear the Lord and gain His perspective of us. The result is that we experience richness, a sense of personal honor, and real life.

———————

How do you view yourself? Dependent, independent, or interdependent? Are you living life at the extremes, or have you found a balance?

Rejoice always, pray without ceasing, in everything give thanks.   —1 THESS. 5:16–18

When tough times come and I realize I'm not giving thanks because I feel hurt, abandoned, and neglected, it is because I have begun to compare what I wanted with what I received.

When the comparison bug bites, I have found it better to go with it, rather than to fight it. The only thing I try to change is what I compare my situation with. I attempt to balance the loss by reviewing what I have gained, and to look at my growth in character. When I compare my circumstances to others', who have more, I choose also to look at those who have less.

Joshua isn't able to breathe without the help of a machine. Someone has to be with him twenty-four hours a day to anticipate all of his needs. He can't speak. Reading his lips and watching his expressive eyes are the only ways of understanding what he wants to communicate. He is totally dependent on other people.

When I am hurt and unthankful I think of Joshua, who is thankful for those who love and care for him. Then I take a deep breath and let it out slowly. It becomes natural again to thank the Lord that I depend on Him for every breath I take.

Getting a clearer picture of my dependence on Him is the best answer I've found for an unthankful heart. It helps me move from self-pity to praise.

I can rejoice and be thankful in whatever place I find myself.

But those who wait on the LORD
Shall renew their strength;
They shall mount up with wings like eagles,
They shall run and not be weary,
They shall walk and not faint.

—ISA. 40:31

Life is full of paradoxes. An incest victim would express it in the following manner: ["I was robbed of my power as a child. I did not live in a home where children were considered worthy of having their own opinions or feelings. I was told, 'Don't be angry.' 'Don't be afraid.' 'Shame on you!' Other people stripped me of the power that a healthy child would have learned.

"I spent many of my adult years feeling powerless and depressed. The harder I tried to be a 'good girl' and please others, the more weary I became. I was still stripped of power. I believed that I was not entitled to any, so I didn't even ask for it.

"As I have struggled through the recovery process, I have been learning that God is so much different than my earthly parents. He not only wants to empower me to live, He wants me to soar. His messages are, 'Enjoy each day as a special gift.' 'Jesus paid the price; you are free from shame.'

"It is actually freeing to admit my own powerlessness. It doesn't mean 'shame on me.' It means I can be free to be who I am, and let God be who He is."] You also might feel beaten down by life. God doesn't want for you to merely exist, but rather to soar like an eagle.

With God's strength I can rise above my problems.

*But, speaking the truth in love, may [we] grow up
in all things into Him who is the head—Christ.*
—EPH. 4:15

The Apostle Paul highlights two essential components of successful communication in growing relationships: truth and love.

These two qualities seem to be opposites. Often a person has the ability to be honest, direct, and to the point. That honesty can even be brutal, as he or she lays it on the line and attackingly cuts down an intimate friend or spouse. There are others who seem to be proficient at the opposite end of the spectrum. They try to be "loving," which for them involves not bringing up something they feel might cause a reaction. They live in hope the problem will just go away, or think they should just pray about it and remain silent.

Honesty without love is destructive, but love without honesty is deceitful.

We need to find a balance. This means speaking honestly in love, and loving by being honest. The blend of truth and love is the answer.

This type of communication is authentic and real. Constructive honesty builds up. Destructive honesty tears down. And at the same time, sensitive speakers are needed. Develop the balance of truth *and* love.

Ask yourself if you demonstrate love in your choice of words, tone of voice, and body language. Do you talk in a way that makes people glad they listened? Is your communication characterized by truth?

Keep sound wisdom and discretion;
So they will be life to your soul
And grace to your neck. Then you will
*   walk safely in your way,*
And your foot will not stumble.
*   —PROV. 3:21b–24*

Wisdom and discretion really go hand in hand. As wisdom is applied to everyday life with discernment and discretion, positive results follow.

The first result is long life. Today we are bombarded with all kinds of theories that promise extended life. Eat oat bran and avoid red meat. Exercise every day. Sleep eight hours every night. These can be helpful, but our overall goal needs to be seeking wisdom from God.

We do not need to live in fear if we have wisdom. We can know that we are safe in God's hands. We will not struggle with sleep disturbances due to paralyzing anxiety or fear if we have grabbed hold of true wisdom.

Often people in biblical times would wear a necklace that had a symbolic meaning. Many people still do that today. Solomon's reference to "grace around our neck" alludes to the fact that a truly wise person will be characterized by grace. A wise person is part of the construction crew, rather than the demolition crew, in others' lives.

Graciousness comes as a result of finding the true wisdom of God. Lord, open me up to see more of Your wisdom.

The Lord is not slack concerning His promise, as some count slackness, but is longsuffering toward us, not willing that any should perish, but that all should come to repentance. —2 PETER 3:9

We read all the hundreds of promises in the Bible about God eventually putting an end to crime, abuse, injustice, and the sinful part of our own soul. And we want it *now,* if not sooner. Why wait? I sometimes get angry with God for not letting me be in control. I think that if I were in control, Jesus would have returned the day I became a Christian!

But this passage reassures us that God won't forget His promises. He will keep every one of them, just as He fulfilled all the ancient prophecies hundreds of years after He made His promises. This passage shows us God's reason for waiting.

God is compassionate and patient. He doesn't want anyone to go to hell, but His righteousness demands it for those who reject Christ. God wishes all would repent. And He not only longs to save our soul, He longs to salvage our lives. When it comes to your personal recovery, God is your biggest fan. He hurts when you hurt. Your victories are His victories.

But God is patient. He operates on a different timetable. We demand an easy instant cure; He demands lifelong cooperation in a spiritual and emotional growth process.

We have a brilliant, compassionate, and longsuffering God who has a master plan filled with wonderful surprises.

For You, Lord, are good, and ready to forgive,
And abundant in mercy to all those who call
upon You.   —PS. 86:5

When I was a child, my mother would often remind me that the two hardest words to say are "I'm sorry." Admitting honestly and directly when I have made a mistake or done something wrong does not come easily. It is especially difficult to say "I'm sorry" to someone who I feel does not understand and who I feel has a tendency to hold grudges rather than to forgive. God is not that type of person.

We can approach God in prayer. It is safe to come to Him with our failure and sin. God is "good, and ready to forgive."

In other words, we don't have to fear praying a prayer of repentance.

God will show mercy. He is willing and wants to forgive. His mercy is possible because the penalty for our sin and failure was paid by Jesus Christ on the cross. That penalty only had to be paid once. If someone is given a jail sentence, he or she only has to serve the time once. Jesus took on Himself the penalty of our sin. The sentence has been served. We can now come to God confidently and honestly and say "I'm sorry," knowing He will be merciful with us.

Thank You, Lord, that I don't have to fear coming to you with my failures. Thank You for being a God of grace.

*Likewise you younger people, submit yourselves
to your elders. Yes, all of you be submissive
to one another, and be clothed with humility,
for "God resists the proud,
But gives grace to the humble."*

—1 PETER 5:5–6

Serenity comes from knowing I do not have to pretend to be something that I am not. Serenity comes from not getting caught in the oneupmanship game, but by being submissive.

Submission has often been misunderstood in Christian circles.

What is submission? Elaine Stedman says, "Authentic submission is not reluctant nor grudging, nor is it the result of imposed authority. It is rather a *chosen,* deliberate, voluntary, love-initiated response to another's need. It is an act of worship to God, whom we serve in serving others."*

Humility is closely aligned with submission. If I'm humble I'm willing to choose submission. I can love.

Often for the codependent, there is a tendency to submit because of feeling worthless or pressured by another's expectations. This is giving in out of a sense of compulsion to prove one's value, or feelings of coercion, rather than true submission.

Submission is a voluntary, love-initiated response. There is serenity in that kind of decision.

I can live today based on my choices rather than being controlled by nonbiblical "shoulds."

*Elaine Stedman. *A Woman's Worth* (Waco, Texas: Word, 1976).

> *The refining pot is for silver and the furnace for gold,*
> *But the LORD tests the hearts.*
> —PROV. 17:3

Life involves disappointments and discouragements. All of us face them at one time or another. Things don't turn out the way we planned them. People let us down. Unexpected events block our progress.

With many of the surprises of life, there are things we can do to change the circumstances. However with those situations that can't be changed, God calls us to accept them.

God uses these as a test for us. He develops and evaluates our character through our reactions to the little irritations of everyday life.

If we can accept that God is testing us through these circumstances to help us grow, it gives us a new outlook on the problems.

Romans 8:28 says, ". . . all things work together for good to those who love God." God does not say some things work together for good; He says all things do. He does not say all things are good, but good things can be the result of all things. Often the good that comes from our difficulties is that our character is strengthened and we grow in maturity.

Lord help me to see the tests of life as Your way of developing, not destroying me.

Lord, who may abide in Your tabernacle?
Who may dwell in Your holy hill?
He who walks uprightly,
And works righteousness.
And speaks the truth in his heart;
—PS. 15:1–7

Sometimes we need courage to take a legitimate risk in life or business. Sometimes we need courage to risk our lives to save another's. Sometimes we need courage to risk rejection.

We also need courage to risk our own character development. We need courage to live a righteous life, even though we may be ridiculed for doing so. Sometimes there seem to be losses for being righteous. The grocery clerk gives you too much change and you are honest and return it. You are "out" that extra money, but is it really a loss? How much is self-respect worth?

We need the courage to be real, speaking the truth in our own hearts. Phoniness seems so much easier. It takes courage and hard work to be real.

We also need courage to be consistent, or to keep our word. To swear something simply means to promise something. When we make a promise, it often turns out to have been a mistake. It hurts to keep that promise and not change our minds. We need courage to keep our promises.

If we strive for righteousness, avoid phoniness, and keep our promises, we will not be moved from our self-respect and serenity.

> *Blessed is the man*
> *Who walks not in the counsel of the ungodly,*
> *Nor stands in the path of sinners,*
> *Nor sits in the seat of the scornful.*
>
> —PS. 1:1

George was progressing up the corporate ladder. He had accepted Christ as his Savior and was active at church. He had a beautiful wife and two children.

One day his boss called him into the office and informed him of yet another promotion. It would require that he spend five planning weekends away with the other achievers in his company. George was thrilled.

The first planning weekend was a real eye-opener. Yes, they did plan, but not much of it had to do with business. They planned which bars to hit, how to get cocaine, and which girls they would make moves on. George was definitely out of his element, but he desperately wanted to be accepted by these men. By the fifth weekend he was just one of the guys.

As Psalm 1:1 says, first we just walk. We allow ourselves to be influenced, but we're just passing through. Then it isn't very long until we're not moving quite so fast. We're standing around and opening ourselves up to a much greater influence. Finally we sit with these companions and become one of the gang.

Maybe you have experienced the truth of this progression. It takes courage and character to leave old friends behind you and find a new circle of friends.

It is easier for someone to pull me down than it is for me to shape them up. Do I need to make some changes in my relationships?

But as it is written: "Eye has not seen,
nor ear heard,
Nor have entered into the heart of man
The things which God has prepared
for those who love Him." But God
has revealed them to us through His
Spirit. For the Spirit searches all
things, yes, the deep things of God.
—1 COR. 2:9–10

My wife was studying for several final exams in her graduate program. In her struggle, she said at the dinner table, "If only I had a photographic memory. Would that ever help me now."

You've said it; I've said it: "If only I had someone else's mind. . . ."

1 Corinthians 2:16 says that we can have the "mind of Christ." We can begin to see and understand in new ways. We can gain new perspectives on issues in life as we integrate Christ's thinking into our own.

God has prepared many things for us. Many of the things are not seen or heard by us at the present time, but they will be revealed to us. The Holy Spirit knows all the deep or hidden things God is doing for us, and He will make these clear to us.

The Lord wants to give us His mind.

Thank You, Lord, that You want the best for me. You know I can misperceive life. Thank You that You want me to have Your mind so I can see life correctly.

As for man, his days are like grass . . . .
For the wind passes over it, and it is gone,
And its place remembers it no more.
But the mercy of the LORD is from
  everlasting to everlasting
On those who fear Him.

—PS. 103:15–16

Those who have grown up in dysfunctional homes consistently report that one of the hardest things to cope with was the unpredictableness in their home. Fun and laughter might greet them when they returned from school, or they might face an angry verbal or physical attack. Things might be OK, and then some word or action would set a parent off and result in physical abuse.

There is a dramatic contrast between human nature and the nature of God. People are changeable. They are like grass: growing and healthy one moment, but soon withered and gone. They are like a beautiful flower which quickly fades as the drying wind passes over it.

In contrast, God is a forever God. He is unchanging. This God who lives forever and is unchanging is also merciful. He will always be fair, understanding, and forgiving in His treatment of us. He will be our eternal friend.

A child growing up in a dysfunctional home never knows if his or her parent will be merciful or mad. God is always merciful!

_____

Thank You, Lord, that there is one place I can go and be greeted consistently with love, understanding, and mercy.

Now may the God of peace Himself sanctify you completely; and may your whole spirit, soul, and body be preserved blameless at the coming of our Lord Jesus Christ. He who calls you is faithful, who also will do it. Brethren, pray for us.
—1 THESS. 5:23–25

The apostle Paul was a remarkable man. He was well educated, a man of conviction, had incredible preaching and persuasive ability, and was a godly man.

He realized, though, that his personal success and his effectiveness in sharing the Gospel of Christ was due to prayer. He traveled all over the Middle East sharing the good news of Christianity.

He was fully aware that we are in a partnership with God. We work together with God. God wants us to be blameless in our spirit, soul, and body, yet our prayer time has a great deal to do with that becoming a reality.

God's love and grace is available to us, but God does not force it on us. He waits for us to come to Him in prayer and invite Him to do His maturing work in us.

Our prayers alone would not bring growth and maturity. God's grace without our acceptance of it also does not promote the process of spiritual maturity. Both God's grace and our willingness to receive His overwhelming grace are needed. God will be faithful to come and work in us. However, He waits for us to extend an invitation for Him to do so.

Ask God to work within you in a new way today. Your prayer motivates Him to work on your behalf.

> *Do not rejoice when your enemy falls,*
> *And do not let your heart be glad when he stumbles;*
> *Lest the LORD see it, and it displease Him,*
> *And He turn away His wrath from him.*
>   —PROV. 24:17–18

Junior high was a very unsettled time for me. I struggled with feelings of inadequacy and uncertainty. I can remember going outside at recess time to a big rock where I would meet my buddies. The topics of our conversation would vary, but would usually focus on some poor seventh or eighth grader who had gotten into trouble. We would laugh at that person for doing something wrong or stupid, or for failing. In our minds this person had fallen flat on his or her face, and we loved it.

In reality, of course, our insecurity was showing. We thought we could be bigger at the expense of someone who was down.

I can still remember thinking anxiously, "I sure hope I don't fall on my face. I don't want these guys to laugh at me."

Peace or serenity comes by not living as I did during junior high. Don't rejoice or gloat when an enemy or friend falls.

Serenity can come as we begin to treat friends and foes with love and understanding in their time of struggle, embarrassment, failure and sin.

Lord, if someone I know has fallen flat on his or her face, help me to choose to lend a hand to help them up rather than walking on them.

We ourselves boast of you among the churches of
God for your patience and faith in all your
persecutions and tribulations that you endure,
which is manifest evidence of the righteous
judgment of God, that you may be counted worthy
of the kingdom of God, for which you also suffer.
—2 THESS. 1:4–5

Last fall I was unable to watch a football game I had been looking forward to. I taped the game on my VCR and went off with two friends for a business meeting. After the meeting they decided to come back to my house and watch the game with me. I purposely did not listen to the radio to hear what the final score was. I wanted to experience the emotions of the game.

We cheered as Los Angeles scored and were discouraged when San Francisco tied the score. In the closing seconds, two of us were on pins and needles, wondering if the Rams could get a field goal, while our third friend sat confidently saying, "Why are you so nervous?"

We later found out why he was so calm. On his way over to the house, he had heard a radio news flash that the Rams had won. My friend knew the final score.

If we endure and accept the trials that can't be changed, if we are patient, then God will reward us at the final judgment. We will be counted worthy for not giving up our faith in the trying times. Our perseverance may not be rewarded here on earth, but the final outcome will be a winning score.

I may not be rewarded today for accepting and persevering through what I can't change. However, the final outcome is settled.

> *Then Caleb quieted the people before Moses, and said, "Let us go up at once and take possession, for we are well able to overcome it."*
>
> —NUM. 13:30

The Lord told Moses to send twelve leaders, one from each tribe of Israel, to check out the land of Canaan and determine if they, with God's help, could conquer it. Now God knew good and well that He could conquer Canaan with or without soldiers. But God didn't choose to do things the easy way, because His goal was not merely to conquer the sinful land of Canaan, but to bring about spiritual maturity in the people of Israel.

Two courageous leaders, Caleb and Joshua, came back and said Canaan would be easy to conquer with God's help. They said it was a land of milk and honey. The people of Canaan were tall and strong, but the children of Israel had God on their side. Caleb and Joshua tried to share their courage with the people. They said, "Let's go take it. The land is ours!"

But the other ten leaders who served as spies gave a different report. They said, "There is no way we can defeat those Canaanites! It is not worth the risk."

The people of Israel went with the majority opinion. They wept and griped at Moses, and griped at God. And they missed out on the opportunity to see God's power in action.

In our own strength, we cannot defeat many "giants" who oppose us. And in most situations, God will not defeat them for us. Our maturity is His goal, so He wants us to spy out life's situations, see the truth, then conquer those "giants" ourselves, with His strength.

"And he will turn
The hearts of the fathers to the children,
And the hearts of the children to their fathers,
Lest I come and strike the earth with a
*   curse."*

—MAL. 4:5–6

God loves children. While the world often sees them as a nuisance or a financial burden, God sees children as significant human beings of great value.

As God looks down from heaven with His eternal perspective and sees the fathers of Malachi's day, the fathers of John the Baptist's day, and the fathers of today, I don't imagine He sees many differences. He delights to see fathers who cherish and nurture their children. Not all do. Some are alcoholics. Some are workaholics. Some are so emotionally damaged they have little to offer their children.

One of the greatest joys life has to offer comes from intimate bonding with our children. Nothing the world has to offer beats loving and being loved, sharing our deepest feelings, and making wonderful memories with our children. God also wants to restore the hearts of children to their fathers. This may include forgiving our own fathers for failing to love us as we need them to.

_____

Make a written, detailed schedule of your week. How much time do you spend bonding to your family? Get some counsel, then change your schedule to fit in with God's plans for you.

> *For the Lord does not see as man sees; for man looks at the outward appearance, but the Lord looks at the heart."*
>
> —1 SAM. 16:7

Israel's first king, Saul, was a very tall, good-looking man. But God rejected him as a king because God looked into Saul's soul and found a bitter, arrogant heart. Samuel was looking for a new king, at God's instruction. God told Samuel to pick one of Jesse's sons.

Samuel looked at Jesse's oldest son and was quite sure it must be him. He was the oldest. He was tall. He looked good. He must be the man. But God looks at the *heart,* the *mind,* the *emotions* and the *will.* God saw a ruddy teenager, the youngest of Jesse's children, who loved God. God chose David not only to be the next King of Israel after Saul, but God also chose to have Jesus be born of Mary, one of David's descendants.

When we were growing up, the best looking teens tended to be the most popular. As adults, good looking people still tend to get the best paying jobs. Psychological research proves this. But not all that glitters is gold. The world looks at the outward appearance, but God looks through us like an x-ray machine and examines our motives.

For the rest of your life, imagine that you are wearing a special pair of glasses that enable you to see your mate, children, friends, co-workers, political leaders, fellow church-members, and the people of the world with physical blinders and spiritual insight. See them the way God sees them.

"Tell the daughter of Zion, 'Behold, your King is coming to you, lowly, and sitting on a donkey, a colt, the foal of a donkey.'" —MATT. 21:5

Who is this Higher Power we depend on for recovery?

Over 500 years before Christ, Zechariah the prophet was inspired by God to predict that the coming Messiah would ride triumphantly into Jerusalem on "a donkey (Zech. 9:9)." About 539 B.C., Daniel predicted that a decree would be made to rebuild Jerusalem in the near future. This was fulfilled on March 5, 444 B.C. (Neh. 2:1–8) by Artaxerxes Longimanus. Daniel also predicted that the Messiah would come to Jerusalem 483 years after that decree, but that the Messiah would be "cut off."

483 years after Artaxerxes made his decree, to the day, Christ entered Jerusalem on a young donkey. A short time later, Messiah was "cut off"—crucified.

When Jesus came, in spite of scores of prophecies about Him in the Old Testament, people expected Him to take over planet earth in *their* lifetime. But instead He died on the cross. They expected angels to carry Him to power over the Roman Empire, but instead He rode into Jerusalem on a young donkey. The real God is unbelievably humble. He paid the penalty for our sins on the cross, then rose again on the third day to prove He was still God and still alive.

In spite of the fact that Jesus is God and can see through our motives, He still considers us worth dying for. Our Higher Power is both a humble servant and an omnipotent King of Kings. He can heal us.

> *So it came to pass in the process of time that*
> *Hannah conceived and bore a son, and called his*
> *name Samuel, saying, "Because I have asked for*
> *him from the LORD."*
> —1 SAM. 1:20

Hannah would have benefited from the Serenity Prayer. Year after year she wept about her barrenness. She would not accept what she could not change. She was bitter and very depressed.

Hannah promised God that if He would allow her to have a son, she would dedicate him to the Lord. She told Eli the priest about her vow and Eli also prayed that God would grant her request. If we study all the prayers of godly people in the Bible, we will see that sometimes God answered yes and sometimes no. He listened to the intent of their hearts as well as their specific requests.

God sometimes answers yes to our intent but fills the request in a way other than the specific way we requested. Sometimes He allows our request despite our wrong motives, and teaches us a beneficial lesson about maturity from it. And sometimes God says later.

In Hannah's case, God said yes to her request and her intent, allowing her to become pregnant. She and her husband had a boy named Samuel, who became an outstanding prophet.

Whenever you find yourself becoming bitter toward God (as Hannah was before getting pregnant), trust God's wisdom. He could easily grant any request you make, but His ways of doing things are sometimes impossible for us to understand.

"Blessed are the poor in spirit, for theirs is the kingdom of heaven. . . . Blessed are the meek, for they shall inherit the earth. . . . Blessed are the merciful, for they shall obtain mercy."
—MATT. 5:3, 5, 7

Chapters five through seven of the book of Matthew are commonly referred to as the Sermon on the Mount, because Jesus was sitting on a mountainside teaching a large crowd. Jesus had offered His kingdom to Israel if Israel would repent, so those who followed Jesus were very curious about the coming kingdom and how they could become a part of it.

But Jesus' sermon did not tell them what they wanted to hear. Instead of telling them about the coming Kingdom, Jesus told them how to live and think. He gave them guidelines for a life of relative serenity.

The legalistic Pharisees were concerned with *outward,* ritualistic, behavioral "rules." Jesus was concerned with *internal* personality traits, such as humility and empathy. That's what "poor in spirit" refers to—humble dependence on God rather than arrogant self-reliance.

Those who appreciate God's mercy, show mercy to those who offend them. The pure in heart are sojourners who are honest enough to admit they continually struggle against sin in their lives.

Serenity does not come from obeying a long list of rules. It comes from taking a continual (at times painful) look at our inner selves.

> *But now, do not therefore be grieved or angry with yourselves because you sold me here; for God sent me before you to preserve life.* —GEN. 45:5

Joseph was a man who certainly had the serenity to accept the things he could not change and the courage to change the things he could. God also blessed him with the wisdom to know the difference.

Joseph was his father's favorite son, and was given a special tunic made of many colors. His brothers felt inferior and became enraged. Sibling rivalry has existed since Cain killed Abel and continues to this day. Joseph's brothers were going to kill him too, but Reuben, the oldest, talked them out of it. So they sold Joseph into slavery instead, and he was carried off to Egypt at the age of seventeen.

I'm sure Joseph wasn't thrilled about this turn of events, but he trusted and loved God and knew that no event could happen in his life without his loving Heavenly Father permitting it.

Joseph eventually became the second in command in the entire nation of Egypt.

It is definitely not what Joseph planned, but he had the serenity to *accept* and *trust* God's will in his life.

Dedicating your life to God like Joseph did as a teenager may cost you a lot of hassles. God promises to help us through our tough times and make them work out for His glory and our ultimate benefit.

*"The blind receive their sight and the lame walk;
the lepers are cleansed and the deaf hear; the dead
are raised up and the poor have the gospel
preached to them. And blessed is he who is not
offended because of Me."*   —MATT. 11:5–6

All of us have doubts from time to time. We have doubts about ourselves, doubts about our loved ones, and even doubts about God.

If we couldn't trust our parents to meet our basic developmental needs (such as loving and being loved, and taking responsibility for ourselves), then how can we trust other authority figures? We all know people who have been hurt as adults because they trusted too much. Where is the balance?

We feel shame when we doubt, especially about whether God really exists or whether He really accepts us. Most addictions are *shame-driven*. We expect perfection from ourselves. Then when we fail, we hide our failure, feeling ashamed.

We need to realize that as committed Christians, we can confess our failures to God and to each other, finding unconditional love and acceptance.

John the Baptist was one of the greatest Christians to ever live. Jesus said so in Matthew 11:11. He was Christ's cousin and knew Him since infancy. John had loving, wonderful parents and a "functional" family. And yet, when he was in prison, about to get beheaded by Herod, he had doubts. Jesus returned a message to John to reassure him, then John died content.

Doubts and failure are a normal part of our spiritual growth.

> *"Be fruitful and multiply; fill the earth*
> *and subdue it."*
> —GEN. 1:28

Every child has vital developmental needs, which are best met by our own parents in the first six years of our lives. If our parents do not meet these basic needs (and no parents are perfect) we become more prone to addictions or anxiety.

Four of those basic needs are popularly called "the Four Bs": Bonding, Boundaries, "Badness" and Boss. Bonding means loving and being loved. Boundaries are often a problem in codependency issues, such as serving God without being a masochistic "rescuer." "Badness" refers to accepting that Christians struggle with their depravity until they get to heaven.

The fourth basic need, the need to be the "Boss" of our lives, has been misunderstood in some Christian circles. Some Christians try to run their lives in their own strength and fall flat on their faces. Others say we should "let go" of our brains completely, and "let God" run our lives like a puppet.

The balance found in the Serenity Prayer and in the Twelve-Step programs is that of becoming "Boss" of the areas of responsibility God places under our authority, while depending on God for courage, wisdom, and strength.

God made man and woman in His own image. He instructed them to become "boss" of the entire world, because He had designed them to be responsible.

"For where your treasure is, there your heart will be also."
—MATT. 6:21

In psychiatric circles, we like to talk about "the Reality Principle": the ability to delay gratification to the appropriate time and place. Wise people have it. Immature people do not.

Sociopaths are extremely immature persons who are impulsive and selfish and experience little, if any, guilt. If they want to feel high, they take drugs. If they feel a sexual urge, they find someone, almost anyone, quickly. If they desire a material possession, they steal it or steal the money to buy it. They complain and pit people against each other just to relieve boredom. They are phony.

God demonstrates that He loves sociopaths, while absolutely hating what they do to hurt their fellow human beings. God loves to show His great power and mercy by saving sociopaths and gradually sanctifying them toward Christlike behavior.

There are some sociopathic tendencies within all of us. We must accept this "badness" in ourselves and cooperate with God in our own sanctification.

Be encouraged not to live for earthly treasures, but by the Reality Principle. If we defer sinful pleasures and live godly lives, we can look forward to the fantastic treasures and pleasures we will have in heaven. Wise men seek the truth and change their attitudes and behaviors to fit in with the truth.

The committed Christian life gives us the most genuine joy, love, peace, and pleasure not only when we get to heaven, but right now.

Then David comforted Bathsheba his wife, and went in to her and lay with her. So she bore a son, and he called his name Solomon. And the LORD loved him.
—2 SAM. 12:24

Who do you love most? God loves you and that person infinitely more. God is never surprised by what we think or do. He knows every evil motive we have ever had, and welcomes us with open arms anyway. He longs for a bonding relationship with us.

If you don't believe this, look at the life of King David. A godly man most of his life, David also had human weaknesses and depravity. His most publicized sin was watching his neighbor's wife take a bath from his roof, having an affair with her, and then arranging for her husband to be killed.

But David repented and rededicated his life to God. God not only forgave David. He called David a man after His own heart.

When God chose the genealogy of His Son, Jesus Christ the Messiah, He included Rahab the harlot. And Matthew openly wrote, "David the king begot Solomon by her who had been the wife of Uriah." God told us to be sure our sins would find us out, and He doesn't cover things up to protect His reputation. He knows the truth about us, and He wants us to face the truth, too. Then He can transform our shame into glory.

The righteous God is amazingly merciful to sinners who have humbled themselves to depend on Christ's death and resurrection to pay for their past, present, and future sins.

"But you, when you pray, go into your room, and when you have shut your door, pray to your Father who is in the secret place; and your Father who sees in secret will reward you openly."

—MATT. 6:6

Before Jesus gave us the Lord's Prayer, He told us how *not* to pray.

Even the good deeds that we do are usually done for a mixture of godly and evil motives. When I show a loved one how to put his or her faith in Christ, I may do it primarily out of love and compassion, but partially so I can brag about it later or win favor with God.

Jesus knew that those same good and evil motives would drive our prayers as well.

The Pharisees loved to pray long and loud in the synagogues or the street corners. I know of a modern-day "Pharisee" who stood on his chair in a restaurant to pray for his meal. I'm glad I wasn't at his table. Jesus said if you pray to get attention, then attention is your only reward.

We should not condemn or reject people who crave attention. We should love them. But when *we* pray, Jesus encouraged us to pray primarily in secret, but also with each other. He wants us to be sincere and unrehearsed, not repeating the same prayers each time. He wants us to tell Him what's on our hearts.

A prayer that God loves to hear is secret, sincere, and submissive to His will. It is also very significant to Him, because He loves you.

Be angry, and do not sin.
Meditate within your heart on your bed, and be still.
—PS. 4:4

When we think of serenity, we think of peace, joy, physical well-being, a clear conscience, meaning in life, mental alertness, humility, and freedom from co-dependent addictions.

The opposite of serenity is depression and anxiety, which results in sadness, decreased energy, trouble concentrating, and a host of other symptoms.

We treat thousands of men and women at our Minirth-Meier Clinics throughout America for clinical depression. Some are caused by various medical disorders, such as hypothyroidism, cancer, and alcohol abuse. But most of these depressions are caused by a spiritual/emotional problem: holding grudges. Many good people are very angry on the inside and do not even know they are holding subconscious grudges. Some Christians have been erroneously taught that getting angry is also a sin, so they fool themselves into thinking they aren't holding grudges even when they are.

In today's passage as well as other places in Scripture, God tells us it is possible to be angry without sinning, but we are to resolve our grudges and vengeful motives by bedtime. Sort through the anger-producing situation and, with God's help, forgive yourself, others, and perhaps even God.

When you feel angry, learn to resolve your anger the healthy way—God's way.

*Enter by the narrow gate; for wide is the gate and
broad is the way that leads to destruction.*
—MATT. 7:13

The reason many men and women go through midlife
crises in their thirties or forties is because that is when
we finally give up on the idealistic notion that life
should be easy and fair. When reality hits, we realize
that we can throw those "shoulds" out the window, because life is always difficult, and frequently unfair.

There is nothing wrong with wanting things to be
easy. In fact, mature people find easy ways to do things
when easy ways exist. But we must accept the reality
that living a successful, serene life is hard work.

Becoming a Christian is relatively easy in one regard, requiring mere faith, and yet it is so difficult in
other ways that a majority of people take the broad
road that leads to destruction. To become a Christian,
one must simply depend on Christ's death and resurrection to pay for his or her sins, just as one depends on
a chair to hold him or her off the ground.

But trusting Christ is extremely difficult if parental
authority figures were not very trustworthy. We see
who God is through psychological "sunglasses" the
color of our parents, especially of our fathers. No wonder trusting Christ is so difficult while so easy. It feels
as if we are giving up control of our lives, and in a way
we are. But in reality, we are gaining control over negatives when Christ enters our lives.

*Jesus, help me accept that Christian growth is a slow, difficult pro-
cess.*

> *"Be strong and of good courage, do not fear nor be afraid of them; for the LORD your God, He is the One who goes with you. He will not leave you nor forsake you."*
>
> —DEUT. 31:6

The Israelites were about to enter into the land God promised them. Moses was still in good health, but because of an earlier act of disobedience God would not allow him to enter the promised land. Moses gave the people a final charge, and then publicly appointed Joshua as their new leader.

Many years earlier, Moses had sent spies to survey the land of Canaan. Joshua and Caleb were the only two who had returned from this mission with a positive report, urging the people to claim the land God had promised them. God was now rewarding Joshua for his courage and trust.

Shortly before Moses' death, God Himself told Joshua to be strong and of good courage because He would be with him. A short time later, God took Moses up on a mountain somewhere in Moab, opposite Beth Peor, allowed Moses to die in His presence, and buried him there.

Joshua and Caleb were courageous leaders in Israel in the years following Moses' death. Their courage was based on two factors: they fought hard in battle, and they depended on the Lord for strength.

You can base your own courage to face life's battles on God's promise to always be with you.

*"They are no longer two but one flesh. Therefore
what God has joined together, let not man
separate."*
                                        —MATT. 19:6

God loves divorced people. God forgives divorced
people. God uses thousands of godly, divorced people
to help others in many various ways. But God *hates*
divorce (Mal. 2:16).

We know of one psychiatry professor who continually surprised us by recommending divorce to many
of his patients. Later on we discovered that he had
grown up in a very legalistic religious environment,
but he didn't have a personal relationship with Christ.
He felt compelled by his tradition to stay with his wife,
so he enjoyed seeing other marriages freely break up.
He finally left his wife for another woman.

Jesus doesn't want anyone to cause a divorce. We
should work hard to preserve our own marriages and
help others we care about to preserve theirs.

But how about the good people who have suffered
unwanted divorces? How about the children of divorce
who feel rejected? How about people like King David
who have an affair, remarry, and recognize later that
what they did was wrong? God loves them all very
much. We should too.

---

*If you are considering divorce, consider committing your marriage to
Christ and getting some marital therapy, preferably by a Christian
therapist.*

> *The secret things belong to the L*ORD *our God, but those things which are revealed belong to us and to our children forever, that we may do all the words of this law.*
> —DEUT. 29:29

If there is really a God, why do so many people suffer? Why is there a murder every minute? Why do good people die painful, prolonged deaths? Why do bad people seem to prosper? Why is sin so hard to resist? Why does God allow people to spend eternity in hell? How could a God of love allow me to have so much heartache?

We have heard these questions hundreds of times, and for most of them we have a very simple answer: we don't know. When we were young, cocky medical students, we thought we knew almost everything there was to know. In fact, for perfectionists like us, saying "I don't know" to students, patients, or even our own children used to be quite humiliating. Perfectionists want to know everything, and uncertainty is anxiety-producing.

But now that we are older, we are getting more comfortable with "I don't know." We trust God. He knows the answers to all those questions. We don't always need to know. If He wanted us to know, He would have plainly told us. He desires us to live a life of faith in Him.

Many secrets are known only by God. Accept that. Trust Him to work everything out fairly in the long run. Learn what He has told us in His Word. Live by it and teach it to your children.

If David then calls Him 'Lord,' how is He his Son?"
And no one was able to answer Him a word, nor
from that day on did anyone dare question Him
anymore.
                                                    —MATT. 22:41–46

Is there really a personal God? If so, who is He? Was Jesus really God? Or was He just a very good man?

Jesus gave the Pharisees a puzzle. Jesus had claimed many times during His three-year ministry that He was God. When the Pharisees said that Jesus was just a descendant of David, Jesus replied that He was both David's son and David's Lord. In fact, Jesus quoted Psalm 110. In that passage, David spoke of Jesus and called Him his Lord.

We have met a number of psychotic patients who thought they were God. We have also met a number of self-centered sociopaths who acted as though they were God. But we have never, ever met a good, sane person who claimed to be God.

Be honest with yourself. If Jesus was not God, He could not possibly have been a good, sane man. He was either psychotic, or a sociopath, or else He was who He claimed He was: Jesus Christ, the promised Messiah, God in the flesh, who existed from eternity with the Father and with the Holy Spirit. It's the only solution to a complex puzzle.

We can deny the truth; or we can accept the only Higher Power who can help us.

> *And Jabez called on the God of Israel saying, "Oh, that You would bless me indeed, and enlarge my territory, that Your hand would be with me, and that You would keep me from evil, that I may not cause pain!" So God granted him what he requested.*
> —1 CHRON. 4:10

We don't know much about Jabez. We know he was more honorable than his brothers. We know he made a request, and that God must have been pleased with it because He granted it.

Since we know Jabez prayed a good prayer that was granted by God, we would be wise to examine it and to pray a similar prayer ourselves. What can we learn from it?

It is OK to ask God to bless us. It is OK to ask God to increase our sphere of responsibility. It is good to desire for God to be intimately involved in our lives. We should pray for God's help to avoid evil. Jabez showed real wisdom when he asked God to keep him from evil so he would not cause pain to anyone.

People who had rigid parents tend to expect God to be the same, demanding that we *earn* His acceptance and our salvation. In reality, God loves us unconditionally. But He blesses us conditionally.

God is angry when we hurt each other or ourselves. His rules are designed to protect us from that very thing. When we honestly ask for His help, as Jabez did, we can be confident in His delight to answer us.

Think of your own personal, original prayer based on some of the principles found in Jabez's prayer. Share it with God.

"Therefore I say to you, do not worry about your life, what you will eat or what you will drink; nor about your body, what you will put on. . . .Which of you by worrying can add one cubit to his stature?"

—MATT. 6:25, 27

Serenity is something Jesus definitely wants us to have, and it must be something we can control, or He wouldn't have told us over and over again, "Do not worry." But "turning off" worry is easier for some people than others to do.

Basically, the more loving and trustworthy your parents were, the easier it will be to trust God to supply your basic needs. If your parents taught you to be independent and responsible, that will also make it easier for you to "turn off" worry as well.

If we are lazy and passive, God will not feed and clothe us anyway. In fact, the Bible teaches that those who don't work should not eat (2 Thess. 3:10). The heavenly Father feeds the birds of the air. Have you ever seen God drop worms into their mouths from heaven? I haven't! God put it in their genetic programming to work at finding food for themselves and their babies. The birds do the work, God provides worms in the ground.

I've never met a patient who could not, with hard work, get over an anxiety disorder. God wants to give us serenity, and we must work toward it.

Remember that our heavenly Father will meet our needs when we are faithful.

> *"You should know in your heart that as a man chastens his son, so the LORD your God chastens you.*
> —DEUT. 8:5

A certain amount of the suffering we experience is necessary. It is part of life. At the same time, much of our suffering is unnecessary. If each of us learned to get in touch with our anger, for example, and forgive, verbalize, and hold no grudges, most depressions and suicides could be prevented. If we trusted God to help us meet our basic needs, and could look honestly at our sinfulness and yet accept ourselves as God accepts us, most anxiety would disappear. If we took proper care of our bodies, we could avoid many physical illnesses.

Some suffering, of course, borders between necessary and unnecessary. God has to chasten us from time to time when we rebel, just as loving fathers discipline their sons and daughters.

We love our children. We want them to grow up to be citizens who are family-oriented, make a contribution to society, are self-sufficient and responsible.

God also loves us very much. He wants us to mature, to see ourselves as He sees us, to help others, to overcome addictions, to love our families, and to enjoy life. It would be nice if all these good things happened the moment we trusted Christ, but they don't. God has to guide us through tough times, just as He led the nation of Israel through forty years of wandering. We can choose not to rebel, but because of our natural tendency to sin, God's discipline is a necessary part of life.

Is it your goal to have a hassle-free life, or a holy one?

*"But you shall receive power when the Holy Spirit
has come upon you; and you shall be witnesses to
Me in Jerusalem, and in all Judea and Samaria,
and to the end of the earth."*   —ACTS 1:8

We need courage for a lot of things in this life. We
need courage to stand up to people who try to take
advantage of us. It takes courage to look at the truth
about ourselves. I have seen many hospital patients
check out of the hospital, blaming the rules or the hospital food for their inability to stay, when it is obvious
they are right on the verge of seeing all their repressed
rage toward a parent or other frightening emotions.

It also takes courage to tell your friends and neighbors how to trust Christ. We all have inferiority feelings, and fear the rejection of others.

These were the very last words Jesus spoke on
planet earth. He was standing on the Mount of Olives
in Jerusalem. When He finished speaking, His body as-
cended slowly up into heaven in full view of His followers. It must have made quite an impression,
because the same disciples who fearfully ran away
when Jesus was arrested to be crucified ended up willingly dying terrible deaths for the Lord after His resurrection and bodily ascension. Some day Jesus will
bodily descend on that same Mount of Olives to begin
His Millennial Kingdom.

*The Holy Spirit's primary role in our lives is to comfort us, to convict
us to sin, and to give us courage to do the things God wants us to do.*

*Therefore a man shall leave his father and mother
and be joined to his wife, and they shall become
one flesh.*
—GEN. 2:24

The most important psychological need we have is for intimate bonding. We need desperately to love and be loved. You can give a baby all the food and clean diapers it needs, but if it doesn't get enough hugs and physical touching, it will not digest its food, will wither up gradually and die from lack of love.

As adults, we still desperately need intimacy. We can't live without it. Ask the P.O.W.s who survived Vietnam how they did it. They figured out ways to communicate with each other by rapping codes on walls, and built bonds of friendship. Healthy bonds with people give us emotional strength and stability.

Many adults have only a superficial relationship with their mates. Sometimes one mate is willing to work at deep communication skills and bonding, but the other mate fears it. In that situation, the mate who desires bonding must rely on close friends for honest fellowship, while modeling good communication to the defensive mate.

God created us for each other. He wants mates to bond spiritually, emotionally, and physically.

*God loves your mate much more than you do. Ask God to help you
change your behavior in such a way that He can love your mate
through you.*

*"But seek first the kingdom of God and His
righteousness, and all these things shall be added
to you."*   —MATT. 6:33–34

This is a vital passage that can eliminate a great deal
of unnecessary pain when properly applied.

We must realize that all humans have inferiority
feelings. Many of us waste a lot of our time and energy
attempting to prove our significance through sex,
money or power. Therefore we must determine daily
to stay out of the rat race. We must choose to give up
all sinful pursuits of illicit sex, living for money, or
prideful power struggles.

Make a daily commitment to gradually become
more and more like Christ (Rom. 8:29) and to serve
Christ (Matt. 6:33). In order to do this, you may need to
rearrange your schedule and your priorities. Spend
time each day seeking to know God as He really is and
bond with Him. Take care of your own mental health.
Work at bonding with your mate and meeting his or
her needs, and bonding with your children and meeting their needs. Use your spiritual and emotional gifts
to benefit others. Take time for both work and play.
Realize that Christians who think they stand are the
most likely to fall. Pray that God will enable you to stay
out of trouble each day.

*If you give up sinful aspects of sex, money and power to become like
Christ, serve Christ, and stay out of trouble one day at a time, then all
these things will be given back to you, in good and meaningful ways.*

And his servant said to him, "Alas, my master!
What shall we do?" So he answered, "Do not fear,
for those who are with us are more than those who
are with them."　　　　　　　　**—2 KINGS 6:15–16**

The year was about 850 B.C. Ben-Hadad II was the King of Syria. He had thousands of soldiers, and had intended to make surprise raids on Israel in order to eventually defeat Israel. But every time he gathered his troops to a secret location, God told Elisha the prophet the place, and Elisha told Joram, the king of Israel. Ben-Hadad was enraged, and thought one of his own men must be tipping Israel off. When he discovered Elisha was responsible, Ben-Hadad decided to attack Elisha first, then Israel.

Elisha told his servant not to fear, because Elisha's soldiers outnumbered Ben-Hadad's. But the servant saw no soldiers for Elisha and thousands for Ben-Hadad. Then Elisha prayed that the Lord would allow his servant to see the truth. God opened his eyes and the servant saw mountains full of angels on horseback and in chariots of fire.

Then God struck the Syrian army with blindness. Elisha led them into Samaria, where they were surrounded by Israeli soldiers. God opened their eyes and Elisha fed them a feast and sent them away in peace. The raiders never returned (2 Kings 6:23b).

Since everything we see here on planet earth appears to have a finite beginning and ending, it is sometimes difficult to believe in an eternal God, angels, and things we can't see. It takes faith.

Give us this day our daily bread.
And forgive us our debts.
As we forgive our debtors.
> —MATT. 6:11

The Lord's Prayer followed by Jesus' surprising statement that if we forgive others, He will forgive us, but if we don't forgive the men and women who sin against us, then God will not forgive us for sinning against Him.

If the Bible is God's love letter to mankind, then it must be perfect, and it is. God does not contradict Himself. Therefore, we can understand confusing Scripture passages such as this in the light of other Scripture passages.

We know from many other passages of Scripture that everyone who places trust in Christ's death and resurrection to pay for sins is saved from all past, present and future sins from that moment on.

But we still sin. And our sin may trigger God's chain of loving disciplinary consequences. We feel guilty, which drains our energy. When we obey God and forgive others or ourselves, God forgives us, and although it may take time, our strength is restored.

Think of three people you potentially have the most subconscious or even conscious vengeful motives toward, then ask God the Father to only forgive you to the extent that you forgive them. It's a humbling thought!

There are many who say,
"Who will show us any good?"
LORD, lift up the light of Your countenance upon us.
You have put gladness in my heart,
More than in the season that their grain and wine
  increased.
I will both lie down in peace, and sleep;
For You alone, O LORD, make me dwell in safety.

PS. 4:6–8

One of David's greatest failures was in raising his son Absalom. Absalom was a good-looking young man. He stood at the gate daily where people came to bring their complaints, listened to their situations as a "friend," and made everyone think that their cause was a just one. He was a manipulator.

Absalom led an uprising. He wanted to kill and re-place his own father as king. David was forced to flee. God protected David, and despite David's orders, one of his faithful men killed treacherous Absalom. David won the battle but lost his son.

As Absalom was hunting him down, David and his men were wondering if there was anyone out there still loyal to him. Have you ever felt that way on a bad day? I sure have. But David was God's choice for king. God loved him and was paying close attention to him. God put gladness in David's heart, even on this terrible day.

Serenity in our lives comes partially from the realization that God loves us and protects us. And if He permits suffering, He will help us grow from the experience.

> *"Pray for those who spitefully use you and
> persecute you, that you may be sons of your Father
> in heaven; for He makes His sun rise on the evil
> and on the good, and sends rain on the just and on
> the unjust."*
> —MATT. 5:44–45

Life does not seem fair, and in many ways it isn't. God makes rain soak the lawns and farms of the just and unjust. We are honest but have financial stresses; our neighbor cheats the IRS and prospers. We have trouble losing weight; our friend never needs to diet. We have been terribly hurt by someone; God asks us to love and pray for him or her.

Is this passage asking us to be masochists? Is it suggesting that we allow others to disregard our feelings and rob us of our dignity? Not at all. In fact, some passages of Scripture warn us to beware of those who would abuse us.

Jesus is saying, Step back, my beloved child. Accept the apparent unfairness of this life, and trust Me to even things out in an eternity. Stop and think about it. Most abusive parents were abused themselves. They were taken advantage of by the very people who should have protected them. They are filled with rage, bitterness and feelings of inferiority.

God *hates* child abuse and every other sin, but He loves every sinner. His great mercy and power can transform the most hopeless life.

Even our enemies are significant to Him and worth saving. Someone may be rude to you today because he or she is hurting in some way. Love that person instead of getting even. Pray for him or her.

> *For You will light my lamp;*
> *The Lord my God will enlighten my darkness.*
> —PS. 18:28

I remember as a child playing a game with my brother in the evening, just before bed. We would race each other down the stairs to our basement bedroom without turning the lights on. Out of breath, we would flop on our beds. The game was that the bogeyman was after us, chasing us in the dark. Whoever was last into the room was the one who might be caught by the bogeyman.

Fear of the dark is common in young children, and even in some adults. But we don't have to live in fear. The Lord turns our darkness into light. We can take courage; we don't have to live in the darkness. He wants to bring His light to our lives.

It would have been far easier and less frightening for my brother and me to have turned on the basement light and been able to see where we were going. God brings a sense of clarity to life. He gives us a clearer perspective of where we are and where we are going. We can also take courage because of the help and strength God gives us to fight and defeat our enemies. What is the enemy in your life? What are you fighting? God wants to give you His strength to face it. God is our refuge, a safe place to turn when we are feeling attacked. Take courage today as you draw near to God.

If you are feeling lost in the dark, God is light. If you need a safe place, God is a refuge.

Your words were found, and I ate them,
And Your word was to me the joy and
rejoicing of my heart;
For I am called by Your name,
O LORD God of hosts. —JER. 15:16

Alan lost his wife of eleven years to cancer. He had a ten-year-old daughter whom he dearly loved, and he decided to take Christmas week off to spend time with her.

A strange thing happened during that vacation. Every morning his little girl would close herself off in her room and wouldn't come out until suppertime. Alan didn't know what to do. Did she not want to be with him? He was hurt and confused.

On Christmas morning, she triumphantly presented her daddy with a package wrapped in newspaper and bows. Inside was a pair of socks she had knitted for him. Her eyes flashed with pride as she said, "Daddy, this is what I was doing each day for you." Alan gathered her in his arms with tears rolling down his face. "Honey," he said, "I love the socks. They're beautiful. But all I wanted this Christmas was time with you."

I wonder how often Jesus weeps over our busyness. He just wants us to be quiet and spend time with Him. He longs for us to approach the Scriptures as if we had a very important date with our beloved.

Lord, please teach me to take time out of my day so You can fill me with Your joy.

> *Therefore let him who thinks he stands take heed*
> *lest he fall. No temptation has overtaken you except*
> *such as is common to man; but God is faithful,*
> *who will not allow you to be tempted beyond what*
> *you are able, but with the temptation will also*
> *make the way of escape, that you may be able to*
> *bear it.* —1 COR. 10:12–13

True wisdom is demonstrated in how one understands and handles temptation. What does the Bible say about temptation? James 1:13–15 tells us God is not in the "tempting" business. He is not the author of temptation. Instead, temptations come from our own subconscious desires.

Today's passage says that we can be tempted when we least expect it. When we are standing firm or think that we are doing well in avoiding sin, we need to be careful lest we fall flat on our faces.

Temptation is also a progressively developing process. An evil desire can creep into our conscious awareness. This thought is followed by being enticed, like a fish drawn from its hiding place toward the wiggling bait on the fisherman's hook. As the thought is focused on, it develops, and finally it is acted out. Sin leads to death. But we do have hope, and it is this: temptation does not need to get the best of us. For each temptation there is an escape. If we call on the Lord, He will not allow us to be tempted beyond our ability to withstand it.

Lord, I need Your help to conquer the temptations of life.

"I am the Alpha and the Omega, the Beginning and the End," says the Lord, "who is and who was and who is to come, the Almighty." —REV. 1:8

Our own reasoning ability is limited by our human experience. Every plant, animal, and person had a moment of conception. Everything we see had a beginning. It is nearly impossible for us to visualize anything or anyone being infinite.

And yet, the recovery programs that really work require dependence on a Higher Power. But who really is the true Higher Power? Down through history, many people have worshiped idols, which were no more than father-projections made of wood, clay, or stone.

But God's Word tells us that Jesus Christ is that True Power. He always has been. He always will be.

Jesus Himself said He is the Alpha and Omega, the "A" through "Z" of eternity. He always existed, but took on a human body for a period of time. What a tribute to His love for us that He would limit Himself in that way. He was. He is now. He is to come. He is the Almighty God, the Son of the Father, and our Higher Power for now and forever.

Jesus, the eternal God, became Jesus, the sacrificial Lamb, but will return in the clouds as Jesus, the Messiah of believing Jews and Gentiles. For now, he guides our lives and our recovery as our Alpha and Omega.

> *For I know the thoughts that I think toward you,*
> *says the LORD, thoughts of peace and not of evil, to*
> *give you a future and a hope. Then you will call*
> *upon Me and go and pray to Me, and I will listen to*
> *you. And you will seek Me and find Me, when you*
> *search for Me with all your heart.*
>
> —JER. 29:11–13

The Israelites were captives in the foreign country of Babylon (now Iraq). They had disobeyed the Lord, and captivity was the price they had to pay. However, this was not a permanent punishment. God promised to restore them to their homeland.

Even though they had blown it, God was not abandoning them. God's thoughts toward them were of peace and not evil. He saw a future and a hope for the people of Israel.

I am not perfect. I sin, and there is a price to pay for it. However, it is not a permanent condition of punishment that I must live under for the rest of my life. God has a future and a hope for each of us. He wants to free us from the captivity of sin.

Is there an area of your life that has a negative hold on you? Do you feel like a captive? Captivity does not need to be permanent. Pray to God and He will listen. If we seek God with all our hearts, we will find Him. And when we find Him, we will be set free from the chains of captivity.

Dear Lord, teach me Your plan that sets captives free. Give me hope to trust in You and love to share Your plan with others.

"And God will wipe away every tear from their eyes; there shall be no more death, nor sorrow, nor crying; and there shall be no more pain, for the former things have passed away." —REV. 21:4

This passage talks about "serenity future." It gives us some "serenity present" because it offers hope for a future where we will be protected from abuse, disease, loss and sorrow of every kind.

This is talking about the eternal state; with new heavens, a new earth, and the New Jerusalem; after the one thousand-year Millennium is over.

God will wipe away all tears for all eternity. That will feel really good to this psychiatrist who has seen so many people suffer.

Jesus will make everything new. The Bible tells us we can't even *imagine* what wonderful surprises Jesus has in store for us.

Those who thirst for spiritual and emotional blessing and intimacy will be able to drink, without any cost, from the "fountain of the water of life." I believe Jesus—the gift-giver, love-giver, and life-giver—is that Fountain.

People through the ages have fantasized about finding a fountain of youth. But someday we will live with the true Fountain of eternal life.

May God grant us serenity now, that is a small sample of the outstanding eternal serenity to come, in which "necessary suffering" will no longer be necessary.

> *Thus says the LORD, the God of Israel: "Like these*
> *good figs, so will I acknowledge those who are*
> *carried away captive from Judah. . . . For I will set*
> *My eyes on them for good, and I will bring them*
> *back to this land.* —JER. 24:5–6

There go those figs again. Figs in the Bible usually represent the nation of Israel, God's chosen beloved people. He talks about them so much in the Bible that I often wish I could have been Jewish. But God has grafted us Gentiles into His fig tree. He loves us too.

In Jeremiah's prophecies, the Jews from Judah were carried away into slavery in Babylon. God has allowed the Jews to be scattered many times out of their homeland, always during times of rebellion against Him.

God made conditional covenants with the Jews in the Old Testament. He sent clear blessings and catastrophes. Sometimes Orthodox Jews wish God would choose somebody else for a while. But God also made unconditional covenants with His people. He promised that no matter what they do, He will eventually bring them back to their land permanently.

In the same way, our own personal restoration is marked by successes and failures, discoveries, and wanderings, periods of insight and periods of denial and psychological blindness. Through it all, we have a God who loves and accepts us unconditionally. His love is always loyal, never-ending.

A good parent loves to see his children grow and mature. So does God. He will always love and accept us.

> *. . . Of which I became a minister according to the gift of the grace of God given to me by the effective working of His power. To me, who am less than the least of all the saints, this grace was given, that I should preach among the Gentiles the unsearchable riches of Christ.*
> —EPH. 3:7–8

Before his conversion, Paul persecuted and killed many believers, so he humbly acknowledges God's incredible grace to save a sinner like him, the least of God's saints. Paul's "dynamite" *(dynameos)* courage was a gift from the Lord at his conversion.

Now Paul had the wonderful privilege of courageously extending to the Gentiles of the world the "unsearchable riches" of the Jewish Messiah. His secondary goal was to explain to the Gentiles, in particular, how the "fellowship" of this mystery will be carried out.

The plans of our living God were made possible because of what was accomplished by Jesus two thousand years ago on the cross. By believing on Him, we have the right to be called children of God. As His adopted sons and daughters, we have His protective love and we now have access to His power. Because of what Christ did we can also have great courage. We know the God of the universe—personally! We can boldly go to the Father as His assertive and confident children, and there find the strength to overcome any obstacle we encounter on earth.

"Dynamite" courage was part of God the Father's plan for our lives. Jesus made it possible. The Holy Spirit enables us. The rest is up to us.

A man's heart plans his way,
But the Lord directs his steps.
PROV. 16:9

I was rummaging through a box of pictures and cards that the children have lovingly created over the years. There were cards with a small handprint and the date. How I treasure these! There were the first attempts at printing their names with the letters upside down and backwards and absolutely beautiful. Finally there were the masterpieces created recently by a ten-year-old and a fourteen-year-old. Steadily life marches on.

Change cannot be stopped. As Christians we choose to follow God's leading even though we don't know where we're going. Oh, we think we know. We create plans but unexpected surprises occur along the way which make it necessary for us to learn flexibility and, also, trust.

How can we prepare to face the unknown challenges waiting around the corner? We can anchor ourselves to the character of God. God is good! God is love! Life will present us with contradictions but, in the midst of them, we can trust God's purposes.

Thank You, Lord, for being trustworthy. Your love and Your character will guide me through all the unknowns of today.

Cease from anger, and forsake wrath;
Do not fret—it only causes harm.
—PS. 37:8

It is one thing to be upset about the evil that goes on all around us. But if we harbor anger and allow it to smolder, we may become emotionally or physically ill.

Getting angry doesn't hurt us if we resolve it quickly. We are told in both the Old and New Testaments to get angry but not to sin. In Ephesians 4:26, the apostle Paul suggests that we forgive by bedtime.

"Do not fret—it only causes harm." Psychiatric research has revealed more about the harm caused by "fretting" or worry, holding grudges or vengeful motives, and other negative emotions. These things cause serotonin and norepinephrine depletions from the brain, causing clinical depression. Some of the symptoms are insomnia, tiredness, poor concentration, and sadness. Other complicated physiological reactions can also take place that decrease our antibodies and lower our resistance to all infectious diseases, including viral cancers.

If we wait on the Lord, we will see justice. The meek will someday inherit the earth. They will be delighted by the absence of evil and abuse—and the abundance of peace.

We need wisdom to know how to deal with anger in a healthy way. Being our own best friend includes protecting ourselves from the ill effects of mishandling our normal day-by-day anger.

Every word of God is pure;
He is a shield to those who put their trust in Him.
Do not add to His words,
Lest He reprove you, and you be found a liar.
—PROV. 30:5–6

How can God be known? Through His Word and His Son.

Perhaps you have heard the story of the bird in search of food in the middle of winter. A kind person, realizing the scarcity of food, had filled the bird feeder. With the continual snow, only a small amount of food would be uncovered in the storm. The caring person noticed a weak bird appear, pecking in the snow. The person felt so helpless. He wished he could communicate to the bird and point the bird to the supply. The individual thought "If I could just become a bird, then I could communicate and let the bird know where to go for food."

In a similar way, God realized our inability to really know and understand Him. Wanting to communicate with us, He decided to send His Son Jesus Christ to become one of us. As a man, Jesus could speak our language and communicate to us what God wanted us to know. God also revealed more of who He was through the written Word of God, the Bible.

There is so much to know about God. I can find out more as I study His Word, which reveals who He is.

For we do not have a High Priest who cannot sympathize with our weaknesses, but was in all points tempted as we are, yet without sin.
—HEB. 4:15

The people in my life that I have felt a real freedom to talk with are incredibly empathetic and understanding. I have felt that they were on my side; that they were for me. In contrast, there are many I would never have gone and talked with because I felt they were judgmental or condemning.

In order to feel safe and share our deep feelings, we need friends who are empathetic, supportive, and caring. If the person we confide in has also gone through a similar experience, that increases our confidence. For example, a victim will often feel safer working with a therapist who has also been a victim.

The Lord is like this for us. He was tempted in every way we are. The Lord is our High Priest. In Old Testament times, the high priest was the one who represented the people of Israel to God. He was their spokesman. Jesus is our representative before God, and He is on our side. We can confidently come to Jesus, since He is for us. He has experienced what we are going through, and He sympathizes with our weakness. Jesus does not condemn us when we come to Him, but in Him we will find mercy and grace.

If I am hesitant to go to Jesus in prayer, it might be because I have not seen who He really is. He is on my side; He went through what I am experiencing; and He is empathetic regarding my weaknesses.

> *The fear of man brings a snare,*
> *But whoever trusts in the Lord shall be safe.*
> —PROV. 29:25

People pleasing is hazardous to our health. Our self-talk bombards us with toxic statements: "I should get along with everyone. If there is any conflict, it must be my fault."

Thinking this way gives other people all the power. We become nonpersons, clones of whoever we are with, dependent on their approval.

What a devastating way to live! It is a slow route to suicide, a first step in the destruction of ourselves. Often people who have allowed themselves to be molded into someone else's image find themselves discarded. The person they have tried so hard to please often finds them boring. No wonder Solomon writes that the "fear of man brings a snare."

People pleasers often feel that they must be God pleasers too. They think God loves them when they're perfect and hates them when they're not. That kind of thinking drives us away from God rather than toward Him.

Trusting God means that I take Him at His Word. I am accepted by God because of what Jesus Christ did on the cross, *not* because of what I do or don't do. Therefore, I am free to be myself.

The New Testament meaning of grace *is "freely given, undeserved, unmerited, unearnable and unrepayable favor." When I trust in that truth, the result is a personal peace that is beyond all understanding.*

They wandered about in sheepskins and goatskins,
being destitute, afflicted, tormented—of whom the
world was not worthy. —HEB. 11:37–38a

Unfortunately, even though laws have been passed to promote equality in America, prejudice in attitude is still prevalent. Have you ever been in a situation where you were in the minority? Have you felt ridiculed and put down based on the difference between you and the majority?

If we are Christians we must accept the fact that we may suffer severe hardships and prejudice. The Christian leaders of history have been stoned, beaten, put in jail, and killed because of their faith in Jesus.

The apostle Paul says in effect, "Why do you think you will not have to suffer? You will. It has been appointed."

There are many who are opposed to what Christianity stands for and are very vocal about it. A friend of ours was on a plane returning from the East Coast and sat beside a man who appeared to be praying. After he finished, our friend inquired as to what he was praying for. The man replied, "I'm praying to Satan to break up the marriages of Christian pastors and leaders."

We will encounter spiritual prejudice and suffering because we are Christians. That fact should not surprise us.

———————

Lord, give me the strength to withstand the suffering I may experience because I love You.

> *He makes my feet like the feet of deer,*
> *And sets me on my high places.*
> —PS. 18:31–33

Growing up in Western Canada, I saw the majestic Canadian Rockies every day. I remember the excitement of seeing a deer or mountain sheep up on the rugged face of the mountain. Usually we would stop, get out our binoculars, and watch the deer and sheep jump gracefully from rock to rock. They were sure-footed even though the terrain was rough. They seemed to move without fear. They were able to climb gracefully to the very top of the mountains.

We can have courage because of what God does for us. He makes our feet like those of a deer. God will make us sure-footed in an unstable world. He will relieve our fears and give us confidence to face the challenges of life. God will arm us with strength for whatever happens. As we place our faith in Him, He is like that mountain. He is solid, strong, and unchanging.

What are you facing today? Are you struggling with fear? Do you feel uncertain? Do your circumstances seem unstable? Take courage in God. He wants to give you the sure-footed feet of a deer. He wants you to feel safe, strong, and confident as you face this day.

What God promises, He delivers. Accept His strength, power, and stability in the midst of your shaky, unstable world.

For the love of money is a root of all kinds of evil.
—1 TIM. 6:8

Steve was a friend who had worked hard and established himself as the head of a manufacturing firm. His company came to be known as a leader in the United States. Steve enjoyed the benefits of the money he accumulated, but he always had time to stop and go to lunch. He would make time if I expressed a need to get together with him to talk over a personal problem. He was alert to ways he could use his money to help those less fortunate. He was a giver. He had control of enormous amounts of money, but the money didn't control him. He loved people more than he loved money.

Brian had made his money through land investments. He was now "retired," but he appeared to be more driven than ever to accumulate more wealth. He seemed consumed with it. You might say, he loved money, but money controlled him. Brian was too busy for his wife, his kids, or anyone. He had long ago forgotten about God. He was an obsessed man.

It is clear that money is not evil, but the *love* of money is the root of all kinds of evil. This greediness has the potential to cause us to stray from our faith.

How do you handle money, or better yet, how does money handle you? Money can be a help or a hindrance. It depends on where we place our love.

Do I need to regroup in my thinking toward money? Is it something I love and focus on? Have I placed money in its proper perspective?

> *Where there is no counsel, the people fall;*
> *But in the multitude of counselors there is safety.*
> —PROV. 11:14

Teens can be a wonderful and frustrating package. Mind you, it's a tremendous pressure to be so young and to know all the answers. Parents are sometimes the last people they will listen to. The wise parent sees to it that a teenager has other adult Christian friends to relate to.

What about adults? Do they need friends to encourage them, support them, and give them guidance? You'd better believe it. Our greatest resource as Christians is the presence of Jesus Christ Himself. The second is the fellowship of God's people.

Proverbs 13:20 says that "He who walks with wise men will be wise, But the companion of fools will be destroyed." We need to choose our companions carefully, for we will become like the people we spend most of our time with.

Ray Ortlund writes, "I don't know about you, but I desperately need men around me who are giant-killers. I have an innate tendency to fear; I need fearless, godly men."

Godly counselors need to be affirmers, but they also need to be courageous enough to exhort and rebuke us. They need to hold us accountable to meet the goals we have set. Godly companions will bring out the best in us.

Who is on your Christ-centered support team? Begin developing those kinds of relationships today.

And when I saw Him, I fell at His feet as dead. But He laid His right hand on me, saying to me, "Do not be afraid; I am the First and the Last. I am He who lives, and was dead, and behold, I am alive forevermore."
—REV. 1:17–18

Have you ever gone to the top of a high mountain, climbed out of your car, and stood there absolutely awestruck with the beauty of nature and your insignificance in comparison? That is a taste of what John felt when Christ showed him prophetic events. Christ would not allow some of these events to be written down. John was awestruck, and fell at Jesus' feet.

Jesus comforted John as He wants to comfort us, by revealing aspects of His nature to increase our faith and relieve our fears.

We don't need to fear Satan in the sense of our eternal destiny, because Jesus holds the keys to death and hell. We should watch out for Satan's deceits and temptations—he goes around like a stalking lion in search of people to abuse with appealing sinful pleasures that end up being destructive. But don't fear Satan relative to God's power. Resist Satan and God will make him flee from you.

Then God told John to write down Christ's revelations for all future generations to read. Christ promised special blessings to all who study and apply the special Book of Revelation.

Lord, help me to trust You now, day by day, as my Higher Power.

> *. . . casting all your care upon Him, for He cares
> for you.*
> —1 PETER 5:7

Speaking in various places often involves carrying boxes of books along with my personal luggage. Therefore, last year I purchased a collapsible cart. Traveling is so much easier now that I don't have to carry all that baggage, but can place it on the cart and roll it.

Many of us carry emotional burdens God never meant for us to bear. We become physically worn out and emotionally drained by the problems.

What worries or anxieties are burdening you? Do you have a financial concern that is getting you down? Do you have an interpersonal problem that turns you inside out? Are you upset by a job problem? Are you concerned about your future? Whatever the problem is, you can cast it or put it on the Lord. God never meant for you to carry it yourself.

The application of this verse can be carried out with an exercise in visualization. Picture your problem as a heavy weight in a gunny sack carried on your back. The road you are walking stretches on for miles. Now visualize the Lord walking beside you. Stop walking! Unload the sack, turn it over to the Lord, and let Him carry it.

It is possible to use prayer as a way of unloading our burdens. We can approach God with our concerns.

It's time to stop carrying the burdens of your life alone. Turn them over to Christ.

"Come, I will show you the bride, the Lamb's wife."
And he carried me away in the Spirit to a great
and high mountain, and showed me the great city,
the holy Jerusalem, descending out of heaven from
God, having the glory of God. —REV. 21:9–10

The book of Revelation was written by John the Beloved while he was exiled on the Island of Patmos. But Revelation 1:1 makes it clear that it is the revelation of Jesus Christ, not of John.

In this passage, John viewed the end of the Great Tribulation. Then one of the angels who caused the seven plagues came to John and showed him a delightful sight—the bride of Jesus, the New Testament church. Then the angel took John to a high mountain to see the New Jerusalem, or he took John to a high mountain that was the New Jerusalem. I believe John saw us, all of Christ's followers. We are the bride of Christ, and we will come back to earth with Jesus to begin the Messianic Kingdom.

On earth we suffer much pain even if we actively pursue personal recovery and growth. Accepting what we cannot change is part of the real world and part of the Serenity Prayer. When I am suffering from the realities I cannot change, I refresh myself with the delightful thought of my future with the Lord.

May God's promise of your bright eternal tomorrow bring you the serenity to bear the pains of things you cannot change today.

> *For He does not afflict willingly,*
> *Nor grieve the children of men.*
> —LAM. 3:33

Inside millions of households, ranging across all social, economic and educational lines, the horrendous crime of child abuse is being committed every day.

Physically abusive parents seem to have many similarities. Instead of dealing with their own negative feelings, they assault their children. Physical abusers often come from violent homes and enter adulthood with unmet needs.

Were you raised by physically abusive parents? If you were you have experienced the horror of being punished to serve your parents' purposes, not for your good. Two important distinctions must be made: the difference between punishment and discipline, and the difference between your earthly parents and your heavenly Father.

Discipline is motivated by love; punishment is the result of fury. Discipline is for the best of the child, while punishment is a reliever of parental poison.

We must also grasp our heavenly Father's character. How incredibly different it is from that of vengeful, insecure child abusers. Our Father disciplines us but does not inflict pain maliciously nor grieve our hearts as does the abusive parent. His compassion and mercy are constantly with us. He has our best interest foremost in His heart.

Lord, thank You for loving me enough to discipline me. Teach me to discipline rather than punish my own children.

The heavens declare the glory of God;
And the firmament shows His handiwork.
—PS. 19:1

One of the highlights for me as a child was the exciting times I had on camping trips in the Canadian rockies. Having grown up on the flat prairies of Canada I still remember the excitement that would build inside me as we drove from Calgary into the majestic, towering mountains. They were rugged, and each mountain different from the next. I can remember building a lean-to and then cooking on an open fire as we waited for the evening to come. As it would get darker, a myriad of stars would begin to appear. It was so dark in the wilderness and the stars were so bright.

Even as a child I was awed by the grandeur of the mountains and night sky. I remember thinking that God sure knew what He was doing when He created our world and set the stars in their place.

God communicates to us through His creation. The God who made such a wonderful, beautiful world also made us. That fact should give us encouragement that the Lord knew what He was doing. At times we might wish He had made us differently, but the Creator of the universe did not make a mistake. We are made the way He wanted us to be made. We are His workmanship.

Stop today and observe some of God's handiwork. Look in the mirror and thank God for how He made you.

> *He has shown you, O man, what is good;*
> *And what does the LORD require of you*
> *But to do justly,*
> *To love mercy,*
> *And to walk humbly with your God?*
> —MIC. 6:8

Tony Campolo tells the story of getting together with his buddies as a young boy to pull a prank. They went to the corner store and changed all the price tags. We can only imagine the confusion that resulted.

Sometimes it feels as if some pranksters have come into our world and changed the price tags. Things are valued more than people. Frantic activity is valued more than serenity. Money is valued more than morality. We value quick thrills more than commitment.

Micah attempted to switch the price tags back. He told the nation of Israel that God didn't want external rituals, He wanted an inward relationship. God wanted the people to obey Him because they loved Him, not because it was a burdensome command.

There are three actions God values in the lives of His followers. He wants them to be fair in their dealings with others. He also wants them to love mercy and carry through on their commitments. God wants His people to walk humbly with Him. He is the source of our love, our serenity and our power. These actions will be so counter to our culture that they will be a manifestation to those around us that we are walking with God.

What does my lifestyle demonstrate that I value?

*Bear one another's burdens, and so fulfill the law
of Christ. . . . For each one shall bear his own load.*
—GAL. 6:2, 5

Codependency is not a new problem. It is just that people are finally becoming aware of problems that have been going on since the Fall.

Codependency is any addiction to persons, substances, things or behaviors. Some people are addicted to rescuing others. They go overboard and do too much for the person they are trying to help. Instead of helping, the rescuer ultimately causes hurt by fostering dependence and selfishness in the one being "rescued." If an alcoholic spends his or her paycheck on wine and then asks you for money, for example, you can best love him by saying no. But you can offer your friendship and your honest confrontation. You can recommend a professional treatment center, or welcome him or her to an AA group or your local church.

Galatians 6:5 says everyone should bear his own load. The Greek word here is *phortion* meaning a normal load, such as a backpack a soldier would carry. Galatians 6:2 says we should carry each other's burdens, but the Greek word is *bare*. It means we should carry each other's legitimate *overburdens*—heavy, crushing loads that are more than a person can carry without help. We sin if we carry someone's *phortion* for them. We sin if we don't help carry a brother's overburden.

May God grant us the wisdom to do what is best for those who request our help.

> *For unto us a Child is born, unto us a Son is given;*
> *and the government will be upon His shoulder. And*
> *His name will be called Wonderful, Counselor,*
> *Mighty God, Everlasting Father, Prince of Peace. Of*
> *the increase of His government and peace there will*
> *be no end.*
>
> —ISA. 9:6

As we consider who God is, we must accept Him in totality. There is the tendency to gravitate to one facet of God and ignore the rest. God is a God of dichotomy. God (Jesus) came in the form of a child, yet He is also a ruler over the government. He is the Judge but also the comforter. He is love and grace but also truth. He acts in judgment and also love. He is the mighty powerful God, yet the Prince of Peace.

We will experience an imbalance if we focus only on one aspect of God. Kelly thought of God only as a judge, and constantly felt put down. Interestingly enough, her own father had treated her this way. Kelly needed to see that God was also grace. Rob, on the other hand, had a father who had never disciplined him and had over indulged him. As an adult now, Rob centered on God's grace and did not accept that God judges wrong-doing. He continued to blatantly get involved in affairs. He felt that God's grace would forgive him, so it didn't matter what he did.

We need to see all of who God is; to view Him in His totality. Truly we have a wonderful God.

Lord, help me to experience all of who You are and not confuse You with my parents.

*Is anyone among you suffering? Let him pray. Is
anyone cheerful? Let him sing psalms. Is anyone
among you sick? Let him call for the elders of the
church, and let them pray over him, anointing him
with oil in the name of the Lord.*
—JAMES 5:13–14

God has designed us to need each other. The "do
your own thing" philosophy ignores the fact that God
has made us interrelated and interdependent.

A young woman shared her testimony at church
about being raised in an abusive alcoholic home. God's
hand on her life was so evident. As I started leaving the
service, the woman in front of me, obviously a visitor,
turned around: "Boy, the people in your church sure
have a lot of problems. We don't have anyone like that
in our church." I wanted to breathe a sigh of relief that I
wasn't attending her church.

We need one another. There is an "us-ness" to the
Christian faith. We are called the body of Christ. The
body is composed of cells. Every cell functions in such
a way that the other cells can operate efficiently. There
is only one cell that operates on its own, cancer.

If we are hurting, suffering, or sick, we can choose
to retreat or reach out and allow others to minister to
us. Only as a result of our vulnerability can others
know our desire for healing.

Learning to receive doesn't appeal to our pride in
the same way that giving does. What a precious gift it
is when we can't give but must only receive.

Lord, teach me how to receive as well to give.

He who trusts in his own heart is a fool,
But whoever walks wisely will be delivered.
—PROV. 28:25–26

Do you ever wonder if the Bible has anything relevant to say to you? A sure sign that the Scriptures are God's Word is that they hit each of us right where we are living.

A proud heart shows up in the way we relate to others. Do you have a need to always be in control? Inside every overly controlling adult is a wounded, shame-driven child.

Trusting in the Lord and applying His principles moves us from the love of power to the power of love. After people have been with us do they go away impressed with our greatness, or full of the possibilities of their own greatness? Do they feel used or understood?

Jesus Christ was the ultimate example of sacrificial, serving love. As His followers, we are to be Christ's channels of love to the people in our lives. We must not refuse to open our minds, our hearts, and our arms. We must share ourselves with others, and embrace who they are. When we relate in this way to others, we enable them to have a clearer and bigger understanding of God. We can make the invisible God more "real," and bring about in each other's lives an experimental awareness of what it means to be deeply loved by Him.

Lord, help me to make You more real to the people in my life today. Show Yourself to them through me.

"For whom the LORD loves He chastens,
And scourges every son whom He receives."
—HEB. 12:6

As a typical child, I got into mischief and from time to time would deliberately disobey my parents. They would take me into the spare bedroom and begin to talk. They would say, "Why did you do this, and what can you do differently tomorrow?" Then they would take out a belt and say, "We are going to spank you," followed by, "We are doing this because we love you."

At the time, those words somehow didn't ring true to me as I sat with my behind stinging. I remember thinking "This doesn't feel like love!"

Now that I have children of my own, that statement makes more sense to me.

In my psychological practice, I am often confronted with individuals who tell of feeling abandoned. They tell of being allowed to do whatever they wanted. They felt as if their parents didn't even care about them.

God demonstrates by his discipline that we are His children. He shows He loves us by caring enough to correct us and teach us how we can act differently in the future. God's purpose for our discipline is that we might be educated by the process. He does not just want to punish us, He wants us to learn to act differently in the future. God's discipline focuses on the future correct deed, rather than the past misdeed.

Lord, thank You that You show Your love to me by disciplining me.

Lift up your heads, O you gates!
And lift them up, you everlasting doors!
And the King of glory shall come in.
Who is this King of glory?
The LORD of hosts,
He is the King of glory.

—PS. 24:9–10

When we lift our eyes and focus on praising our Lord, something powerful happens inside of us. Our perspective changes. We realize that we are not alone. The Lord is present. He has been here the entire time. He will find a way to use every problem in our lives for our growth and His purposes.

Lifting up your eyes doesn't mean that you have to retreat to a quiet place. You can choose to do that if you wish. It is wonderful when we are able to pull away to adore the Lord. But it is not a prerequisite to lifting our eyes. It is possible to praise God in the middle of our circumstances. We can practice God's presence no matter where life takes us.

How many people has your life touched already today? What kind of a difference would it make if you lifted each of those people into God's presence? What if at the same moment you were saying, "hi" you were lifting your eyes to the Lord and saying, "Lord thank You for this person. Make him or her aware of Your presence today." I can guarantee that we all would have an attitude change.

Lord, thank You that I can lift my eyes and focus on You in such a way that I will be empowered to be Your force for wholeness in my world.

*And let us consider one another in order to stir up
love and good works, not forsaking the assembling
of ourselves together.*   —HEB. 10:24–25

Jimmy Durante was asked to perform at a veterans'
benefit. Because of his busy schedule, he agreed to
perform, but only for ten minutes. The evening arrived
and Durante went on stage. He began his monologue
and the crowd cheered him on. In the front row were
two seasoned veterans who had been in the first World
War. One had lost his right arm, and the other his left.
The two were sitting alongside each other, and
Durante couldn't help but notice them. After his jokes,
these two men who could not clap on their own would
turn and clap together. Durante was so moved that he
performed for thirty minutes. When he finally walked
off the stage, the sponsor asked why he had extended
his performance. Durante told the man to look through
the curtain. The two men were still clapping.

We were not meant to live as islands in our Christianity. We need the support and encouragement of
others. We are not meant to go it alone. Assembling
together can be done in a church fellowship or a support group. More and more churches today are pro-
moting involvement in small groups. By being
involved we can "spur one another on toward love and
good deeds."

_____

*Consider joining a small group to be supported and encouraged and
then reciprocate in kind.*

> *Who can find a virtuous wife?*
> *For her worth is far above rubies.*
> —PROV. 31:10

Some people think the Bible degrades women, but I believe it does just the opposite. Jesus lived in a very male-dominated age, and yet taught that in heaven there will be equality between males and females. God used the prophet Malachi to warn men that if they abused their wives in any way, He would not answer their prayers.

And here in Proverbs 31, the Holy Spirit guided the author to write a glowing description of a wise and godly woman. Today's verse is followed by a long list of qualities that identify her.

Not only is she virtuous and valuable, she is trustworthy, consistently good, resourceful and responsible. She is wise, independent, and enterprising. She is strong—both physically and emotionally. She feels good about the things she buys and sells, and has confidence in her own judgment.

She is not too proud to work hard, or to serve the poor and needy. She "wears" emotional strength, honor and rejoicing all over her personality. She says wise and kind things. She fears God, and her children and husband feel blessed to live with her.

Think of specific things you can do to help bring an end to the abuse and misuse of women and to spread the biblical view of their great worth to the God who created them.

He is despised and rejected by men,
A Man of sorrows and acquainted with grief.
And we hid, as it were, our faces from Him;
He was despised, and we did not esteem Him.
Surely He has borne our griefs
And carried our sorrows. —ISA. 53:3–4a

In our culture, there are many times when we want to associate with the hero, the leader, and the beautiful people. We sometimes hope that we will feel better about ourselves by our association with such figures.

Jesus chose a different image for Himself than the top rung of society. In His physical appearance Jesus was not particularly outstanding or attractive. Rather than being the hero, Jesus was despised and even rejected. He experienced sorrow and grief.

Jesus chose the image of the unlovely. He chose to identify with where most of us live on a daily basis, in order that we could identify with Him. Jesus did not want us to have to escape from the realities of life and try to get next to a superstar. Jesus took on human form and suffered the rejection and disappointments of life. He suffered through everyday trials, but lived victoriously through them. He did this in order that we also would be able to face our reality honestly and squarely, and with the Lord's help be victorious. Jesus identified with us so we could identify with Him.

People are drawn to Christ because He is a real person who lived as we live. If we are like Him, we will be approachable and attractive to others not because of the image we project, but because we are real.

Return to the LORD your God,
For He is gracious and merciful,
Slow to anger, and of great kindness:
And He relents from doing harm.
—JOEL 2:13

A baby is totally dependent on its parents for its physical, emotional, and spiritual survival. The quality of nurturing it receives leaves the child with a feeling of belonging and of being worthy.

But what if this baby is abandoned, beaten, neglected, criticized, or resented? The child's ability to trust is shattered. In order to protect itself the child adopts an "I don't need anyone" position. Healthy relationships are no longer pursued. Internal barriers keep others away.

Many of us have experienced this internal agony. It blocks us from further intimacy. If we marry at all, that marriage is full of pain and isolation. If we chose not to marry we often go from one unhealthy relationship to another.

We have much to grieve. With the help of a Christian counselor we need to let our heart break. The tears, the anger and the incredible sadness must be faced. All the barriers we have erected to protect ourselves from intimacy must be brought down.

When we come to the absolute end of ourselves, we also find ourselves ready to face our Lord.

When my father and my mother forsake me, then the Lord will take care of me.

*But I saw no temple in it, for the Lord God
Almighty and the Lamb are its temple. And the city
had no need of the sun or of the moon to shine in
it, for the glory of God illuminated it, and the Lamb
is its light.*
                                   —REV. 21:22–23

Sometimes I feel all alone. Sometimes I feel discouraged. At times like these, serenity seems a figment of someone's imagination. Then I read passages like this one. It motivates me to keep helping others whenever I feel discouraged about myself. It gives me a sense of dignity and serenity on the days I feel inferior or lonely. I am a carpenter's kid from Michigan who will someday be a prince in the New Jerusalem.

The New Jerusalem won't have a temple. The Father and the Son will be its temple, and their glory will light up the whole city. When God gave the Ten Commandments to Moses, Moses' face shone with the reflected light for three days and people couldn't even bear to look at him. Imagine what it will be like to stand in God's actual presence!

My teenagers will love the New Jerusalem because they'll get to stay up all night every night—their new bodies won't need to sleep. And the gates will stay open day and night. There will be no thieves to come and steal our treasure. Only true believers will be allowed to enter.

Do you ever feel discouraged, lonely or insecure? Does serenity seem far away on those days? Meditate on God's extraordinary plans for your future. It will do wonders for your peace of mind.

> *Precious in the sight of the LORD*
> *Is the death of His saints.*
> —PS. 116:15

I have had the experience of counseling and supporting individuals who are grieving the loss of a loved one. Often it is a time of shock, bewilderment, and confusion. Then there is the pain, anger, and depression that follows the realization of their personal loss. In times of discouragement the tendency is to ask the question, "Why, God? Why are you allowing this?" I can't answer this question, but it is true that God views death differently than we do. It is part of His plan.

As a young child, I can remember running underneath the quilting frame which was placed on four chairs in our living room. I looked up at the jumble of different colored threads and patches of material, and asked my grandmother what that tangled mess was. It sure didn't make sense to me from my perspective.

Imagine my surprise the first time she picked me up and let me see the quilt from the other side, from her viewpoint. Now all the threads, patches, and colors blended together in a beautiful pattern.

Our earthly viewpoint on death may be like looking at the underside of the quilt. God has a different view. He says the death of His children is precious in His sight. My guess is that for Him, it is like a happy family reunion. A son or daughter has come home.

Only when we have faced the reality of our death are we really prepared to LIVE!

Love has been perfected among us in this: that we may have boldness in the day of judgment; because as He is, so are we in this world. There is no fear in love; but perfect love casts out fear, because fear involves torment. But he who fears has not been made perfect in love. We love Him because He first loved us.
—1 JOHN 4:17–19

How much of every day do you spend in worry or paralyzed by fear? How would your life be different if all fear was removed?

Wouldn't it be wonderful if something happened deep within you that would give you such inner confidence, calmness, and security that you would never be afraid of anyone or anything in the future?

Wouldn't it be exciting if you had a spiritual, emotional, and mental experience that was so significant you found no tendency to retreat to anxiety, worry, fear, or guilt?

In this passage John reminds us that this can be a reality. He says "Perfect love casts out fear." If we are experiencing God's perfect love, we can begin to live, and living is risking.

Bruce Larson puts it this way, "To be saved means to be so secure in God's love, present, and future, that I have no need to be safe again."

Lord, teach me to love perfectly and to cast away my fear.

> *Let all bitterness, wrath, anger, clamor, and evil*
> *speaking be put away from you, with all malice.*
> *And be kind to one another, tenderhearted,*
> *forgiving one another, just as God in Christ also*
> *forgave you.*
> —EPH. 4:31–32

None of us wants to spend the majority of our time feeling out of control, overwhelmed by our emotions, cornered by our circumstances, whipped by our guilt and "if onlys," and frozen by our fantasies. But that's where many people are before they decide to become part of a Twelve Step Program.

As we learn to take responsibility for our choices, we will become *responders* rather than *reactors*. A reactor is full of bitterness, wrath, anger, loud quarrelling and evil speaking, because a reactor is overinvolved in other people's problems. He or she lives for and through other people. Under all that fury and obsession is a hurting, frightened child.

In contrast, a responder understands that we are responsible only for ourselves, our actions, and our words. At the same time, we are free to love others, not rescue them.

What a change this brings to our relationships. Rather than trying to control other people, we learn to be honest and to clearly communicate our needs.

We learn to be kinder, more compassionate and forgiving toward ourselves, and others. We speak words that are helpful and edifying.

Recognize when you're reacting. Replace your reactions with healthy choices.

"I, wisdom, dwell with prudence,
And find out knowledge and discretion.
The fear of the LORD is to hate evil;
Pride and arrogance and the evil way
And the perverse mouth I hate.
Counsel is mine, and sound wisdom;
I am understanding, I have strength.
—PROV. 8:12–14

All true wisdom comes from the God who created our brains. Therefore, as you read Proverbs 8 of "I, wisdom" personified, substitute the words, "I, God."

If we have God's type of wisdom, we will have common sense. We will also have discretion.

True wisdom is not just mental, but moral. If we reverentially fear the Lord, we will detest evil, pride, and arrogance. Neither will we have a foul mouth.

If we have wisdom, we will both give and seek wise counsel and sound judgment, because we will have understanding and insight into our psychological dynamics. We will also have God's strength.

Kings, rulers, princes and judges who do well on earth do so by applying God's wise principles, whether they know it or not. Non-Christian psychiatrists who work wonders on their patients are those who are also applying the principles of the Bible although they have arrived at those principles through research and reason. All truth is God's truth.

Those who love God's wisdom, God will love, and those who seek God's wisdom diligently will find it.

Now to Him who is able to keep you from
  stumbling,
And to present you faultless
Before the presence of His glory with exceeding joy,
To God our Savior,
Who alone is wise,
Be glory and majesty,
Dominion and power,
Both now and forever.
　　　　　　　　　　　　—JUDE 1:24–25

Introductions can be a dull formality or they can be enthusiastic and full of life. They say something about the person giving the introduction as well as the individual being introduced.

How do you think Christ would introduce you to God the Father? Christ can present you as faultless. How ludicrous, you might say. I certainly am not perfect. I've blown it many times. The Bible would endorse that fact for all of us. It says "We have *all* sinned." However, because Christ paid the penalty of our sin and put on us Christ's righteousness, we appear faultless to God.

Christ also is able to present us to God with joy. So often we have the tendency to feel as if God is angry and displeased with us. We often feel those around us are unhappy with us. However, we are a joy to Christ and that is how He would present or introduce us to God.

What an encouragement that thought is. I can't wait to be introduced. How about you?

Christ sees me as faultless and I bring joy to Him.

Give ear, O LORD, to my prayer;
And attend to the voice of my supplications.
In the day of my trouble I will call upon You,
For You will answer me.
Among the gods there is none like You, O Lord;
Nor are there any works like Your works.
—PS. 86:6–8

Gary had high hopes for a promotion. He had dramatically increased his sales of a particular pharmaceutical drug, which put him next in line to become a regional manager. Suddenly, the Federal Drug Administration froze sales until more research could be done on that medication. That also put a freeze on Gary's promotion.

Gary's friend, Art, called on the phone soon after this and asked what he was doing. Gary replied quickly that he had been praying. "Is it *that* bad?" asked his friend.

For many people, prayer is a last resort. We certainly can call on God in times of trouble. But as we mature, prayer can be part of our everyday life. We can pray when we are on top of the world, as well as when it feels like the bottom has dropped out of our world. God will be there when we call, and He will answer.

You will often hear it said, "It does not matter who you worship: Confucius, Mohammed, Joseph Smith, . . . as long as you are sincere." Don't believe it. There is no other god but the Lord God.

May God grant me the wisdom to pray when I am feeling serene and also to courageously come to Him during times of crisis.

*And this is the testimony: that God has given us
eternal life, and this life is in His Son. He who has
the Son has life; he who does not have the Son of
God does not have life.* —1 JOHN 5:11–12

A Wall Street Journal article reported on a survey in
which men and women were asked, "What is it that
you fear the most?" The number three fear of all par-
ticipants was the fear of death. The fear of failure
ranked number one, and the fear of loneliness was
number two.

1 John 4:18 says that "perfect love casts out fear."
Perfect love has only the good of the person being
loved in mind. Perfect love was demonstrated when
God sent His only Son Jesus Christ to die in our place.
Fortunately that wasn't the end of the story. Jesus was
the ultimate victim of my sin, but God wasn't going to
leave Him a victim forever. Death had no power over
Him. Resurrection was God's answer to the worst that
human beings could dish out.

If I accept Jesus Christ as my Lord and Savior, I have
eternal life. That frees me from my fear of death.

Something else happens too. I am welcomed into a
caring, supportive group of believers. Together we
support each other as we discover what it means to
follow Jesus. We no longer need to fear loneliness.

The incredible power that raised Christ from the
dead is also available to me today. That power can
bring good out of even my most devastating failures.
Therefore I don't have to fear failure.

Because of Christ I do not have to fear failure, loneliness or death.

Take away the dross from silver,
And it will go to the silversmith for jewelry.
—PROV. 25:4

Each summer my wife and I like to go to the Sawdust Festival at Laguna Beach, which is close to where we live. Artisans of every kind display their creative artwork. Many of them set up and actually make their specialty right on site. There are potters, glass blowers, oil painters and sometimes even a gold or silversmith.

The silversmith will take the rough pieces of silver and silver ore and heat them in the fire. By so doing the impurities can be removed from the silver. Often the process is repeated several times. The goal is to extract the pure silver.

Most of us are like the silver ore. We have parts that need to be refined and reworked. The imagery of the silversmith helps us realize that God can and will send some trials to refine us and make us into more valuable silver.

Can you accept some of the problems you are facing as God's way of making you into a better person?

Lord, help me to accept that the problems I face can refine me. Thank You for making me more like You.

I will bless the LORD who has given me counsel;
My heart also instructs me in the night seasons.
I have set the LORD always before me;
Because He is at my right hand I shall not be moved.
—PS. 16:7–8

Have you ever battled for the solution to a problem? You honestly didn't know which way to turn. You felt trapped. You fell into bed at night exhausted and perplexed. Perhaps you spent most of the night tossing and turning. Suddenly at around three A.M. you found yourself wide awake, and you knew the answer.

Jacob had an experience like this. He had deceived his father and stolen his brother Esau's birthrite. Esau was pursuing Jacob, and Jacob was fleeing for his very life. He was guilty and he knew it. That evening he had a dream. When he awoke he cried out, "The Lord was here and I didn't even notice."

Our greatest resource in times of stress is God Himself. If Jesus Christ is your Lord and Savior, He is closer to you than the things that irritate you, for they are outside of you. If we can grasp the depth of His truth, God will become the very center and heart of our life rather than just an addition to an already busy schedule. God is interested in every aspect of my life.

When food color is added to icing, all of it turns the same color. When we make Christ central, everything is colored by Him.

I want to bless the Lord who guides me. Because He is my guide, I don't have to race through life in a frenzy.

"Why do you spend money for what is not bread,
And your wages for what does not satisfy?
Listen diligently to Me, and eat what is good,
And let your soul delight itself in abundance.
—ISA. 55:2

Our present generation, like most others, appears to be in a constant search for satisfaction. The philosophy of our culture sells us the idea that if we have the perfect body we will be satisfied. The sales pitch for satisfaction also comes from the promise of owning the right car, buying the right house, or living in the right area of the country. Other messages of the media suggest that if you are dissatisfied in your marriage or other relationships don't waste any more time on it. Discard that unfulfilling relationship and go in search of the perfect person.

Today's passage is saying in effect, "Hold it! Don't go wasting your money on all these things that don't satisfy." Rather come to Christ who offers real life to you, not in exchange for any dollar amount.

Christ offers us life, real and abundant life, as a free gift. Christ said "I have come that you might have life and have it more abundantly."

Lord, when my soul is hungry for love and thirsting for significance, help me to feast on intimacy with You and drink the water of Your Word.

> *Therefore do not let sin reign in your mortal body,*
> *that you should obey it in its lusts.*
>
> —ROM. 6:12

Sin keeps us running in circles. In our pursuit for love, we will often try anything rather than stop to face ourselves. No matter what we try, we keep running into a deep sense of shame when the fix wears off. It has been said that we determine our choices and then our choices determine us. Nowhere is this more true than in the cycle of addictions.

It all begins when we are in pain. The pain might be the result of low self-esteem, shame, dissatisfaction, stress or simply the sheer boredom that life can bring. We follow the lusts of our choosing and the result is a temporary anesthesia. The trouble is, that choice creates consequences—more remorse, greater guilt and intensified pain. More guilt and shame, more remorse, and more anesthetic. The cure has become a curse.

But we are not condemned to a downward out-of-control spiral. At any point we can face ourselves and choose to feel the pain. We can understand that pain and we can give over what can never be. Then we are ready to ask Jesus to face the pain with us.

It will be a tedious process, but eventually we will gain new self-perceptions. We will establish new supportive relationships. In every aspect of our being we will become instruments of righteousness rather than destruction.

Lord, when I feel hurt, lonely, anxious or tired, help me face reality, to commit it to You and to make the necessary changes.

Bless the LORD, you His angels,
Who excel in strength, who do His word.
Heeding the voice of His word.
—PS. 103:19–20

Do you remember when you first fell in love? Just having your eyes meet brought a tingle to your spine. Thoughts of him or her filled your every moment. You couldn't wait until the next time you would be together again. Anyone who would listen soon learned how precious this person was to you. You blessed their name constantly. You let the person know they were adored.

The years have passed, and perhaps you have now been married five, ten, twenty or more years. How do you talk about one another now? How do you talk to each other now? Do you bless one another, curse one another, or just ignore each other? The opposite of love is not hate. It is indifference. It happens when we stop actively blessing each other.

Perhaps this is why the Lord wants us to bless Him at all times. The Lord delights in our praises, and He also is aware of what the act of blessing Him does for us. When we bless God we are reminded of all He has given us and done for us. He forgives our iniquities, heals our diseases and redeems our very life from destruction. He satisfies our deepest hunger—the need to be loved unconditionally. He is righteous, just, merciful, gracious, slow to anger and abounding in mercy. He deserves our praises.

You, oh Lord, are worthy of praise! Today I want to bless You through my attitudes, words and actions.

> *Now the Spirit expressly says that in latter times*
> *some will depart from the faith. . . . forbidding to*
> *marry, and commanding to abstain from foods*
> *which God created to be received with thanksgiving*
> *by those who believe and know the truth.*
>
> —1 TIM. 4:1

Those of us who are trying to recover from addictions are caught in a real dilemma. Our recovery requires dependence on a Higher Power. It also works best if we are intimately involved in supportive, insightful growth groups within our local church. And yet today's passage warns us to beware of man-made "religion."

What we see here is that before Christ returns, many believers will depart from the faith. Their children may grow up in Sunday school but never even hear that salvation is by grace through faith (Eph. 2:8–9). Religious leaders will be forbidden to marry, and people will be instructed not to eat certain foods for "religious" reasons. Paul taught us not to pay any attention to all these rules and rituals. We are living in an age of grace, where all things are permissible, though not all are expedient.

Jesus said the Bible is perfect. He said not to put our faith in religion or religious leaders. Even Paul complimented believers who took notes on what he taught them to search the Scriptures for themselves to see if he was right. We can trust God's Word.

We should avoid religious codependency, but not the loving believers
who can support us.

Let another man praise you, and not your own mouth;
A stranger, and not your own lips. —PROV. 27:2

Jeff didn't know the meaning of serenity. He was on his way up the corporate ladder, and he was sure that if he paused for even a moment he would be passed over. What a talker Jeff was. If you were willing to listen, he was more than eager to tell you about the new contacts he had made and the opportunities awaiting someone of his caliber.

Contrast Jeff to the man who does his best in the endeavors he undertakes, but who is also interested in the people he works with. He enables those around him to be the best they can be. He can rejoice over others' joys. If someone gets a promotion he doesn't assume that it is a slap in his face.

Jesus Christ was equal with God, yet he chose to come to earth in humble human form. He didn't come to rub shoulders with the big wigs of society, but to save people who knew they had a need. He held no academic degrees, came from an unpretentious family, and never traveled more than seventy-five miles from home. He *did* build personal character that was different from anything the world had ever seen. He really cared about others, though He never lost sight of who He was. In fact, He put His life on the line for His friends. God exalted Him. He was given a name that was above all names, a name which causes us to confess that He indeed is Lord.

What kind of recognition do I seek? The person who takes recognition doesn't get it. Recognition is returned by those who feel valued.

> *. . . since it is a righteous thing with God to repay with tribulation those who trouble you.*
>
> 2 THESS. 1:6

Sally was so typical in her comments toward a fellow worker at her place of employment. As she discussed her difficulty in the counseling office, she threw up her hands and said, "I am just going to have to teach Sharon a lesson; I'm going to make her hurt too!"

We all have within us the tendency to want to get even. Chuck Swindoll, a well known author and preacher, tells the story of pulling into a crowded parking lot and bumping the car next to him as he opened his door to get out. A man happened to be in the car. Chuck checked to make sure that he had not left a mark, leaned down and said "I'm sorry" to the man in the car. As he reached the sidewalk in front of the store, something inside him said "Turn around." He did, only to see the man get out of his car, walk to the other side, and deliberately open his door against Chuck's car three times. Chuck felt like going back and punching the man's lights out. Then he envisioned the next day's newspaper headlines: "Pastor Kills Man in Parking Lot," or worse yet, "Pastor Is Killed by Man in Parking Lot."

We have all felt the desire to get even.

This passage, however, says to let the Lord take your case and represent you. He will keep score and will bring tribulation to those who trouble you.

God will balance the scales of justice. I can set aside my feeling for revenge.

"... 'Not by might nor by power, but by My Spirit,'
Says the LORD of hosts."
—ZECH. 4:6b

At the time when these verses were written, Israel was in the process of rebuilding the temple. They had faced obstacles and were still confronted with some. Zerubbabal, the governor of Judah, reminded the Israelites that military strength or human manpower alone would not be enough to accomplish the completion of the temple. What was needed was Spirit-empowered workers under the direction of God's appointed leader.

1 Corinthians 3:16 says that *we* are God's temple. This is where the relevance of this historical verse from Zechariah can have meaning for us.

If we are the temple of God, how is the building process (or growing, maturing process) in our lives going to be accomplished? Just as the completion of the temple in Judah could not be completed by "might" and power, the same is true of the building process in our lives. We've all known people who tried to change their spouse's life by force, by might. They tried to force and coerce their mate to change. But change and growth do not happen by outside force, but by inner working of the Holy Spirit. We need to be inwardly controlled rather than outwardly manipulated.

Are you open to letting God's Spirit work in you and complete the building process He desires?

The next time I feel like changing someone else, I will ask the Lord what He wants to change in me. I will pursue how He wants me to grow.

> *Servants, be obedient to those who are your*
> *masters according to the flesh, with fear and*
> *trembling, in sincerity of heart, as to Christ.*
> —EPH. 6:5

Corporations in the United States report that they lose millions of dollars each year due to poor employee morale, absenteeism (much of which is not due to actual physical illness), and lack of motivation. Companies are willing to spend large sums of money to train their managers to motivate employees for more effective output.

What is your attitude toward your company? What kind of work ethic do you have? Do you go through the motions, or do you take pride in your work?

Paul challenges us to change the way we work by adopting a new idea. We are really working for Christ. We should view it that way.

If you do, you will not have the tendency to be laxidaisical and half-hearted in your work. You will not just try and get by with the bare minimum, or just do what you think will be noticed to please a boss.

Instead, work with a heart-felt commitment. Ingrain in your thinking that you are doing this for the Lord and not just for your employer. Work on your attitude and remember God has placed you in your job to help you grow. Make the most of it. Do your best. Give it your all, remembering who it is you are really working for.

Lord help me to remember that the majority of my success depends on my attitude. Help me today to have a positive attitude.

"Hear instruction and be wise,
And do not disdain it."
—PROV. 8:33

Big tears slid down Emily's cheeks. No sound came from her throat. The only clue to her inner anguish was there on her face. Every morning the child would be left at Grandma's. And every day the three-year-old would remain at the window, watching, waiting, and wondering where mommy was.

Have you ever wanted something or someone as much as Emily wanted her mother? Solomon created a word picture of a man seeking wisdom. He watches daily for it. He waits for it. When he hears wisdom he listens to it.

Emily had a hole in the core of her being. She desired attention and affection from her mother. Unfortunately, her mother, for her own reasons, was incapable of giving love. Emily's need will only be satisfied when she discovers Jesus Christ who will give her a picture of God's unconditional love. She will only feel God's love as it is shown to her by her brothers and sisters in the body of Christ.

Do you need wisdom? Are you wondering what to do in a relationship? Perhaps there is a business decision facing you. The Lord gives wisdom if we will search His Word for His principles. Our desire for wisdom is only as great as our willingness to search for it.

Lord, in my relationships and decisions, help me to seek Your perspective.

> *Come, and let us return to the LORD; for He has*
> *torn, but He will heal us; He has stricken, but He*
> *will bind us up. After two days He will revive us;*
> *on the third day He will raise us up, that we may*
> *live in His sight.*
> —HOS. 6:1–2

In seminary, I was fascinated by all the prophecies in the Bible. The fulfilled ones reinforced my faith. The unfulfilled ones gave me hope and excitement and more determination to make some tough emotional and spiritual choices in my own life.

Many passages, like today's, have a dual meaning. They have a future prophetic meaning which is often unclear, like the pieces of a puzzle. But they also have a daily, here-and-now application.

Scholars believe this prophecy applied to the destruction of Jerusalem in A.D. 70. Since one day with the Lord often means a thousand years (2 Peter. 3:8), some speculate that it also predicted Jewish revival after two thousand years. That would make the Messianic restoration of Israel very soon.

But in addition to its prophetic meaning, these verses have an application to our lives today. They teach us something about what our Higher Power is really like. He allows suffering, but He heals us too. He lets us become emotionally and spiritually broken when we sin, but He longs to bind us up. He has a "salvaging" plan for our daily recovery.

God is much more concerned with your recovery process than you are, but His methods are complex and His future plans for you are often mysterious.

*"It shall come to pass
That before they call, I will answer;
And while they are still speaking, I will hear.*
—ISA. 65:24

A number of years ago, I went through an upsetting time with my place of employment. I was verbally attacked in front of the board who made decisions on employment. I was in a state of shock as I left the meeting. I went home, and later that night wrote my letter of resignation. I felt hurt, misunderstood, and put down. My self-esteem hit an all-time low.

That night I cried out to God, "Why is this happening? What do You have for me in the future?"

The next day in the mail there was a letter from a Christian College and Seminary in Canada, offering me a position as Dean of Student Development. The letter had been mailed one week before this incident occurred. I felt a strong sense that God was answering my cry from the night before.

God says, "Before they call, I will answer." He is there and so interested in our life that He gets the answer coming even before we ask. That kind of God can give us confidence to come and pray to Him, and make our requests known. He hears and understands even while we are still speaking. He has our best in His heart.

I do not need to hesitate in bringing my needs to a God who is eager to help.

> *And I saw a new heaven and a new earth, for the
> first heaven and the first earth had passed away.*
> —REV. 21:1

Some believers are so heavenly minded they are no earthly good. A person can spend all day every day waiting for eternity and ignore the orphans, widows, and homeless all around them. We have work to do for the Lord. Serenity is something we must strive for now.

On the other hand, why did God put so many passages in the Bible about blessings in our life to come? Again, there is a balance. Hang a carrot in front of a donkey and he will help you plow your fields for hours. In the same way, this donkey (me!) gets really motivated to help others when I have a new heaven and a new earth to look forward to.

Someday God will destroy this old polluted world and create a new one. Those neat things about our eternal future are a "carrot" to motivate us, to help us get our momentary pain and suffering in perspective.

I often ask myself during a crisis, "What difference will it make a hundred years from now?" But serenity comes not only from looking forward to walking and talking with God in person. It also comes from the realization that He lives with us right now. We are His people. We are already significant. Serenity also comes from hard work. The hard work of helping those in legitimate need, and the hard work of faithfulness in our own recovery process.

True serenity comes from bright hopes for the sweet by-and-by, balanced with hard work in the here and now.

Now no chastening seems to be joyful for the present, but grievous; nevertheless, afterward it yields the peaceable fruit of righteousness to those who have been trained by it. —HEB. 12:11

My wife and I are currently rearing six teenagers. We understand the meaning of this passage. We could have given our children hassle-free upbringing, never disciplining them for anything, and giving in on everything they wanted. And when they were young they would have thought it was the right thing for us to do. They didn't want rules, limits, chores, or consequences for open rebellion.

But now that they are all committed Christians, they can usually see that the discipline we gave them when they were younger was "necessary pain." The more mature they get, the more they accept the concept of "necessary pain."

It's not any different with us and God our Father. Just when we think we are as committed to obeying Him as a believer can possibly be, we commit a foolish sin. God our Father lovingly disciplines us through the Holy Spirit's conviction or a passage of Scripture. He may also use our mate, a child, a friend, a sermon, or a book we are reading.

Whatever happens, we can be sure it is for our good. God's purpose is to make better, more godly people out of us, just as we discipline our sons and daughters to refine their character.

You and I will never *outgrow our need for God to correct our course from time to time.*

The LORD is my rock and my fortress and my deliverer;
My God, my strength, in whom I will trust;

—PS. 18:2

My friend and I were backpacking in the Grand Tetons. The climb had been challenging, the scenery breathtaking and the companionship comfortable. It was near dusk and we were descending to our camp. Suddenly a thunderstorm broke out. We ran for cover and stayed there until we thought the storm was over. From our cleft in the rock, we watched the most spectacular light show we had ever seen. It was magnificent. We could actually see the lightning striking the fields below.

When all seemed calm again, my friend and I ventured out from our place of safety. We made our way onto a flat ledge. We were walking along, when suddenly lightning struck without warning. A tree, about twenty feet in front of us, was split in two. In seconds we were back in the cleft of the rock.

In this passage, David paints a word picture when he calls the Lord his rock. He believed that taking refuge in the Lord provided more safety and security than hiding in a man-made fortress or behind a huge rock.

Are you battling disappointments, relapses, discouragement or loneliness? Whatever the enemy, our Lord has defeated it. He is the victor. With our Lord, death isn't even the final chapter. He is our stability in the storms of life.

Lord, I want You to be my stability in an unstable world.

"For as the rain comes down, and the snow from heaven,
And do not return there,
But water the earth,
And make it bring forth and bud . . .
So shall My word be that goes forth from My mouth;
It shall not return to Me void.   —ISA. 55:10–11

Do you enjoy sitting inside your house while the rain patters against your windowpane? Perhaps you have a favorite spot next to a roaring fire while the snow waltzes to the ground outside. Both rain and snow fall from the heavens to enable other things to grow. Seeds sprout, flowers bloom, trees bud and the planet is refreshed. Not one drop of rain or one snowflake is wasted.

So it is with the Word of God. It never returns to God having accomplished nothing. Just as the rain and snow cleanse the earth, so God's Word cleanses those who hear it. In Psalm 119 we discover that not only does God's Word cleanse us and keep us from sin, it also revives us, strengthens us, and saves us. Because it is truth, it sets us free.

Many of us feel lost and confused because we have been trying to put our lives together without our instruction manual. The loving Creator of the universe has written us a love letter. What an incredible difference there would be in our lives if we would delight in reading it.

_____

God has promised to reward those who diligently seek Him. His Word will always accomplish something in my life.

> *Let each one remain in the same calling in which*
> *he was called.* —1 COR. 7:20

Real wisdom comes in not acting impulsively. Our options need to be carefully researched and evaluated before a decision is made. Nowhere is this more true than in situations involving a job change.

The humorous story is told of a farmer who was frustrated with how the weeds continued to grow in his fields of corn. As the story goes, he was resting beside one of his fields and looked up into the sky. He saw in the clouds what appeared to be 2 large capital letters: "P" "C". He began wondering what that might stand for. Then the thought hit him: "P" "C" stands for "Preach Christ." He sold his farm and went off to be a preacher. He really failed at that. On his way back to the farm, the thought hit him. The "P" "C" he had seen in the clouds must have meant "Plant Corn."

With every job there are some parts that are not fulfilling or stimulating. This passage throws out a caution to us to hang in there and not impulsively make job changes because of some immediate problem. Remain in the calling that fits you. Don't hop from one job to another.

You may be in a job that is not highly suited for you. Instead of impulsively quitting, make the most of it, but begin putting out feelers in others areas. Send resumes and make appointments as you look for a better job.

Lord give me wisdom in finding a job suited to me. Enable me to be faithful where I am until such a position is available.

The eyes of the LORD are in every place, keeping watch on the evil and the good. —PROV. 15:3

One of the songs we used to sing in Sunday school went like this:

Be careful little eyes what you see
Be careful little eyes what you see
For the Father up above is looking down in love
So be careful little eyes what you see

There were also verses about taking care what our ears, hands, and feet do: "Be careful little ears what you hear . . .", "Be careful little hands what you do . . .", "Be careful little feet where you go. . . ."

Solomon knew the truth we sang in that children's song. He said, "Don't forget that the Lord is *everywhere*." He says that God knows and sees everything. He is aware of all we do, both evil and good. How does He see you living? What goes on behind the closed doors of your home or office? Remember, God sees it all. And He loves you. He wants you to think right and do right so you can stand unashamed before Him. He wants us to live openly, unafraid of being watched. He is our loving Daddy who keeps an eye on us and offers us shelter when we're in trouble.

Addictions are the result of enormous denial. They lead to a phony life. True recovery comes from an honest, open life of sincerity before God and man.

*And on the seventh day God ended His work which
He had done, and He rested on the seventh day
from all His work which He had done.*

—GEN. 2:2

There are times in all of our lives when we feel frustrated, overwhelmed, pressured, or "burned out." We glance at our calendar to see when our vacation will finally get here, or dream of a weekend away somewhere. My wife and I arranged one just this morning. We look forward to seeing some old friends and "resting."

When we trust Christ as Savior, we "rest" from depending on good works to save us, depending only on Christ's work on the cross.

But we do good works anyway, even though it doesn't earn us salvation, because we love God, love to help people, and look forward to rewards in the future Messianic Kingdom, the "Sabbath Rest" of Hebrews 4 and Psalm 95.

May God grant us rest from depending on good works to save us, and rest from trying to confide in our own strength alone to survive this life.

If a wise man contends with a foolish man,
Whether the fool rages or laughs, there is no peace.
—PROV. 25:21–22

There are times when it is better to break things off with someone who constantly wants to cause conflict. These individuals will use ridicule at times to stir up strife. At other times they will break out in intense rage. Both of these tactics intimidate, manipulate and keep other people in inner turmoil.

Often the adult child of an alcoholic (ACA) will experience this kind of controlling action on the part of a parent as he or she tries to address the pathological family system. The ACA finds out in therapy how the interactions in his or her family were dysfunctional. If the ACA approaches a family member and tries to talk about it, often the response is one of ridicule and laughing it off, or the other extreme of intense rage. By either response the ACA is frustrated, intimidated and controlled. The result is that the ACA is left in a world of turmoil, lacking any real serenity or peace. There are times when we have to set boundaries and move on rather than constantly trying to pursue talking with such a person.

Solomon in his wisdom succinctly says "there is no peace" with such a person. If you desire peace, don't allow yourself to constantly get into arguments with such a person.

_____

There will be individuals with whom I don't get everything resolved. I need to move on if they keep tension between us.

> *You therefore must endure hardship as a good*
> *soldier of Jesus Christ.*
> —2 TIM. 2:3

Whether we are "blown away" by the circumstances of life has a lot to do with our expectations.

For example, if I believe that life owes me a living even if I don't work, I'm setting myself up for a disappointment. If I think I should never be sick, I am numbed by the doctor's report that I have cancer. If I expect life to be fair, I am hurt by the unfairness that I see.

One of the reasons a soldier can be effective is that he receives training for real combat situations. In their training, soldiers are taught to expect difficulties and hardships. They learn ways to cope with them.

Get ready for the hardships. Expect them, accept them, and endure them. Life is like combat. We will have battles to fight and hardships to endure.

We will be able to endure times of hardship if we have a single-mindedness or focus. The enduring soldier is one who is centered on the problem to be fought and not on the demands of civilian life.

What are your expectations for life? Are hardships part of what you are assuming will come? Are you preparing yourself for those hard days?

Hardships in life come to all of us. Our success in dealing with them depends on our expectations and our personal preparation for them.

He sent from above, He took me;
He drew me out of many waters.
He delivered me from my strong enemy,
From those who hated me,
For they were too strong for me.
They confronted me in the day of my calamity,
But the LORD was my support.
He also brought me out into a broad place;
He delivered me because He delighted in me.
—PS. 18:16–19

Many adults today still suffer from feelings of abuse and abandonment they experienced in early childhood. The media has made us so much more aware of abuse. Abuse may be active, such as hitting, kicking and throwing things. There is verbal abuse which tears a child apart with words. There is also passive abuse which is more subtle. This may be a workaholic parent who has no time for his or her kids. The children feel alone, abandoned and neglected.

God the Father is not an absent parent. He is there to support us when we need it. When we are being confronted and attacked, God delivers us from our strong enemy. When we are surrounded by those who hate us, He is with us. When we feel overpowered by strong individuals, He is beside us. When we feel no one likes us, we can rest assured that God delights in us.

Because of the good Heavenly Father we have, we can take courage. We can have hope to face the future.

Even if you had a difficult childhood, God believes in you and wants to be your good, supportive Heavenly Father. He will always be there for you.

> *For this is the will of God, your sanctification: that you should abstain from sexual immorality; that each of you should know how to possess his own vessel in sanctification and honor, not in passion of lust, like the Gentiles who do not know God.*
> —1 THESS. 4:3–4

For immorality to thrive, two things need to be present: the absence of a relationship, and the desire for heightened excitement. Whether one is consumed by pornography, manipulated through multiple affairs, or driven by dehumanizing desires, the obsession is more valued than the relationship.

On a deeper level, the person involved in immoral actions confuses sex with nurturing. The insatiable need for sex never leaves him or her feeling loved, cherished, or cared for. At the core of his or her very being, this person feels unloved and used.

Oh, the rage that results from this insight! The person may internalize it and experience depression or externalize it and become calculating, manipulative, and ruthless. Underneath all this fury is incredible sadness.

God wants us to enjoy sex within marriage. Our expression of love to each other can be a taste of the divine on earth if we agree with Scripture that sex is one of God's good and perfect gifts. As Christian couples we can have the security of a committed relationship and the thrill and adventure of romance with our mates, if we choose to make this a priority.

Within the bonds of marriage sex can be a marvelous, freeing gift from God. Outside of marriage it is a destructive dead end street.

> *"Give instruction to a wise man, and*
> *he will be still wiser;*
> *Teach a just man, and he will*
> *increase in learning.*
> —PROV. 9:9

Have you ever tried to give counsel to someone who really didn't want it? They asked you for advice, but they really wanted sympathy.

Sometimes as therapists we are called in to work with a client because he or she wants a Christian counselor. The trouble is, once we suggest that some of this person's dysfunctional patterns must be rejected and replaced with concepts such as love, forgiveness, and personal responsibility, the client isn't always so sure about the Christian therapist. They balk at novel concepts like mutual submission in the place of arrogant manipulation. It hurts when someone suggests that blaming is choosing to "be lame." Perhaps it threatens us to open ourselves to a perspective, other than our own. It can be a shock to face ourselves honestly.

Erica was involved in many relationships devoid of peace. For years she asked God why, until she finally admitted she was not being honest with herself. She would often seek our scriptural principles, then do whatever she felt like doing. Now she wants to obey the mandates of Scripture.

Her choice of men has changed, as well as what she wants in a relationship. Her moral standards have also changed, and she can finally face herself in the mirror.

As Solomon learned, "If you are wise, you are wise for yourself."

> *Jesus spoke these words, lifted up His eyes to
> heaven, and said: "Father, the hour has come.
> Glorify Your Son, that Your Son also may glorify
> You, as You have given Him authority over all flesh,
> that He should give eternal life to as many as You
> have given Him. And this is eternal life, that they
> may know You, the only true God, and Jesus Christ
> whom You have sent."* —JOHN 17:1–3

Today's passage demonstrates the interaction between God the Father and Christ, His Son. Jesus began
what has become known as the Lord's High-priestly
Prayer with the acknowledgment that the time had
come for Him to die on the cross.

Jesus looked on the positive side of His impending
death, asking the Father to glorify Him so He could use
His death and resurrection to glorify the Father.

Jesus was given authority over every human who
ever lived, but only gave eternal life to believers,
whom God the Father had given Him. Eternal life involves knowing the Father, the only real God, by knowing Jesus Christ, who was sent by the Father.

The Greek word for "knowing" the Father and the
Son is *ginoskosin*, which implies the deepest kind of
intimacy. In this context, it means that Christ wants to
have an intimate emotional and spiritual relationship
with His bride, the church of believers.

---

*God desires to love us intimately, and wants us to truly know and love
Him.*

Why do You stand afar off, O LORD?
Why do You hide Yourself in times of trouble?
                                        —PS. 10:1

Psalm 10 is a beautiful psalm of social justice, written by King David. David saw how the evil people of his world—like the evil people of our day—were constantly looking for ways to take advantage of the helpless. He pleaded with God to deal with the wicked and protect the helpless.

We have all wondered at times why God allows so much suffering, especially by the innocent and helpless. Why doesn't He stop it right now? Why does He seem to be so far away during times of tragedy and abuse?

Like David, we may long to call on God to arise from His throne to lift His hand in judgment upon the wicked and to defend the humble. Most of the cruel and malicious people in our world have sociopathic personalities. They renounce God, resent authority, and live in complete denial of the consequences of their behavior.

In His timing, God will grant our prayers for social justice. He will punish the unrepentant evildoers of the world, and help the helpless and fatherless.

God grant me the serenity to bear the social injustices I cannot change, the courage to help change the social injustices I can, and the wisdom to know the difference.

> *Now all things are of God, who has reconciled us*
> *to Himself through Jesus Christ, and has given us*
> *the ministry of reconciliation, that is, that God was*
> *in Christ reconciling the world to Himself, not*
> *imputing their trespasses to them, and has*
> *committed to us the word of reconciliation.*
> —2 COR. 5:18–19

Burnout has been called the disease of the eighties, the disease of modern life. Researchers have isolated some variables that lead to burnout. One of the major factors that leads to burnout is unresolved conflict; conflict can be seen in actual physical and emotional "wars" that go on in homes and marriages. Or the conflicts may be silent, and the same emotions are experienced inwardly as a person struggles with anger and resentment. Unresolved conflicts can also happen in a job setting, at a business deal, or between countries. The fact remains that unresolved conflicts are all too common, and they are severely damaging.

A world full of tension and fighting needs individuals who can bring resolution and reconciliation between two warring factions. We can also use these peacemaking opportunities to help individuals find personal reconciliation with God.

We can be ambassadors of Christ and promote peace in a contentious culture. It is not always easy, but resolution and healing and wholeness can take place if we are willing to strive for peace.

Lord help me to bring peace to the broken relationships in my world, beginning with my own.

Rest in the LORD, and wait patiently for Him;
Do not fret because of him who prospers in his way,
Because of the man who brings wicked schemes to
pass. —PS. 37:7

Jack sat in the psychologist's office unloading his story. "I just don't understand why the mean, deceptive, self-centered guys at our company seem to flourish. It is just not fair. I was trying to be conscientious and do my work but these guys undermined me. They told lies about me and last Friday I was laid off. I can't believe it."

The Psalmist reminds us that it is really no use to fret, worry, or be envious of the workers of iniquity. "They will be cut down like grass." Their time is coming, so be patient. The final chapter has not been written.

There are many things in life that don't seem fair. Therefore we are faced with a choice to react and fret, or to rest and be freed. We are challenged to choose the second option and rest in the Lord. That resting is truly a freeing experience.

Have you faced an unfair situation? Have you been unfairly criticized? Don't give up! Develop realistic expectations that include a degree of unfairness. Develop staying power. After tactfully verbalizing your feelings to the appropriate person, determine to forgive. Keep doing the best job you can do whether or not the situation is corrected. Trust in the Lord.

When things go wrong, don't go with them. Trust in the Lord and rest in His promises. Be assertive but wise.

"O Death, where is your sting? O Hades, where is your victory?" The sting of death is sin, and the strength of sin is the law. But thanks be to God, who gives us the victory through our Lord Jesus Christ. Therefore, my beloved brethren, be steadfast, immovable, always abounding in the work of the Lord, knowing that your labor is not in vain in the Lord. —1 COR. 15:57–58

The Rapture of all believers has been described in many passages of Scripture. Because of that blessed hope, we can say with the apostle Paul, who was killed for his faith, "O death, where is your sting?"

The three greatest fears humans have are the fear of failure, the fear of abandonment, and the fear of death. Faith in Jesus Christ and belief in God's Word can give us courage to face all three of these fears.

Death came into the world as a result of sin. In Romans 6:23, we read that "the wages of sin is death." The law of God shows us how far short of God's standard we fall and reveals the "strength" of our sinfulness.

But Christ brought victory over sin and death by His resurrection. Now our own resurrection is certain, whether it be by death or by the Rapture.

The certainty of our resurrection, as believers in Christ, will increase our courage to be steadfast and immovable, and to keep abounding in the good deeds that further His kingdom here and now on earth.

Through Christ we can be courageous and steadfast, knowing that our labor is not in vain.

Blessed is the man
Who walks not in the counsel of the ungodly,
Nor stands in the path of sinners,
Nor sits in the seat of the scornful.

—PS. 1:1

When I was ten years old, my mother taught me today's passage. We memorized it together. Just her fellowship made it fun and worthwhile. She also taught me what it meant.

She warned me to be careful because I would naturally become more and more like whoever I spent time with. She encouraged me to meditate daily on Scripture, and said that if I did that one thing for the rest of my life, God would make my life prosperous and useful to others.

I also remember going to Camp Barakel in upper Michigan for a week. It was my only camp experience because we couldn't afford very many luxuries like that.

Every morning, we had to go out in the beautiful Michigan woods all alone with our Bible for about 15 minutes. We developed the habit of reading and thinking about one small portion of God's Word each day.

The combination of those two events—my mom teaching me Psalm 1 and my camp counselors patiently bearing with me, loving me, and teaching me to have daily devotions—changed my life. Daily meditation on His Word has always pulled me back to the right path when I have started to drift away.

Daily meditation on God's Word will change you more than anything else you could possibly do, other than trusting Christ to save you.

> *Jesus said . . . , "'You shall love the LORD your God with all your heart, with all your soul, and with all your mind.' This is the first and great commandment. And the second is like it: 'You shall love your neighbor as yourself.' On these two commandments hang all the Law and the Prophets."*
>
> —MATT. 22:37–40

Sarah came into therapy severely depressed. She would sleep most of the day and her eleven-year-old daughter was left with the responsibility of caring for her eight-year-old sister. When I talked to Sarah about her relationships, she was quick to say she had many friends. However, as I probed further I discovered that not one of them knew the severity of her depression. Sarah felt she couldn't bother her friends, or God, with her problems.

Without attachment to God and to others, we cannot function as we were designed. We need to bond. Jesus reduced the entire list of commandments into two, each centering on relationships.

Essentially, if we really understand what this means, if we develop a deep relationship with the Lord and with others we will in the process keep the other commandments.

Are you bonded to God? Do you also have a close supportive friend you can completely confide in?

The most important thing we can do in life is to work on building a close relationship with God and with other people.

There is hope and strength in loving God and other people.

He spoke, and it was done;
He commanded, and it stood fast.
—PS. 33:9

A sense of awe overtakes me when I walk along the sand by the ocean. The crashing waves and water seem to stretch on forever. God spoke and all of creation came into existence. That is cause for worship!

The same God who created our universe by His word can recreate our personal worlds through His written Word. Romans 12:2 says that we can be transformed by the renewing of our minds. That renewal depends on our meditating and applying God's Word.

Steve's father cursed his very existence and sexually abused him. Steve remembers fists in his face and the excruciating pain of being thrown against the wall. Eventually the Child Protective Services removed Steve from his home.

One day as a teenager he accompanied a friend to church. For the first time in his life he heard about God's love for him. As appealing as the message of God's love was, the part about God being his Father made him want to throw up. Steve's eyes were blinded to God's love, grace and forgiveness until, with the help of a Christian therapist, he faced the pain in his past. Together they searched the Scriptures and found verses that helped Steve eventually accept God as his loving, perfect Father.

Creator of this universe, recreate my personal world so that my thoughts and actions are in line with Your Word.

> *"And shall God not avenge His own elect who cry out day and night to Him, though He bears long with them?*
> —LUKE 18:7–8

If we spent our entire lives on a deserted island, we would never be hurt by another human being. But we would suffer loneliness that would be worse than any pain we would be likely to receive from other people. We could also easily lose our sanity. Our lives would have no meaning.

We are better off living in the real world with real people—even though we are bound to be hurt from time to time. We also cannot help but occasionally hurt the people around us.

But God reminds us over and over again to do what we can to avoid hurting others, accept the reality that it will happen sometimes, and turn all vengeance over to Him. The Bible says we will be forgiven in the same way that we forgive.

God knows everything including the innermost thoughts and motives of every person. When we let go of our own desire for vengeance and turn it over to God, He will convict our offenders through His Holy Spirit. If they are willing to repent and be forgiven, God will forgive them—just as He has forgiven us. If they don't repent, the matter is still no longer in our hands. We can, and must, trust the Lord to deal with them in His wise and just way.

Lord give me the humility to apologize when I have hurt someone. And when I have been hurt, give me the strength to forgive.

You have given the commandment to save me,
For You are my rock and my fortress.
—PS. 71:3

On November 15, 1989, I had an automobile accident in which my car flipped upside down and landed that way. Both cars were totalled, yet no one had even a scratch.

As my custom is when I drive alone, I was listening to the New King James Version of the Bible on tape. Psalm 71 was playing the moment my car hit—the tape stopped there.

But listening to Scripture gives me serenity every day, and it did that day. I was calm throughout the accident. I was prepared to live or die, and was only curious as to which would happen. I have to admit, I was visibly shaken *after* I crawled out and saw what had happened.

I got the tape out of the cassette player before they towed the car, and listened to it that night right where it stopped on this passage. I wanted to see what God wanted to teach me by allowing this to occur. These passages reminded me that my life is in His hands, moment by moment. I need to be able to say, like the apostle Paul, that my reason for staying alive is to serve Christ and that if I die before the rapture occurs, that will be a real blessing.

On November 15, 1989, I was about due for a reminder.

———

I don't look forward to more of those kinds of reminders, but I accept whatever reminders God chooses to send me.

> *For we know that the whole creation groans and labors with birth pangs together until now. And not only they, but we also who have the firstfruits of the Spirit, even we ourselves groan within ourselves, eagerly waiting for the adoption, the redemption of our body.* —ROM. 8:19–23

When I die, the first thing I want to do is enroll in the University of Heaven, with Jesus as my professor. I hope there won't be too many students in my class. I have so many "why" questions for Jesus I will probably keep Him busy for quite a while.

When Adam and Eve rebelled in the Garden of Eden, God cursed all of His creation. Animals started attacking and eating each other instead of all being vegetarians. Mosquitoes started pestering people. Thorns appeared on rose bushes. Many animals became dangerous to humans. Why? I don't know—that's one of the questions I will ask Him.

Unfortunately humans also became dangerous to each other. Child abuse and peer abuse were right around the corner. Human suffering. Human shame. Addictions to kill the pain.

As humans who care about others and about ourselves, we groan within ourselves when we see the effects of corruption in nature and in mankind. For now, we accept our limitations, do what we can to help, and eagerly await a new earth and a new "us."

We are not perfect yet, but our God is! He will do things through us that we could never do ourselves.

As for God, His way is perfect;
the Word of the LORD is proven:
He is a shield to all who trust in Him.
For who is God, except the LORD?
And who is a rock, except our God?
—2 SAM 22:31–32

The Lord had delivered David from the hand of his enemies and from Saul. Our passage for today is a portion of David's special psalm of thanksgiving.

David knew a lot about the deceitfulness of the human mind, including his own. He observed Saul's ambivalence and paranoia, and he struggled with his own sinful urges. He prayed often for God to show him his own innermost thoughts, so he could mature spiritually. He also meditated on Scripture every day and night, and called God's Word a lamp to his feet. When people went places at night during those times, they tied a special lamp to their feet so they could see where they were walking. This certainly gives us a clear image of what God's Word does as we read it and apply it to our lives.

God's ways are perfect, and His Word was proven true in David's life. God gives strength and protection to true believers, and with His help they can face any obstacle.

David's strength and power were gifts from God, who guarded his life. God gave David the joyful energy to run like a deer, setting David on spiritually and emotionally high places.

The courage to live an addiction-free life comes from God.

> *Let us walk properly, as in the day, not in revelry*
> *and drunkenness, not in licentiousness and*
> *lewdness, not in strife and envy. But put on the*
> *Lord Jesus Christ, and make no provision for the*
> *flesh, to fulfill its lusts.*   —ROM. 13:13–14

Certain sins have a way of making themselves at home in our lives. We get so used to their presence, we often don't give them much thought. By habit or by denial, we continue to indulge ourselves—to make provision for the flesh.

This passage confronts such an attitude head-on. It is high time for us to make a change. We are not victims of our habits; we have the power to throw them away and begin again. And we can protect ourselves from their hold on us by wearing the armor of God's truth.

The apostle Paul reminds us that we are on a journey, and our destination is heaven. Knowing that we will meet our Savior face-to-face motivates us to delay the temporary gratification of sin.

We may struggle with temptation to get drunk, or to satisfy our cravings or appetites right away and encourage others to do the same. Perhaps we are in the habit of griping about people or things, or pitting people against authority figures.

If we allow ourselves to fantasize about sin, we will eventually give in to it. We are encouraged instead, to "clothe" ourselves with loyalty to Christ and to avoid sinful thoughts so one thing won't lead to another.

Resisting sin is hard work. Sinful subconscious thoughts are natural. Developing loving motives and behaviors requires the help of our Higher Power.

The steps of a good man are ordered by the LORD,
And He delights in his way.
Though he fall, he shall not be utterly cast down;
For the LORD upholds him with His hand.
—PS. 37:23–24

If our steps are "ordered by the Lord," does He direct, like a puppeteer with a puppet, every step we take?

I don't believe God wants puppets. He has delegated much authority to us. Philippians 4:13 says "I can do all things through Christ who strengthens me." God is intimately acquainted with all we do. Nothing happens to us without His purposeful or permissive will. Some Christians believe He only directs us morally and leaves all the other decisions up to us. Others think He uses many circumstances to guide us to a certain job or mate or city. I don't know exactly to what extent He influences our decisions, and I may not know until I get to heaven. But in the meantime, I will continue to live my life based on what I believe I can do that would be in line with all Scripture and would be most helpful to others.

God delights in our lives even though we fail Him at times. When we sin, we may feel discouraged and wonder why God uses us at all. But God loves us anyway. He will lift us up, brush us off, and delight in us as we walk in His steps.

Thank You, Lord, for Your involvement in my life. Without Your hand to hold me, I would surely fall.

> *He gave testimony and said, 'I have found David the*
> *son of Jesse, a man after My own heart, who will*
> *do all My will.' From this man's seed, according to*
> *the promise, God raised up for Israel a Savior—*
> *Jesus. . . ."*
> —ACTS 13:21–23

When the Jews were ruled by judges back in Old Testament days, they wanted a king so they could gain the respect of other nations. God didn't want them to have a king, but permitted them to select Saul.

When God removed Saul, He raised up King David.

David loved and served God faithfully most of the time, but failed Him miserably other times. And yet God said of him, "I have found David the son of Jesse, a man after My own heart, who will do all My will." Amazing grace, how sweet the sound, and how profound! David's great faith in and love for God covered a multitude of sins. God the Father looked on the repentant king and saw Jesus' robe of righteousness wrapped around him. David was covered by the blood of his future Messiah.

David made plenty of mistakes. Like the rest of us, he committed countless sins, and had to live with the consequences. Yet God forgave David and chose his genetic line to bring us the Messiah—Jesus Christ.

You cannot be too sinful for God to accept, if you trust Christ as Your Savior. Like David, you are wrapped in Jesus' robe of righteousness, and He loves you.

*The snares of death confronted me. In my distress I
called upon the LORD, and cried out to my God.*
—PS. 18:5

My patients hate it if they catch me glancing at my
watch during their session. They know I'm already
thinking ahead to my next patient. But if I bring up
death and dying for us to discuss together, *they* start
glancing nervously at their watches! They can't wait to
get out of there.

Many patients develop anxiety symptoms or even
panic attacks after the death of a loved one. The death
reminds them how relatively powerless they are over
their own death and the death of their friends and family. They also think of the good relationships they
could have had with the deceased, but didn't.

David wasn't dying yet when he wrote this psalm,
but he was facing potential death from Saul and other
enemies. In his distress he called out to the Lord for
help. David knew he was in danger, but he also knew
God was still in control of the situation. God gave David
tremendous courage and protection because of David's
prayers.

David's cry came before God the Father, somehow,
as all of our sincere prayers do. God not only comforted David's fears, but also postponed David's ultimate death, delivering him from his momentary crisis.

Death is an important part of life. The more we pray
about it and get it in perspective, the more meaningful
our own life can be.

I hope and pray for a useful, productive life and a meaningful death.

> *But the fruit of the Spirit is love, joy, peace,*
> *longsuffering, kindness, goodness, faithfulness,*
> *gentleness, self-control. Against such there is no*
> *law.*
>   **—GAL. 5:22–23**

The Holy Spirit influences our lives, convicting us of areas of sin and developing positive qualities in our lives. These qualities are known collectively as the fruit of the Spirit. Serenity is one of them.

The first three are attitudes of the mind.

• Love—a self-sacrificing love.

• Joy—a deep, inner rejoicing regardless of circumstances.

• Peace—serenity in the face of adversity and suffering.

The second three are behaviors toward others.

• Patience—forbearing and forgiving even when provoked, without harboring vengeful motives.

• Kindness—doing good deeds for others, acts of benevolence.

• Goodness—doing what is right before God, and helping others even when they don't deserve it.

The last three are personal qualities.

• Faithfulness—reliability.

• Gentleness—considerate of others.

• Self-Control—mastery over fleshly impulses, such as overeating, and sexual sins.

Becoming a Christian develops within us the wonderful qualities of life—the fruit of the Spirit.

> *For yet a little while and the wicked shall be no*
> *more; Indeed, you will look diligently for his place.*
> *But it shall be no more. . . . The Lord laughs at*
> *him, For He sees that his day is coming.*
> —PS. 37:10–13

Take a look at that neighbor who is dealing illegal drugs to kids. Observe that woman at the office who is sleeping with two of her bosses to get promoted. Or the person who ripped you off in a crooked business deal. These people live on borrowed time. God will not allow the wicked to go unpunished.

But true believers are meek in the sense that we have humbled ourselves before Almighty God and said, "Be merciful to me, a sinner." And God promises over and over that *everyone* who calls on Him for salvation will be saved. He won't reject anyone. He died to save sinners. Not only to save us from hell, but to make us His own adopted sons and daughters.

We inherited *eternal life* the moment we trusted Christ. We already have it now and for all eternity. Our grateful obedience will be rewarded. Our reward for obedience and repentance may not seem great in this life, but our peace now and our life with God later is beyond imagination. He deserves our highest praise for raising us from the mire of our own sinful natures to be like Him.

So don't be jealous when good things happen to those who don't follow the Lord. Accept the momentary injustice. God knows their day is coming.

The meek will have abundant peace now and inherit the earth later. Keep it all in God's perspective.

> *Who can understand his errors? Cleanse me from secret faults. Keep back Your servant also from presumptuous sins.*
> —PS. 19:12

In 1800 a committed Christian psychiatrist in Germany named Johann Christian Heinroth wrote that recovery depends on a Higher Power giving us the courage to overcome the addictive influences of our "flesh." Heinroth coined the word *ego* to describe the decision-making part of our personality one hundred years before Freud wrote about the ego.

Heinroth also coined the word *psychosomatic* to tell how stress and sin lead to disease. Heinroth credited the Bible for his belief in secret sins. He taught that recovery from addictions required insight into these secret thoughts, feelings, and motives, as well as God's help. His teachings were relatively obscure until AA's Twelve Step program revived what was true all along. Freud said our ego is a slave to our fleshly desires (the id), so just stay out of trouble and quit feeling guilty about your selfish tendencies. Freud also called religion the universal neurosis of mankind. The world loved Freud's easy pragmatism and made him the "father of psychiatry" while they wrote off Heinroth.

King David said we don't understand our errors and secret faults and presumptuous sins. David wanted not only his behavior to be blameless before God, but also his words and thoughts. David wanted to improve from the inside out.

Our secret thoughts must be courageously faced and dealt with if we expect to recover from our addictive behaviors.

What profit has the worker from that in which he labors?

ECCL. 3:9

"Quilters" is a musical about women's lives as they cross the United States in a covered wagon. The quilts they create become magnificent biographies of these women's lives.

In the muslin bag of scraps, carried by each woman, one might discover material from a wedding dress, a baby bonnet, sturdy overalls. Each scrap holds the possibility to be something beautiful if it is combined with another.

After a devastating prairie fire, the grandmother figure muses that life hands different scraps to all of us. What we do with these scraps, piece by piece, determines the pattern our quilt will take.

Life does hand scraps to all of us, doesn't it? Some are fine, delicate, and beautiful. Others feel rough, coarse, and tough.

Perhaps we wish we had different scraps in our muslin bags. If only we had been born into a loving family, if only our marriage hadn't ended. The trouble is that wishing won't make it so. "If only's" always lead us to despair.

We need to change our perspective. We can piece the scraps of our lives together so that the pattern will be a thing of beauty.

Lord, I give you the scraps of my life. Help me to create a beautiful quilt out of these torn pieces of cloth.

> *Go therefore and make disciples of all the nations,*
> *baptizing them in the name of the Father and of*
> *the Son and of the Holy Spirit, teaching them to*
> *observe all things that I have commanded you.*
> —MATT. 28:19

The passage for today is called "The Great Commission." Jesus wants us to make disciples of people of all nationalities—no prejudices on His part! When people trust Christ, He wants them to commemorate His death, burial, and resurrection by being baptized in water. This reflects His own resurrection and demonstrates belief in the triune God.

According to Ephesians 2:8–9, faith, not works, produces salvation. But Christ has commended us to use this outward symbol, baptism, to show the world the complete inner change God has made in us. It is an important commandment.

What Christians often overlook is that recovery is one-third of the Great Commission. We are to teach, disciple, exhort, and love people all over the world. Christ came not only to save us from the penalty of our sins, but also to sanctify us from the power of our sinful tendencies and addictions.

Helping the homeless is great. Feeding the starving nations is a moral obligation. Cleaning the environment God created is wonderful. But nothing compares to guiding a loved one to the truth.

It is my assignment to show my friends and family the truth God has shown me.

The LORD brings the counsel of the nations to nothing; He makes the plans of the peoples of no effect. —PS. 33:10

Several armies of ants were competing for crumbs on the kitchen floor in the house where they lived. Each thought its own colony was the most important and should get the crumbs. Finally, they called a truce. The kings met and argued over who was greatest. While they were arguing, the owner of the house noticed them and stepped on them.

Some leaders who meet in summit conferences around the world, are godly. Others are proud, haughty ants. God could step on them all. Their plans mean almost nothing because God's plans overrule theirs. His plans are eternal. And God blesses nations that honor His principles and His people.

America was founded by courageous leaders who wanted religious freedom. But as President Reagan once said, "Freedom of religion in America has become freedom from religion." Evangelicals are often discriminated against. We must fight back by whatever peaceable means are available.

God will not allow nations to defy Him, but He will save those who call on Him for salvation. This same God is concerned with your personal restoration. He is never too busy to listen to a humble heart.

The God who is small enough to live inside your "heart" is also big enough to control the world.

> *"Two men went up to the temple to pray, one a*
> *Pharisee and the other a tax collector. The Pharisee*
> *stood and prayed thus with himself, 'God, I thank*
> *You that I am not like other men . . . or even as*
> *this tax collector. . . .' And the tax collector,*
> *standing afar off, . . . beat his breast, saying, 'God,*
> *be merciful to me a sinner!'*
>
> —LUKE 18:10–12

One of the primary themes of the entire Bible is pride versus humility—arrogant frustration versus serenity. False pride results in frustrated expectations.

The religious leader stood to pray so people could see him. Because I often study body language, I can imagine this Pharisee standing up, squeezing his eyes shut, dramatically brushing back his perfect white hair, raising his hands high, and praying loud and long. The purpose of his prayer was to show what a neat guy he was.

Contrast this with the prayer of the repentant tax collector. Study his body language. He stood in a temple corner. He was praying to God, not man. His eyes were lowered because he was ashamed.

Jesus tells us this man went home justified, accepted in the sight of God. The Pharisee didn't.

In our own lives, recovery requires humility, lowering our arrogant expectations and seeing ourselves as God sees us.

———————

God, show us the truth about ourselves, balanced with the realization that we are of great value to You, in spite of our sinful nature.

*So teach us to number our days, That we may gain
a heart of wisdom.* —PS. 90:12

Several days before the car accident that influenced
my perspective, this verse stood out to my godly
mother-in-law. She feared something bad would happen to one of her children or their mates, and prayed
every day for me personally the week of my accident.
She didn't tell a soul about it until several days after the
accident.

Some people would attribute my mother-in-law's experience to E.S.P. I believe what people attribute to
E.S.P. is more likely the work of the Holy Spirit, convicting us of sin, and godliness, and our own mortality.

In the days following my car crash, I learned several
important things.

• My days are numbered here on earth. By the time
you read this, I may be gone. Or I may live fifty more
years. I don't know, but God does.

• If I assume that I will live beyond today, I am a
presumptuous fool.

• If I assume my wife or children or close friends
will certainly all live to see tomorrow, I am a presumptuous fool. Their days are numbered too.

• I will commit my life to God early each morning,
one day at a time, asking what He would want me to
do that day.

• I will plan as though God will give me a long life,
but try to live as though today were my last day. One
day, it will be.

God give me the serenity that comes from living one day at a time.

> *And we know that all things work together for*
> *good to those who love God, to those who are the*
> *called according to His purpose.* —ROM. 8:28

I have seen Romans 8:28 used by many believers to bring recovery to other believers. It has helped me all through my life when I have needed to accept things that disappointed me. If I had no expectations, I would never be disappointed, but I am human, so I frequently expect too much.

I think to myself, *It will all work out. I will grow from this. I may even be glad it happened someday.* Seeing ultimate growth from trials helps me recover from them more quickly and accept what I cannot change.

Joseph didn't like being sold into slavery by his jealous brothers. But God used it to make Joseph second in command to the king of Egypt. God made all things work together for good in Joseph's life, even though Joseph didn't understand God's long-term plan at the time.

If my goal each day is to cooperate with God's long-term plan for me, rather than trying to manipulate God into cooperating with *my* long-term plan, then daily crises are less painful. They are mere stepping stones to something better.

We can trust in God's plan for us. We can claim the comfort of Romans 8:28 as we grieve our losses. God can turn them to good.

*Only may the LORD give you wisdom and
understanding, and give you charge concerning
Israel, that you may keep the law of the LORD your
God. Then you will prosper. . . . Be strong and of
good courage; do not fear nor be dismayed.*
—1 CHRON. 22:12–13

David was turning over his kingdom to his son Solomon. David encouraged him to obey God's principles if he expected to prosper. God's blessings are conditional, but, to those who have faith, God's love and salvation are unconditional.

Nick was a suicidal patient of mine. He was financially successful but in deep emotional pain. In his thirties, his parents still controlled him. Like Solomon, his personal recovery required the courage that comes from God.

Nick bolstered his own courage and serenity levels by looking at the positive yet realistic side of things. He accepted the fact that some of the things he feared may come true, but most of them won't. He learned to respond appropriately and lovingly to others. Nick slowly reprogrammed his parental messages and also worked through the painful process of forgiving his parents.

Nick quit being so dismayed by lowering his expectations. He learned to expect fallen humans to be fallen humans . . . and love them anyway. He didn't have to let them step on him. He has finally gained courage to go on with his life.

May God grant us the courage to follow His wise steps to recovery.

> *Whenever I am afraid,*
> *I will trust in You.*
> PS. 56:3

Why are we traumatized by change? Could it be that we're afraid of failing? Yet to be human is to fail. So why do we seek safety above all else?

If we are to overcome our fear of failure, and with it our fear of change, we have to affirm that failure is neither fatal nor final.

Based on Romans 8:28 we can affirm that God wants to bring good out of even our failures. Failure has taught all of us what doesn't work. Sometimes failure helps us to discover a new direction for life. A gentleman who failed at real estate founded a fledgling business called McDonalds. After Nathaniel Hawthorne was fired as a customs clerk, he wrote the novel "The Scarlet Letter." Lastly, failure always makes us more sympathetic and less judgmental of others.

It isn't enough to develop a positive attitude about failure. We must replace our fear of the unknown with faith in Christ. When a child fears a shadow in his room at night, the only cure for the fear is to turn on the light. As our lives become illuminated by the light of Jesus Christ, we find security despite change.

Lord, illuminate my life with Your love and light.

The days of our lives are seventy years; And if by reason of strength they are eighty years. Yet their boast is only labor and sorrow; For it is soon cut off, and we fly away. —PS. 90:10

Amanda ate, spent money, and acted out sex impulsively. She was unusually selfish, and yet she was suicidally depressed. Her attitudes and behavior were the opposite of what would actually be best for her happiness and peace in the long run. She lived to "feel good" right now. Her recovery required a great deal of making new decisions about her values, attitudes, and behavior.

A high percentage of Amanda's thoughts were about short-term plans. A very low percentage would have been about things she had seen and learned in her distant past, or current events in light of eternity.

You may be short-sighted like Amanda. But to God, a thousand years are the equivalent of our remembering what happened yesterday!

In our seventy to eighty years on earth, we are born, grow up, go to school, get a job, work, sleep, and worry. We suffer losses and disappointments, and we feel sorrow over them. Then we die.

Without God, our short years here would be almost meaningless. Some nonbelievers (and believers) look at the emptiness of life and commit suicide. Amanda almost did before she recovered from her depression.

Make each day worthwhile and meaningful— serving God, loving and being loved, one day at a time.

Please do what is best for you in the long run.

> *God demonstrates His own love toward us, in that*
> *while we were still sinners, Christ died for us. Much*
> *more then, having now been justified by His blood,*
> *we shall be saved from wrath through Him.*
> —ROM. 5:8

We must depend on God for the power to recover. But who is that God? What is He really like?

We see a lot about the character of the real God in this passage. God looked down on us from heaven, from eternity past, and saw us as spiritually weak and ungodly. And yet, at just the right time, God took on a human body in Bethlehem, lived a perfect life, and voluntarily died for us.

Now, it is true that some people have given their lives for others. This is the greatest expresssion of love. But usually they do so for a highly respected, "righteous" person. God's love is greater. When we rebelled against Him, Christ died for us. He wanted to reestablish a relationship with the powerless, the ungodly, the sinners. Jesus is intimately involved in our recovery process now and daily intercedes for us with the Father (see Heb. 7:25).

He saved us from hell; He continues to salvage our lives. When God tells us in one passage that salvation is not of works, then tells us to work out our salvation, He isn't contradicting Himself. As believers we are saved from hell, but God also intends to sanctify our lives by teaching us good works and helping us daily in our recovery process.

Jesus wants to give us the wisdom and power for recovery from our
addictions. We can gratefully accept His daily help.

> *"Our Father in heaven,*
> *Hallowed be Your name.*
> *Your kingdom come.*
> *Your will be done*
> *On earth as it is in heaven."*
> —MATT. 6:9–10

This is the first half of the Lord's Prayer. We could actually call it the Disciple's Prayer, because it is a model of how *we* should pray to God.

Jesus began with worship, showing reverence for the Heavenly Father. As a perfect, loving, all-powerful God, the Father deserves our respect.

Jesus also taught us to make a mysterious request: "Your kingdom come." What is God's kingdom? Is it a spiritual kingdom that exists now, a future literal Messianic Kingdom here on earth, or an eternal kingdom in heaven? It quite likely includes all three.

God will accomplish His will whether or not we ask Him to. But in the very act of seeking His will, our lives are put in proper perspective. If we ask sincerely, the Father will grant us wisdom to know His desires for our lives each day as we take part in helping others and in building His kingdom on earth. We also look forward to a literal one thousand-year Millennial Kingdom here on earth, ruled by Jesus. The Father's eternal kingdom is in heaven. As believers, we will dwell in all three. Ask God to guide you in your role in His kingdom.

It is beyond our ability to comprehend God's eternal perspective. May God grant us enough of His insight to devote our lives daily to His will and to His kingdom.

And his servants came near and spoke to him, and said, "My father, if the prophet had told you to do something great, would you not have done it? How much more then, when he says to you, 'Wash, and be clean'?"
—2 KINGS 5:11–13

Naaman was a very proud man who had no peace. He was the commander of the entire army of the King of Syria, Ben-Hadad II (860–841 B.C.), but he was dying of leprosy, an infectious disease that causes the skin to rot until the body literally falls apart. It was humiliating for a five-star general to ask for help, but Naaman was desperate. He went to the prophet Elisha, whom God had given the ability to perform miracles. Elisha gave Naaman some strange and unpleasant instructions: wash yourself seven times in the muddy Jordan River, and God will heal you.

Rather than being delighted that a cure was coming, Naaman was furious. He had expected Elisha to bow down to him, heal him with a magic touch, and be honored at the privilege.

Naaman's servants persuaded him to humble himself and dip in the muddy Jordan seven times, and as Elisha had predicted, God restored Naaman to perfect health.

We can never obtain the benefits of serenity until we fall on our faces before Almighty God and fearfully confess our sinful pride. Naaman was completely cured of his leprosy by a God who loves to reward the humble and forgive the proud when they turn to Him and repent.

The LORD is slow to anger and great in power.
And will not at all acquit the wicked.
　　　　　　　　　　　　　　—NAH. 1:3a

Judy had been raised in a Christian home. In fact, her father had been a pastor. Judy could quote me any Scripture I wanted to hear, and yet her life was crumbling around her feet. Her first marriage ended after she had multiple affairs. Each time an affair was over, she would confess it to her husband. He would agonize over the reality facing him and then finally forgive her. Judy would be flattered by yet another man's attention, and before she knew it she was involved in another affair. Finally her husband had had it. He filed for divorce. Now in her second marriage, Judy had taken off her wedding ring and was telling her new husband that she felt like having another affair.

I asked Judy how she could live such a fragmented life. It was as if she were two people. One quoted Scripture, and the other had no sexual restraint. Judy's reply saddened my heart. She said, "Oh, well, God is gracious. He will forgive."

Cheap grace! Judy is a Christian. She has asked Jesus Christ to be her Savior, but she will have no peace on earth because she hasn't also made Him her Lord. She will suffer consequences for her willful rebellion.

Our Lord is gracious, loving, accepting, and forgiving, but He also is Holy. He hates sin, because of what it does to His children.

When I accept God's love and God's demands I acknowledge Him as both my Savior and Lord.

> *I would have lost heart, unless I had believed*
> *That I would see the goodness of the LORD*
> *In the land of the living.*
> *Wait on the LORD;*
> *Be of good courage,*
> *And He shall strengthen your heart;*
> *Wait, I say, on the LORD!* —PS. 27:13–14

Corrie Ten Boom tells the story of how her father responded when she opened her heart to him and said that she was afraid of the trials and persecutions she still might face. This happened during the Second World War. Corrie had been hiding Jewish people in her home so the Nazis would not take them to the concentration camps. Many times, she told her father, she felt as if she might not have the stamina to stand up to the impending persecutions.

Her father assured her by asking her to remember vacations on the train as a little girl. Corrie remembered her dad giving her the train ticket just at the moment she would step onto the train. Not before, not after, but at the moment she needed it.

As we wait on the Lord, He will give us the courage and strength we need. He will be there with the ticket, as Corrie's father was, at the precise moment that we need it.

Do you believe that? Can you take courage in His promised strength to meet your need?

God's timing in meeting our needs is precise. It is not ahead of schedule, but it is also never too late.

*And at the end of the time I, Nebuchadnezzar,
lifted my eyes to heaven, and my understanding
returned to me; and I blessed the Most High and
praised and honored Him who lives forever.*
—DAN. 4:34

Even in Old Testament times, the just were saved by faith. The Law didn't save anyone; it only educated people about the extent of their "badness." Today's passage describes what happens to a proud political leader who listens to his own press clippings.

Nebuchadnezzar was that kind of proud leader, and for a while, he ruled the world. He was the King of Babylon. He got so proud that God drove him into a psychotic state. Nebuchadnezzar thought he was a bird for seven years. His officials ran the kingdom for him.

Finally, God allowed Nebuchadnezzar to regain his sanity. His officials turned the Kingdom back over to him, and this formerly arrogant ruler of the world was now a believer in the living God of Israel.

There is a lesson to be learned here. Nebuchadnezzar would never have changed his ways without God's supernatural intervention in his life. But God doesn't force anyone to change. Nebuchadnezzar could have angrily denounced God when he regained his sanity. But he humbled himself before Almighty God and repented. He publicly announced his psychosis and supernatural recovery, giving God the glory.

Our greatest threat in life is not being victimized by a criminal or being tricked by Satan. The greatest threat to our well-being and success in life is our own arrogant pride.

For by grace you have been saved through faith, and that not of yourselves; it is the gift of God, not of works, lest anyone should boast.

—EPH. 2:8–9

Yvonne was a severe codependent who always tried to please those around her. She would do almost anything to gain others' approval. She squelched her own ideas and opinions out of fear of upsetting someone close to her. She constantly set aside her needs and desires and then felt manipulated by others. In essence she had come to believe that her worth was dependent on what she did or didn't do. If she could perform well enough, others would accept her.

The apostle Paul clarifies in today's passage that we become acceptable to God not on the basis of our works, but by the grace of God. Paul's message to Yvonne would be, you can never do enough to merit salvation. Forget trying to earn it. Salvation is a free gift, and God is not keeping a score card on whether we have done enough to earn it. "Works" do not make it; rather, salvation is a gift we receive.

If you are like Yvonne, God says you can quit striving to be perfect and to do everything to gain others' approval. He declares that you are acceptable and loved. Now accept God's grace demonstrated in salvation. Depend on what Christ did on the cross to save you.

———————

I can be set free from the treadmill of endlessly trying to prove I'm OK. I can depend on Christ instead of myself, and be saved for eternity.

But He was wounded for our transgressions,
He was bruised for our iniquities;
The chastisement for our peace was upon Him.
And by His stripes we are healed.
All we like sheep have gone astray;
We have turned, every one, to his own way;
And the LORD has laid on Him the iniquity of us all.

—ISA. 53:5–6

Years ago in the southern states there was a young boy who was caught stealing food for his family. He was a frail boy and struggled with almost constant colds and flu. He was thrown into jail and waited for his day in court. Finally, the day arrived. After the case was presented, the judge declared that the boy receive forty lashes and be placed in jail for two weeks.

The little boy's mother cried out, "My boy is too sick. Please have mercy. I'm not sure he can survive a severe beating."

In the courtroom that day was a man who had befriended this sickly child. He had come to witness the trial. He approached the front of the court and said, "Honorable judge, I will take this boy's place. Give me the lashes, and I'll serve the time too."

The judge granted his request. The penalty had to be paid. The little boy was released. Jesus took our penalty of death rather than making us suffer because of our iniquity, just as the loving man did for the sickly boy.

———————

Spend some time thanking God for taking your place as He died on the Cross for your sins.

Confess your trespasses to one another and pray for one another, that you may be healed. The effective, fervent prayer of a righteous man avails much.
—JAMES 5:16

Joan and Jim were childless for years despite constant medical efforts and huge expense to get pregnant. Desperate, they asked the elders of their church to anoint them with oil and pray for them to conceive. Eighteen months later, they gave up and adopted a baby boy. Four months afterward, they became pregnant with a little girl. Years later, they are as thrilled with their adopted son as with their biological daughter.

However, there are also times when God does not heal the physical ailment but wants to change us through prayer. I had a sister who was handicapped and bedridden. She could not walk or talk, feed herself, or control her movements. She was in diapers until she died at the age of thirty. On several occasions, my parents had a group come and pray for Carole's healing. The Lord did not answer that prayer the way we asked. However, prayer changed *us*. We were comforted by the support and concern of others who prayed.

God is still God, whether or not He answers our prayers our way. God will bring change as we pray. Sometimes the change will be in the circumstances and sometimes we will have matured even if the situation remains the same.

Prayer will bring change. Lord, help me to have confidence in that and come to You in prayer. Help me to also courageously make myself accountable by honestly sharing my faults with trusted friends.

"You will keep him in perfect peace,
Whose mind is stayed on You.
Because he trusts in You.
—ISA. 26:3

God created us as spiritual beings. The Ten Commandments state we are to worship no other than the true God of the Scriptures.

Sometimes we worship other people. We watch soap operas, read paper back novels, and spend hours fantasizing about what it would be like to be someone else.

Sometimes we worship things. We surround ourselves with gadgets, in beautifully furnished homes, while driving the best machines anyone can make. But we are still empty inside.

Sometimes we worship ourselves. We think we are wise, all-powerful, and perfect. If we deceive anyone, it certainly isn't the people we live with. We are fooling only ourselves.

Only the worship of God fulfills our humanity. If we worship anyone or anything else, we lose our ability to function as whole human beings. The way to peace and serenity is the way back to the God who made us.

God does not want us to consider Him just another duty to be added to an already frantic schedule. He wants to be at the heart of our experience. The result is a wholeness, peace and serenity that is unattainable any other way.

Lord, make me aware that every relationship, every commitment, and every contact today can be an act of worship to You.

> *My brethren, count it all joy when you fall into*
> *various trials, knowing that the testing of your faith*
> *produces patience. But let patience have its perfect*
> *work, that you may be perfect and complete,*
> *lacking nothing.*   —JAMES 1:2–4

When I first read James 1:2, I remember wondering how anyone could be joyful about trials and problems.

James is not saying however, that we should be joyous *for* the trials but rather *in* the trials. There are rich advantages from these testings. Trials, rightly taken, can produce the quality of endurance. We develop strength of character and faith through persistent endurance.

Often there are problems and trials that we can't run from or can't change. We have to come to the place of accepting them. We must, as the Serenity Prayer states, "accept those things we cannot change."

Our attitude in accepting the trials can have significant impact on the final result. We can get caught in self pity, and pout. We could get angry over the problems. We could try to escape in addictions to blur the reality of the trials, or we can "consider it joy."

The personal impact of trials depends highly on my reaction to problems. The choice is up to me.

The Lord is my strength and my shield:
My heart trusted in Him, and I am helped.
—PS. 28:7

What gives you the ability to face the enemy? Whether the enemy fires at you behind battlefield bunkers or from behind closed doors down office hallways, what gives you the strength to face the battle? Where do you find your courage?

False courage comes in six-packs or bottles with childproof lids. Real courage comes from knowing you're wearing your battle armor and you aren't fighting alone.

When David went after Goliath he knew the odds were in his favor. He trusted his ability to hurl rocks at much smaller targets and hit them every time. Most importantly, he knew he never fought alone. He had courage because his battle companion was the Lord. ". . . The Lord, who delivered me from the paw of the lion and from the paw of the bear, He will deliver me from the hand of this Philistine" (1 Samuel 17:37). David walked into battle with strength of heart, a solid plan, and an awesome sense of God's presence.

If you need to be courageous today, then armor up, think through a plan, and pray through the plan. Remember God is ready to walk with you into every situation you face. If you ask Him to join you, you'll never fight alone.

Lord, when I'm afraid, when courage seems out of reach, help me to think of David. Help me get used to wearing the armor You've supplied. Show me that I am fighting side by side with You.

> *Therefore submit yourselves to every ordinance of man for the Lord's sake, whether to the king as supreme, or to governors, as to those who are sent by him for the punishment of evildoers and for the praise of those who do good. For this is the will of God, that by doing good you may put to silence the ignorance of foolish men—as free, yet not using your liberty as a cloak for vice, but as servants of God.*
> —1 PETER 2:13–16

A sociopath has complete disregard for the rules of society. The sociopath has no remorse for what he or she does, and constantly mistreats others.

We live in a culture and society that does have order. The government has set up ordinances and laws that we need to obey. God wants us to honor all people, to recognize authority figures in our world, and to follow what they legislate.

We are not above the law, as the sociopath tends to feel. We cannot just do what seems good in our eyes. We need to respect others around us and consider their personal needs. To do this is not enslaving.

We feel a deep inner freedom when we know we are living in accord with the laws of God and man. We can go to sleep with a clear conscience. Is there some law that frustrates you, and you have chosen to disregard it? You will be set free inside if you decide to obey and follow it. That is God's way. Obey all laws and Honor everyone.

The purpose behind God's laws is not punishment and restriction, but peace and liberation.

*And I saw that all labor and all achievement spring
from man's envy of his neighbor. This too is
meaningless, a chasing after the wind.*
—ECCL. 4:4, NIV

Solomon could have had anything he wanted from
God, and he requested insight so he could rule his people well. And he got it. And it was very depressing for
awhile.

Solomon learned that apart from God, " . . . all is
vanity and grasping for the wind" (Eccl. 1:14b). Every
human he studied was spinning his or her wheels in a
race to compete for a feeling of significance that never
lasted. Solomon himself had tried sex, power, and
money and found them all vanity.

The more insight he developed into human depravity and his own "badness," the more grief and sorrow
he experienced. He saw that everything people did
was out of a sense of competition with their neighbor.
He saw that insecurity was a bottomless pit that could
not be filled.

But God loved Solomon. He wouldn't give Solomon
all that painful insight into human nature without giving Him solutions to teach his people. Solomon learned
that the meaning we have in life comes from serving
God.

---

*May God grant us insight into our own nature, the courage to face
ourselves, and the wisdom to find meaning in life through serving
Jesus Christ.*

> *"For My thoughts are not your thoughts, nor are
> your ways My ways," says the* LORD. *"For as the
> heavens are higher than the earth, so are My ways
> higher than your ways, and My thoughts than your
> thoughts.*
> —ISA. 55:8–9

When we don't know something we go to the closest
thing that resembles it. But when it comes to learning
about God there's nothing to compare Him to. The
only thing we can be sure of, is that God is different
than the way we have pictured Him in our minds. His
ways are higher than our ways, and His thoughts are
higher than our thoughts.

If you really love somebody, God loves him more. If
you really want to do right things, God wants that even
more. If you really hope for the success of another person, God hopes that much more. Your best thoughts
don't even touch the basement of God's thoughts. Your
thoughts and God's thoughts are worlds apart.

So how do we really find out what God is like? Jesus
came to show us. Jesus wasn't a messenger, He was the
message. He came to reveal the very nature of God.

". . . The WORD became flesh and dwelt among us"
(John 1:14a).

If you really desire to know who God is, then you've
got to get to know Jesus. He's the only one *who* can
share with you the high ways and high thoughts of God
because He thinks just like His Dad.

*Lord, please share with me the serenity and excitement of thinking
Your thoughts and living Your ways.*

> *"I know that You are a gracious and merciful God, slow to anger and abundant in lovingkindness, One who relents from doing harm. Therefore now, O Lord, please take my life from me, for it is better for me to die than to live!"*   —JONAH 4:1–3

The example of Jonah in this passage is an interesting example of how much emphasis we place on having our own agenda take place and the anger that follows when it doesn't happen as we planned.

Jonah had gone to the wicked city of Nineveh and told the inhabitants that God would destroy their city in forty days. The people received his warning and repented. God changed His mind and had mercy. However, Jonah really wanted to see the city of Nineveh blasted and destroyed by God. He was eager to see God act in judgment.

Their repentance brought great joy to our merciful God, but it wasn't good enough for Jonah. He was angry. He was embarrassed and actually became suicidal. He asked God to take away his life. But God loved Jonah too. He forgave Jonah and brought him back to his senses.

His prayer to God was full of self-pity and anger. God in His wisdom did not answer this prayer and do what Jonah requested. God had Jonah's best at heart.

Do you have it all planned out as to how God should work in your circumstances? Can you trust that God's response to your prayer will be for your best?

Dear Lord, when I am being judgmental at times when You desire mercy and forgiveness, please forgive me and show me the truth.

> *In the middle of its street, and on either side of the river, was the tree of life, which bore twelve fruits, each tree yielding its fruit every month. And the leaves of the tree were for the healing of the nations.*
> —REV. 22:1–2

This is a puzzling passage about an eventual "Serenity Tree" in the New Jerusalem. The tree or trees will bear twelve different fruits, one for each month. They will be known collectively as the "Tree of Life." The leaves of the trees will be used for the healing of the nations during the Millennium.

Being a psychiatrist, I hope God allows me someday to dispense medicinal leaves from the Serenity Tree to people who suffer from mental and physical illnesses. It will be wonderful when serenity becomes that simple.

Unfortunately, many of our patients expect us to be able to do that right now. They think serenity comes in a leaf or a pill or a bottle. They don't want any Twelve Step program. They don't want to hear that recovery is a lifelong process. They think recovery means perfection—no more pain. And they fantasize that I should bring about their recovery for them, not just guide them as a professional on a tough path they will walk for themselves. In the Millennium, I will finally be able to deliver what idealistic people expect today.

Someday, God will give mankind constant serenity. But for now, He gives us recovery programs with sometimes difficult steps.

You also be patient. Establish your hearts, for the coming of the Lord is at hand. Do not grumble against one another, brethren, lest you be condemned. Behold, the Judge is standing at the door! My brethren, take the prophets, who spoke in the name of the Lord, as an example of suffering and patience. —JAMES 5:8–10

The typical reaction in the midst of suffering and struggle for many people is to grumble and complain. The root of the grumbling often centers on a comparison game that is played.

If we are struggling financially, we look at another couple who seems to be doing well financially and complain that we are not like them. They may in fact be struggling in some other area. The apostle Paul encouraged us not to compare ourselves with others.

We are also challenged not to gripe and focus on our problems and sufferings, but instead to follow the example of the prophets. The prophets stuck their necks out and pointed people to Christ. They were patient in the midst of the suffering they encountered because of the message they were sent to give.

James wants us to focus on the Lord's coming rather than on the suffering of the present. What is holding your gaze and catching your eye? Are you expectantly watching for Christ's return or wallowing in self-pity because of your circumstances?

Grumbling leaves me a grump! Gazing on Christ gets me over the bump! Lord, thank You for the serenity and joy that come from serving You with the perspective of Your eternal plan in mind.

> *In You, O LORD, I put my trust;*
> *Let me never be ashamed;*
> *Deliver me in Your righteousness.*
> *Bow down Your ear to me,*
> *Deliver me speedily;*
> *Be my rock of refuge,*
> *A fortress of defense to save me.*
> —PS. 31:1–2

Who do we trust? We decide. We choose. We make our moves. Is it your bank account, your IRAs, your chances for future company advancement, or someone who is higher up the success ladder?

The psalmist said he had chosen to place his trust in the Lord, because the Lord is a refuge. He responds quickly to us and rescues us. The Lord is a rock of refuge and a strong fortress.

Along the ocean coast, vicious storms and strong winds can make sailing treacherous. The waves can build and threaten to swamp a boat. A skilled skipper will in such times try to find a harbor or protected bay. Usually the bay is calmer because of the jutting land mass or jetty which breaks the force of the waves.

God is such a protection for us in the storms and crises of life. By placing our trust in the Lord we can be delivered. We trust in the Lord, because of who He is and what He does on our behalf.

Are you facing a crisis today? Why not choose to place your trust in Jesus.

It is my choice as to where and in whom I place my trust. I will not be disappointed by placing it in Jesus.

For "He who would love life
And see good days,
Let him refrain his tongue from evil,
And his lips from speaking deceit."
—1 PETER 3:9–11

Trying to get revenge and paying back evil for evil typically escalates a problem. There is a tendency within us to out-do what the other person has done to us. How many times have you heard the phrase, "Just you wait, I'll show him." The result is a snow-balling effect as the negative interchange increases.

Peter challenged us in these verses not to pay back an insult. We do not try to get even for three reasons: 1. it hurts the other person; 2. it hurts us; 3. it hurts our relationship.

Someone who is insecure enough that they have done evil to us is usually further damaged if we hurl back insults toward them.

Attacking behavior is much like a boomerang that has a way of coming back to get us. We can experience real life and good days if we refrain from trying to get revenge. We can come to love life by not speaking evil of one another.

A relationship is often broken by the escalating pattern of attacks, counter-attacks and further revengeful acts. We ought instead to pursue peace.

———

Lord, I can handle being wronged rightfully and love life, or spitefully and hate life. Please help me to be tactfully assertive but insightful and forgiving.

> *Each one should test his own actions. Then he can
> take pride in himself, without comparing himself to
> somebody else.*
>
> —GAL. 6:4, NIV

At Minirth-Meier Clinics throughout the country, we treat tens of thousands of patients. Our primary goal is to help each of them gain insights into themselves. We, as therapists, cannot change anyone, nor should we. People can only change themselves, and only if they want to. But if we love people, we will want them to see the truth about themselves, their codependent relationships, their abilities to resolve conflicts, and their significance in God's eyes.

If we admit to the Lord that we need wisdom and insight, He will give it to us. Galatians 6:4 is one of my favorite verses in the whole Bible. In it, Paul commands us to study our own psychology.

We should not compare ourselves to others, but rather test our own actions to see if we are becoming more like Christ. Paul instructs us to take pride in ourselves. The Greek word for "pride" is *Kauchēma,* which does not mean arrogant pride, but rather personal exultation over what God is doing in your life with your cooperation. You should be proud of that effective teamwork with Christ.

May God grant us the wisdom to see ourselves as we really are, so we can use the truth to set us free from a wide variety of unnecessary pains.

"Heaven is My throne,
And earth is My footstool.
Where is the house that you will build Me? . . .
But on this one will I look:
On him who is poor
And of a contrite spirit,
And who trembles at My word."

—ISA. 66:1, 2

One of the things my wife and I enjoy is to tour the majestic cathedrals and churches in cities we visit. It is fascinating to study the architecture, to see the light coming through the exquisite stained glass windows, and see the unique ways the churches are decorated. If you were constructing a place where God would dwell, what would it look like?

We are the temple in which God desires to live. What does God desire for His living quarters? What is His wish for the interior of our being? Isaiah the prophet suggested three things.

Be humble. Have a realistic view of yourself. Realize who you are in Christ Jesus. You are a person of value and worth.

Be contrite. This means to be thoroughly deeply sorry for your sin. God does not want you to pretend you don't have sin. You can confess your sin to Him and He will forgive.

Take God's Word seriously.

God wants us to have a humble spirit that will value and follow the truth laid out in Scripture.

Search yourself today for specific things you can do, with God's help,
to make beautiful your inner temple.

> *Likewise you husbands, dwell with them with understanding, giving honor to the wife, as to the weaker vessel, and as being heirs together of the grace of life, that your prayers may not be hindered.*
> —1 PETER 3:7

Have you ever felt your prayers were not being heard or answered? Your prayers could be hindered because of the way you are treating your spouse. Wives are the weaker vessel only in the sense of physical size and strength. Husbands are to respect that difference.

This verse specifically tells husbands to be "considerate" of their wives. This means to treat them with understanding and knowledge. How well do you know and understand the deep spiritual, emotional, and physical needs of your mate? Are you asking questions? Do you pursue getting below the surface in your interactions?

We are to treat our spouses with respect, and as fellow heirs of God's grace. The wife is not an heir below her husband, but an heir *with* him. There is an equality of value, worth and significance. The challenge to us is to value, respect and treat as an equal those special people God has placed in our lives. We are equal as we stand before God. Let's not try to keep our spouse one down. That is not God's way. If we do, the bottom line is that our prayers will be hindered.

I can improve the effectiveness of my prayers by my attitudes and actions toward my spouse.

"Blessed is the man who trusts in the Lord,
And whose hope is the Lord.
For he shall be like a tree planted by the
waters,
Which spreads out its roots by the river,
And will not fear when heat comes;
But her leaf will be green,
And will not be anxious in the year of drought,
Nor will cease from yielding fruit.
—JER. 17:7–8

Those of us who place our trust in the Lord will be stable. We do not need to give in to overwhelming feelings of anxiety, for through all the seasons of our life we will be productive.

How should we live as a result of this marvelous promise? First of all, we need to put our trust firmly in the only solid reality in our universe, Jesus Christ.

Then we need to ask ourselves some tough questions. How much time in the last week did I spend worrying and fretting? What did all my anxiety accomplish? It would be more productive to meditate on this promise and thank God for it than to worry about things over which we have no control.

Christ experienced great anguish in the garden just prior to His death on the cross, but He is the only one who ever lived a life free from the anxiety and worry that stems from fear of facing the truth about ourselves. The closer we get to Him the more we will experience a sense of wholeness, meaning and peace.

Worry fragments me into pieces. Worship enables me to be at peace.

> *Therefore, laying aside all malice, all guile,*
> *hypocrisy, envy, and all evil speaking, as newborn*
> *babes, desire the pure milk of the word, that you*
> *may grow thereby, if indeed you have tasted that*
> *the Lord is gracious.* —1 PETER 2:1–3

When I get up and look in the mirror some mornings I'm faced with a disheveled, red-eyed, unshaven reflection. It's not the way I like to think of myself. I need a cup of coffee just to recover from the shock.

God's Word can be a mirror to reveal our spiritual self. As we read God's Word sometimes we begin to see deceit, hypocrisy, envy, anger, and slander in ourselves. We can then make changes.

God's Word enables us to get a clear picture of ourselves spiritually. That picture isn't always rosy. However, if we feel we never have to take a hard honest look at ourselves, we live in denial.

God's Word helps us see clearly the reality about ourselves. However, it doesn't stop there. God's Word shows us that God is good and He wants to help us grow and mature as we drink of "the milk of the Word" just as a baby grows as it is fed nourishing milk.

God's Word has what we need to grow spiritually and fight off evil forces.

God's Word can help us grow up by allowing us to see areas in ourselves that need to change.

Pull me out of the net which they have secretly
laid for me,
For You are my strength. Into Your hand I
commit my spirit;
You have redeemed me. O LORD God of truth.
—PS. 31:4–5

Mike was having business problems. Financially, he had never been at a lower point. He confided in his next door neighbor. The neighbor committed himself to secrecy. A week later at his son's ball game, Mike had the humiliating experience of having one of the dads say, "Hey I hear you're hitting the bottom financially, buddy. I'm sorry." Mike felt naked in front of all those other dads. His confidence had been betrayed.

When Jesus hung on the cross He suffered from the external wounds, the crown of thorns, the spikes in His hands and feet, the sword in His side, and the lashes on His back; but there was also an internal wound. It had been placed there by a kiss of betrayal.

Sir Winston Churchill was quoted as saying, "Success is never final. Failure is never fatal. It is the courage that counts." When our confidence is in God's love, betrayal does not need to be fatal. It stings. It's unfair. But so was Christ's death on the cross. Easter morning was God's answer to the cross. It can be the answer to the betrayal we have felt as well.

Courage is a direct result of seeing the cross.

Be sober, be vigilant; because your adversary the devil walks about like a roaring lion, seeking whom he may devour. Resist him, steadfast in the faith, knowing that the same sufferings are experienced by your brotherhood in the world.
—1 PETER 5:8–9

We as Christians live in a world in which there are evil forces that attack us. Peter visualized Satan as a vicious lion on the prowl for its next meal.

There are individuals who see a demon or evil force behind every bush and who become obsessed with evil in everything around them. The opposite kind of individual also exists in our world. This is the person who doesn't really believe there is any evil threat around them. We should not be obsessed with evil, but in a balanced way be alert to it.

As you spot the evil, resist and stand firm in your faith in Jesus. We do not need to live in fear. We can face evil, and with the backing of our faith in Jesus and His Word, take a stand.

Let's not be blown away by evil, but let's be alert to its reality. Let's stand confidently in the Lord and resist the evil around us.

Jesus has overcome evil. That is why we can stand confidently in Christ against it.

*When God gives any man wealth and possessions,
and enables him to enjoy them, to accept his lot
and be happy in his work—this is a gift of God.*
　　　　　　　—ECCL. 5:19 (NIV)

Whatever the Lord has blessed us with financially is to be received with gratitude and used to honor Him. No matter what your financial statement is, there is some way every day that you can give something back.

Jethro Mann runs a lending library of bikes. When he retired a friend gave him a few broken bikes. He was talented at fixing things, and at the age of 63 he built his first bike.

Suddenly an idea occurred to him. There were many children in his neighborhood who wanted bikes but couldn't afford them. He went to flea markets, junkyards, and thrift stores looking for salvageable bicycle parts. He filled a two-story backyard warehouse with 450 bikes that he built from all the parts. Then came the fun part. He opened the door of his warehouse to the neighborhood children. They could check out a bike in the morning, and return it at sunset. The warehouse operated on an honor system.

Some mornings Jethro can be found working in his bicycle warehouse at two o'clock, making sure that all the bikes are safe and ready for the eager children who will be there the next morning.

What has God given you? Can you give something back?

———————

Lord, Help me to remember that all good and perfect gifts come from You. Show me how I can give something back.

> *"Blessed be the name of God forever and ever,*
> *For wisdom and might are His.*
> *And He changes the times and the seasons;*
> *He removes kings and raises up kings;*
> *He gives wisdom to the wise*
> *And knowledge to those who have understanding.*
> —DAN. 2:20–21

Before Nebuchadnezzar became a believer in the living God, he had a dream. But he didn't tell anyone what it was. His astrologers claimed they could interpret dreams and tell fortunes, and Nebuchadnezzar demanded that they tell him what his dream was, and what it meant. He would kill them all if they didn't come through.

Daniel was a wise believer and was not a phony like the astrologers. He knew only God could show him what Nebuchadnezzar's dream was, so he prayed and God granted his request.

Daniel blessed the God of heaven for some of His excellent attributes and God gave him wisdom. Daniel did not depend on himself for insight.

Truth dwells with Him. He sees the truth about all things.

We have a God who loves to give wisdom to us if we, like Daniel, ask for it.

"And should I not pity Ninevah, that great city, in which are more than one hundred and twenty thousand persons who cannot discern between their right hand and their left, and also much livestock?"
—JONAH 4:11

Jonah was embarrassed and angry. God had told him to go to Nineveh and tell all the inhabitants that the city would be destroyed in forty days because of the evil going on. After some extra persuasion and a smelly ride in a large fish, Jonah obeyed God and walked through the city proclaiming God's words of doom.

Jonah wanted to see the people die. He felt his credibility was at stake. The people of Nineveh were cruel. Wooden stakes lined the road to the city with dead bodies of foreigners impaled on them. But God looked with pity on 120,000 children in Nineveh who were too young to tell their left hands from their right.

To Jonah's amazement, the people of Nineveh believed God and repented. They prayed that God would have compassion. God heard the cry of the people.

God answers our prayers knowing many factors that we don't understand at the time.

> *Then he said to me, "These words are faithful and*
> *true." And the Lord God of the holy prophets sent*
> *His angel to show His servants the things which*
> *must shortly take place. Behold, I am coming*
> *quickly! Blessed is he who keeps the words of the*
> *prophecy of this book."*
> —REV. 22:6–7

Revelation is the only book of the Bible that promises special blessings (including serenity) to all those who read and heed it. Obviously, there are messages that speak directly to us in the twentieth century in Revelation. One of them, I believe is that we should reserve our worship and praise for the only One who truly deserves them.

John fell down in front of the angel who showed him the vision. The angel was angry because he was only a servant of Christ and His followers; he wasn't God, and he said that he was a servant to the prophets and to us, the followers of Jesus. It amazes me that God has even instructed His angels to hold us in high esteem.

Some scholars invent symbolic meanings for nearly every statement in Revelation, missing out on God's literal plans for our future. Their pride tends to make simple things complex, overruling the simplicity of God's love and His plans for us. We can forgive past abusers more easily when we have an eternal perspective on life. We can deflect inferiority feelings when we read the truth about our future as God's children.

When your serenity is slipping, study God's Word for the present and future blessings He has promised you.

For this is commendable, if because of conscience toward God one endures grief, suffering wrongfully. For what credit is it if, when you are beaten for your faults, you take it patiently? But when you do good and suffer for it, if you take it patiently, this is commendable before God. For to this you were called, because Christ also suffered for us, leaving us an example, that you should follow His steps.
—1 PETER 2:19–21

Healthy parents train children early in life that there will be consequences which will follow the choices they make. If I choose to speed on the freeway, it is likely that I will receive a speeding ticket. If I decide not to go to work for a month, I will not receive a paycheck.

If we suffer and endure it because we have done something wrong, that really isn't commendable. However, the real test for us comes in how we bear up under the pain of suffering for doing good. What happens after you conscientiously give your all on a project and then someone critically attacks it? What happens when your motives are right but someone misjudges them? The real test of character is how we handle suffering even when we have done nothing wrong. This is the way we prove our character.

Lord help me to realize I may experience suffering even if I am doing what's honorable. Help me respond with a Christ-like attitude.

Blessed be the LORD.
For He has shown me His marvelous kindness in a
* strong city!*
For I said in my haste,
"I am cut off from before Your eyes";
Nevertheless You heard the voice of my
* supplications.*
—PS. 31:21–22

Pete's marriage of two years lay in ashes around his feet. His young wife, the child of an alcoholic, agreed to come in for counseling once a week for three months, in order to work on their relationship. The following weekend she went out and had an affair. Pete was sitting in my office weeping uncontrollably. When I shared with him that God wanted to be there for him during this time, Pete gasped, "How could He? I have only cried out to Him in the crisis times of my life."

Apparently David was feeling the same way when he wrote this psalm. He had been racing through life, overcome with his responsibilities, feeling totally cut off from God. David hadn't had time for God, but God heard David's prayer and delivered him from his trouble. Even though David felt unfaithful, God demonstrated His faithfulness. David's heart was strengthened and his courage increased as a direct result of God's intervention.

In quiet times, noisy times, frantic times, peaceful times, silent times, joyful times, depressing times, all times . . . I thank You Lord, that You are with me.

*. . . as His divine power has given to us all things
that pertain to life and godliness, through the
knowledge of Him who called us by glory and
virtue.* —2 PETER 1:3

Bob went to our pastor and inquired if today's verse
meant that he should not go to a doctor or psychologist. The pastor told him that the verse has often been
misinterpreted to mean that psychology and medicine
are not needed and should be avoided. What this verse
does say is that spiritual vitality and godly living can
be reached through an intimate knowledge of Christ.
Christ is the source of spiritual power and growth. The
focus of this passage is on spiritual life rather than our
physical or emotional life. In the verses that follow, we
find clues as to how to continue to grow in our spiritual
life. We are to add to our faith, virtue, knowledge, self-
control, perseverance, godly living, brotherly kindness
or concern for others' needs, and love.

The entire passage encourages us to draw on the
Lord's power to continue to change and to develop
character.

———————

*God's power is our resource for a healthy developing character. In
which of the seven areas listed above do you need Christ's power to
keep growing?*

> *For when they speak great swelling words of
> emptiness, they allure through the lusts of the flesh,
> through licentiousness, the ones who have actually
> escaped from those who live in error. While they
> promise them liberty, they themselves are slaves of
> corruption; for by whom a person is overcome, by
> him also he is brought into bondage.*
> —2 PETER 2:18–19

Wisdom involves not allowing ourselves to get into a repetitive negative cycle. There are so many patterns in life that can be repeated time and time again, but are destructive to us.

The codependent often finds him- or herself letting others overstep their boundaries and control him or her. The codependent tends to be angry about the manipulation, but out of fear of being abandoned continues to be misused.

The alcoholic continues to drink even though he or she knows the negative results it brings. The person with an eating disorder continues to abuse his or her body with either too much or too little food. We become a slave to whatever masters us. It can be that we are addicted to another person, alcohol, drugs, food, exercise, or work.

In contrast to being mastered by these, we can exercise wisdom and get help to break the cycle.

What is mastering you now? What continues to control you and keep you in negative self-destructive patterns? It is time to make changes.

> *"How long will the vision be, concerning the daily sacrifices and the transgression of desolation, the giving of both the sanctuary and the host to be trampled under foot?" And he said to me, "For two thousand three hundred days; then the sanctuary shall be cleansed."*
> —DAN. 8:13–14

Our personal recovery requires our humble dependence on God, our Higher Power. But what is He like? What are His plans for me? Today's passage is one of those vague prophecies that will be obvious someday. But I love these; they are a real challenge. They show me what a wonderful and wise God we have. He has a master plan for all people for eternity.

Antiochus IV Epiphanes destroyed Jerusalem, plundered the temple treasury, and desecrated the temple itself, about four hundred years after Daniel predicted it. In 167 B.C., he declared himself to be a god and forced the Jews to eat swine in the temple, ending Jewish sacrificial worship.

The 2,300 days may refer to each evening and each morning that would pass before Judas Maccabeus refurbished the temple and restored Jewish sacrifices in 164–163 B.C. It may also refer to sacrifices in the Messianic Kingdom beginning again around A.D. 2100.

Nobody knows the day or hour of the Lord's return. But it is reassuring to know we have a brilliant God with a definite plan and that each believer has an important part in His future.

God has already proven He is real by fulfilling past prophecies. He knows what He is doing even when we don't understand.

> *Now this is the confidence that we have in Him,*
> *that if we ask anything according to His will, He*
> *hears us.*   —1 JOHN 5:14

We can approach God in prayer with a confidence that if what we are asking is in His will, He will answer it.

Several years ago the farmers in the midwest were experiencing a severe drought. It had been weeks since it had rained and the corn crops were going to have to be plowed under if they didn't receive some moisture.

A group of believers decided to call a community wide prayer meeting to ask God to send rain on Friday. As the people began to gather at the little country church on the appointed evening, a little girl came walking up the road carrying her umbrella.

Not one of the adults had such practical faith and confidence that God would answer their prayer. Maybe this is why Jesus said that unless we become as a little child, we can't enter the kingdom of heaven (Mark 10:15). God wants us to take Him at His Word. He has promised He will hear and answer all our prayers that are in His will.

What do you need to ask God for today? Do you believe He will answer? Are you prepared for His abundant response to your request?

Lord, when I pray in Your will, please hear me and give me confidence in Your answer. And when I pray out of your will, hear me but convict me.

For thus says the LORD of hosts: "once more (it is a little while) I will shake heaven and earth, the sea and dry land; and I will shake all nations, and they shall come to the Desire of All Nations, and I will fill this temple with glory," says the LORD of hosts. "The glory of this latter temple shall be greater than the former," says the LORD of hosts. "And in this place I will give peace," says the LORD of hosts.
—HAG. 2:6–9

This passage describes a future Temple of Peace where God Himself will be our peace for a thousand years. People will bring treasures from all nations to help build the temple to its new dimensions and to see Christ. It will be a more glorious temple than the one Solomon built. It will be a place of international worship and peace.

The God whose goal is to have a Temple of Peace someday also wants to bring personal serenity into our lives right now. When you are anxious, God grieves. He longs to bring you comfort. God calls Himself the "Comforter" and the "Prince of Peace."

Psychiatrists relieve anxiety disorders through insight-oriented therapy and dealing with those insights biblically. God is the Source of all true insights. For Him to plan an eventual Temple of Serenity only seems logical.

Both today and tomorrow, God has your peace as one of His highest goals.

> *Beloved, do not think it strange concerning the fiery trial which is to try you, as though some strange thing happened to you; but rejoice to the extent that you partake of Christ's sufferings, that when His glory is revealed, you may also be glad with exceeding joy. If you are reproached for the name of Christ, blessed are you, for the Spirit of glory and of God rests upon you. On their part He is blasphemed, but on your part He is glorified.*
> —1 PETER 4:12–14

Have you ever been the honored guest at a surprise party? In my experience of being completely surprised on two occasions, I can report that it is embarrassing. Being caught off guard feels awkward.

Whether the surprises of life are planned to make us happy or they are unplanned natural disasters, before we can begin to deal with them effectively we need to accept them.

When suffering surprises you, I hope it's because of your stand for Jesus. It always surprises me that there are those who hate God's message of love and truth so much they strike out at anyone who tries to share it. Learn to accept it, so you will be free to love them and respond in grace instead of reacting to their surprise attack.

After acceptance, rejoice! If it's a "good" surprise, enjoy it. If it's a painful surprise due to honoring God with your life, then rejoice. Even your enemies will be able to see the Lord changing your life.

Lord, When I'm surprised, help me to accept the situation knowing You're in control and nothing ever surprises You.

I sought the LORD, and He heard me.
And delivered me from all my fears.
—PS. 34:4

What do we do when we feel the tentacles of icy fear grip us by the throat? First we need to focus on our faith, not on our fears. Fear does not originate with God. Therefore, we need to crowd the fears out of our mind by being full of faith in the reality of the Holy Spirit, in our Lord and Savior Jesus Christ, and faith that God has a purpose for our lives. His purpose for us is not security. Whenever we choose fear over faith or the security of the past over the insecurity of the present and future, we are not obeying God.

Faith always proceeds the miracle. It wasn't raining when Noah built the Ark. Fear is a chasm separating us from what we really want in life. There is an old Chinese proverb that states "If you deliberate fully before taking a step, you may spend your entire life on one leg." Our faith is in God. What could God do through you if you were totally committed to Him and not afraid to try? Try the thing you most fear. God will rid you of your fear only as you move out and face it.

Faith overpowers fear as I stop making security my God.

> *"Nevertheless I have this against you, that you have left your first love. Remember therefore from where you have fallen: repent and do the first works, or else I will come to you quickly and remove your lampstand from its place—unless you repent.*
>   —REV. 2:4–5

One of the most common statements I have heard in my office over the years of marital counseling is "I just don't love her anymore."

The enthusiasm and excitement has been replaced by mere existing. Communication continues to diminish as each partner pulls away from the other. The result is an isolated marriage relationship.

John, in these verses, challenged us with regard to our relationship with God to return to our first love.

First of all we must remember and reflect on those special times we shared. Instead of focusing on all the negatives, remember the positive.

Secondly, repent or ask forgiveness for your part in letting the relationship get complacent. That process involves honestly looking at yourself in the mirror rather than pointing the finger and blaming your mate.

Finally, do some of the things you used to do at first in your relationship. Surprise your mate. Add some sparkle by letting your partner know you were thinking of him or her.

We can practice these same steps in our relationship with God.

Is there a relationship I need to rekindle? Why not start today!

Let us hear the conclusion of the whole matter:
Fear God and keep His commandments,
For this is the whole duty of man.
—ECCL. 12:13

Solomon, the wisest man who ever lived, wrote a book on what life is all about, the book of Ecclesiastes. Much of the book appears to be pessimistic. His summary on life without God is that everything is meaningless. In essence, all human endeavors lack ultimate value, and really amount to nothing.

After discussing this fact at length, however, Solomon ended his book with the two verses in our reading today. His conclusion is that meaning is found in a life that reverences God and is willing to follow His commandments. God's commandments were not given to be negative and restrict us. Their purpose was to lay out for us a pattern of life that could enable us to experience a more fulfilling existence. The commandments were written to bring more joy and happiness to us. God is not against us. He is for us.

Where are you in your search to find meaning and significance in life? Are you disillusioned with life? Have you given up on people? Does your routine seem meaningless? Is the Lord part of your life? He can make a difference.

The meaning of life involves including the Maker of Life, Jesus Christ. Seeking to become like Him and to serve Him wholeheartedly will open your door to a meaningful life.

> *And after the sixty-two weeks Messiah shall be cut off, but not for Himself; and the people of the prince who is to come shall destroy the city and the sanctuary. . . . Then he shall confirm a covenant with many for one week; but in the middle of the week He shall bring an end to sacrifice and offering.*
>
> —DAN. 9:26–27

This prophetic puzzle tells us a lot about how God, our true Higher Power, thinks and plans. Most of it has already been fulfilled.

A week in prophecy is often seven Jewish years (360 days each). Daniel said there would be a command to restore Jerusalem, and 483 years later, Messiah would enter Jerusalem. On March 5, 444 B.C., Artaxerxes Longimanus ordered the temple rebuilt. Exactly 483 years later, Jesus rode a donkey into Jerusalem the week before His crucifixion. Some skeptics say Daniel was a lucky guesser!

Daniel also predicted the temple would be desecrated again by the Antichrist during the Tribulation. The "prince" will make a covenant with "many" (usually taken to mean Israel), then he will desecrate the temple. The Great Tribulation will begin. It will end with the Battle of Armageddon and Messiah's second coming.

When I was a skeptical graduate student, prophecies like this one convinced me to "get my act together" and serve Jesus Christ, the coming Messiah. I hope it will have the same impact on you.

Our Higher Power is not a myth or father-projection. He is a real person who controls all events, past, present, and future.

But as for me, I watch in hope for the Lord, I wait
for God my Savior; my God will hear me.
—MICAH 7:7

Micah the prophet lived in evil times. Violence was rampant and loyalty was rare. He saw suffering everywhere. Judah was particularly corrupt. The judges and political leaders took bribes, and the rich and influential got what they wanted at everyone else's expense. Sound familiar? God sent the Babylonians to defeat Judah.

But Micah kept watch for the Lord. He waited in hope. Micah prayed for his people with realism and optimism. He knew judgment was coming. But he also knew that the Lord would eventually restore his broken people.

I love to go to the California coast at evening and watch the sunset. I feel as if I am at the end of the world. When the sun goes down over the ocean, the stars and planets shine brightly. I stare at those stars and wonder if the Lord will return tonight. I keep watch and wait for Him. I hope for Him.

The world is growing more prosperous . . . and more corrupt. I care deeply about people and frequently grieve over all the suffering we experience in this life. I pray for God to grant specific and immediate relief for my patients and friends, either here and now or to come back and take us all home. I wait for Him to answer in His timing.

Let's all pray together for God to end this world's suffering rapidly.
Let's also claim Micah 7:7 as we pray for those we love.

> *And he said to me, "Do not seal the words of the*
> *prophecy of this book, for the time is at hand. He*
> *who is unjust, let him be unjust still; he who is*
> *filthy, let him be filthy still; he who is righteous, let*
> *him be righteous still; he who is holy, let him be*
> *holy still."*
> —REV. 22:10–14a

The Lord's return is nearer than it ever was before. Probably the basic level of corruption in the world will not change much prior to the rapture. There will continue to be righteous and unrighteous, users and used, abusers and abused. The Alpha and Omega will end things on an uplifting note, but until then we accept having an imperfect world and do the best we can to maintain an attitude of serenity as we continue to make a contribution here and there.

If we continue to do the Lord's commandments, He will bless us in many ways. We will see the sparkle in the eyes of those whom we have helped. We will get a hug from those we love. We will get surprising blessings in the present and even more surprising blessings at the Judgment Seat of Christ and in the Messianic Kingdom. There is a hymn I love to hear that says, "It will be worth it all when we see Jesus. Life's trials seem so small, when we see Him."

God grant me the serenity to accept the suffering in the world that I cannot change, the courage to change the suffering that I can, the wisdom to know the difference, and the hope that You will soon return to correct it all.

But let none of you suffer as a murderer, a thief, an evildoer, or as a busybody in other people's matters. Yet if anyone suffers as a Christian, let him not be ashamed, but let him glorify God in this matter. —1 PETER 4:15–16

Some people and situations hurt us. Jesus told us to expect and accept suffering, that it is unavoidable.

Peter, however, makes a distinction: he says we can experience *unnecessary* suffering when we violate other people's boundaries. He specifically warns us against meddling in others' affairs. He says we will suffer unnecessarily if we have wronged someone else, stolen from, defrauded, or killed someone. He challenges Christians not to suffer for sinful behavior and endure that shame and guilt.

Christians also suffer necessary pains of various kinds: the death of a loved one, unavoidable illnesses, undeserved financial surprises, unwarranted rejection. We tend to erroneously feel ashamed for this kind of loss. We develop false guilt during our grieving process. If we suffer for our commitment to God, we should glorify Him in it and thank Him for the opportunity to identify with Christ's pain.

Am I suffering because I am a pain in someone else's life, or is my suffering a result of some necessary pain through which Christ shines?

> *God is our refuge and strength.*
> *A very present help in trouble.*
> *Therefore we will not fear. . . .*
> —PS. 46:1–2a

It has been said that "fear always springs from ignorance." What are you afraid of? Who are you afraid of? It has been said that fear is the strongest negative emotion. It has a paralyzing, immobilizing component. However, if as Emerson said, fear comes from ignorance, then fear should alert me to the fact that I need to gain some new input and insight on what it is I fear.

Fear can be the warning light that I don't have all the facts. It's time to go on a search. The psalmist had faced his fear and realized it was not the enemy. He saw that he did not need to fear or be afraid of anyone, because God was his refuge and strength. God is here in the present to help in our trouble.

He is our light, our salvation, and our deliverance.

The psalmist didn't deny the problem. He clearly saw the situation he was in. He raised his focus and saw God who was greater than the difficulty.

Focusing on the person of Christ and His power keeps me from panic in the midst of problems.

"Nevertheless I have a few things against you, because you allow that woman Jezebel, who calls herself a prophetess, to teach and beguile My servants to commit sexual immorality and to eat things sacrificed to idols. And I gave her time to repent of her sexual immorality, and she did not repent. Indeed I will cast her into a sickbed, and those who commit adultery with her into great tribulation, unless they repent of their deeds."

—REV. 2:20–22

If there is one area where Christianity typically has received "bad press" it is in the sexual area. Many through the centuries have charged Christians with being narrow-minded and prudish.

God wants us to enjoy sex. He has approved of it completely, because He created it. When God commands us to keep our sexual experiences for our marriage, He is not trying to be narrow. On the contrary, He knows how the sexual area can be most rewarding and fulfilling. When affairs and adultery take place, partners are left crushed, angry, and hurt. Relationships are often ended. Families are fractured.

Is God negative then for giving the warning against adultery? God wanted Jezebel to repent and change her behavior, but she refused. He could not allow her to continue. God was concerned others might be misled and suffer the consequences. He desired each to experience the best in their sexual relationships.

God gives us all kinds of freedom with regard to what we do sexually within marriage. However, He is very narrow about with whom we do it. He challenges us to keep it for our spouse.

If we say that we have no sin, we deceive ourselves, and the truth is not in us. If we confess our sins, He is faithful and just to forgive us our sins and to cleanse us from all unrighteousness.

—1 JOHN 1:8–9

The truth is that we are both good and bad. Our friends have outstanding strengths that attract us, but they also disappoint us at times. We are created in God's image and have talents and abilities, but we also let ourselves down when we fail. None of us are all good or all bad. True wisdom comes from accepting that we are both good and bad.

Jeff came into therapy after trying to build an image that he was all good. He could not tolerate the idea of having any weakness or failure. He pressured himself to always be perfect. For Jeff this "all or nothing" thinking set him up for a fall. And like Humpty Dumpty in the nursery rhyme, the fall came. He felt absolutely helpless and hopeless. He not only saw how he had failed, he now felt like a total failure. Jeff was deceived by denying that he had sin. His perfectionistic tendencies and inability to tolerate weakness, failure, and "badness" both in himself and in others finally brought Jeff to the hopeless point of suicide.

We can admit we are bad because God has a solution for that. Our failures can be forgiven and we can go on to face life. We don't have to pretend to be all good. We can be *real* and allow the Lord to *heal*.

Thank You Lord, that You accept me the way I am, so I don't have to pretend to be something or someone I am not.

"But you, Bethlehem Ephrathah, though you are little among the thousands of Judah, yet out of you shall come forth to Me the One to be ruler in Israel, Whose goings forth have been from of old, from everlasting."
—MIC. 5:2

The prophet Micah predicted the character of our Immanuel.

First, Micah uses an analogy of Jesus as a Shepherd. The shepherd protects his sheep from wild animals and thieves. He guides them to food and safety.

Second, Micah talks about the Lord's power. Israel was struggling as a nation and needed a strong leader and renewed hope. The Messiah would be their hope.

Jesus is also a glorious Messiah, standing in His Father's majesty. Israel needed someone to look up to.

Finally, Micah refers to the Messiah as the one who will bring peace. Israel was constantly at war with surrounding nations. They did not feel secure, but Micah reminded them better days would come. The Messiah would bring protection, power, prestige, and peace.

Aren't these the elements our culture cries out for today? Christ can bring these to our lives. He has given us His Word and His church to encourage and protect us. We have His supernatural protection and His Spirit's peace. We have all we will ever need in Jesus.

We have a Higher Power who came to earth to protect us, empower us, honor us, and give us peace.

> *And they cried with a loud voice, saying, "How long, O Lord, holy and true, until You judge and avenge our blood on those who dwell on earth?"*
> —REV. 6:10

Some believers feel guilty for praying for God's vengeance on abusers, but King David prayed for it often. These tribulation martyrs in Revelation will be perfect, living in the presence of the Lord, and yet they pray for vengeance. It must be acceptable to pray for God to dispense justice on our abusers. But we must remember that God has the freedom to forgive those abusers who repent and come to Him.

Some people who have been abused take vengeance into their own hands. They look for ways to get even. They may even break the law to do it. Revenge becomes their obsession. When we take justice into our own hands, God allows us to suffer the consequences. We are not God and we have no right to judge other sinners. We will be judged ourselves.

Other abused individuals internalize all the pain inflicted on them by others. They may feel that somehow they deserved it. Or they may simply stuff their rage deep inside and eventually sink into depression.

In our passage today, we see that the abused and martyred tribulation saints will call out to the Lord, stating their case and admitting their pain. But they will leave the matter in His hands. He will deal with evil. He wrote it into His own job description!

May we release our vengeful desires and let the Lord carry our grudges.

And let him who hears say, "Come!" And let him who thirsts come. And whoever desires, let him take the water of life freely. —REV. 22:17

It had been a long day backpacking in the National Park on Vancouver Island in the August heat. Along with a group of six other skilled climbers, I had made my way through the rugged brush as we attempted to climb one of the incredible mountains. Each of us carried fifty-pound packs with our personal gear and food. It was now 5:00 P.M. We stopped and reviewed our contour maps, and took a compass reading. The deep gully just ahead of us appeared to be the all-year-around stream marked on our map but it appeared to have dried up.

What were we to do? I felt the twinge of fear inside. We needed water.

We decided after surveying the map to climb higher to a small lake marked on the map. We estimated it would take about three hours. We were already tired. Finally after dark we arrived at the lake. The growing anxiety subsided and a peace began to flow over me.

Today's passage talks about the serenity we can experience as we come to the "water of life." Just as the water quenched our thirst and brought a sense of serenity to our weary bodies that day in the mountains, so Jesus, the "water of life" can restore our thirsty, needy souls.

Why go trudging on, emotionally and spiritually thirsty? Drink from the water of life. Let Christ satisfy your thirst.

> *But may the God of all grace, who called us to His*
> *eternal glory by Christ Jesus, after you have*
> *suffered a while, perfect, establish, strengthen, and*
> *settle you.* —1 PETER 5:10

Many times our heart's desire and request to God is to have immediate gratification and immediate relief from our suffering. The verse today reminds us that sometimes God chooses to let us experience suffering for a while to strengthen us.

Max Cleland was an American soldier who tragically lost an arm and both of his legs in the Vietnam War. He could have returned home to his country a physically and spiritually broken man. However, he saw beyond the disability to making something of his future. His book entitled, *"Strong in the Broken Places,"* is a moving story of a man who grew in greatness. He accepted his reality but determined to move beyond it. His character deepened.

Another friend of ours lost an arm, also in the war, but returned to school and became a psychologist so he could reach out and hug others with his caring spirit and his words of comfort. God promises the believer that suffering and pain will finally end when we go to be with the Lord in heaven.

Pain usually is not fatal, and our suffering is not yet final.

*By awesome deeds in righteousness You will
answer us, O God of our salvation. You who are
the confidence of all the ends of the earth. And of
the far-off seas: Who established the mountains by
His strength, Being clothed with power: You who
still the noise of the seas, The noise of their waves,
And the tumult of the peoples. They also who dwell
in the farthest parts are afraid of Your signs . . .*
—PS. 65:5–8a

Awesome. That's how the bigness of God's deeds can
be described. All of nature shows how awesome God
is. Thoughts of the greatness of God can assist us in
having a new level of courage. God continues to be an
awesome God today. We can take courage because He
wants to be active in our lives. That makes this awesome God a personal reality. This fact can give us courage to keep growing, not to give up, and to fulfill the
potential God has placed within us.

*Take courage today, since the awesome God has chosen to be your
friend.*

> *"I know your works, that you are neither cold nor hot. I could wish you were cold or hot. So then, because you are lukewarm, and neither cold nor hot, I will spew you out of My mouth."*
>
> —REV. 3:15

One of the characteristics of someone who is severely depressed is a flat affect. What this means is that they show little emotion. This kind of person does not respond with enthusiasm to anything. They are "blah." Even when surrounded by the celebrations of Christmas there is no display of emotion.

The Church in Laodicea had become complacent. They showed no vitality and no life. They were lukewarm spiritually. In their feasts as well as in their religious sacrifices, people in the ancient world customarily drank what was either hot or cold, never lukewarm. Therefore this distasteful "lukewarm" label had a real impact. The imagery is poignant. They needed to find true richness, they needed to cover their shameful nakedness with clothes and put salve on their eyes so they could have spiritual sight. The church was unconscious of its real need.

The warning comes to us today to be alert to our spiritual life, to see clearly our spiritual situation, and not to get complacent in our materialism.

Lord at this time of the year when we are bombarded by materialism, help us to have spiritual eyes to clearly evaluate our personal lives.

> *"The heart is deceitful above all things.*
> *And desperately wicked:*
> *Who can know it?*
> *I, the LORD, search the heart.*
> *I test the mind,*
> *Even to give every man according to his ways.*
> *And according to the fruit of his doings."*
> —JER. 17:9–10

Our hearts are deceitful. The *heart* includes our mind, our emotions, and our will.

We can be deceived by our thoughts, feelings, and actions. Psychology has labeled these ways we deceive or lie to ourselves *defense mechanisms*. There are many defense mechanisms that can be used.

We can repress our true feelings and pretend we are fine when we are desperately hurting. Rationalization is a way we avoid the truth and make the unacceptable appear acceptable. Projection is another defense mechanism involving blaming others for our own shortcomings. Denial is the refusal to see what really exists or to accept that it is true. There are many other defense mechanisms, but all of them are ways we lie to ourselves.

The truly wise person is not afraid to lay his cards on the table and face the facts. A wise person will hate his or her iniquity rather than hide it. The wise person can face him- or herself rather than live a life centered on defense mechanisms.

Lord, help me to see myself clearly. Help me to hate my own sin but love the sinner, just as You do.

The LORD will take vengeance on His adversaries,
And He reserves wrath for His enemies;

—NAH. 1:2

God is committed to protecting what is His. He gets angry at those who try to attack, hurt, and undermine His family. He takes vengeance on abusers.

From time to time the newspapers will carry a story of a father who rises in the middle of the night and shoots an intruder who has broken into his home. Most people wouldn't consider this dad to be brutal, or would blame him for taking extreme measures to protect the lives of his family.

We Christians are the family of God. God is our Father, and He is committed to protecting us.

Have you experienced the reality of the security and protection the Lord offers? Don't be shocked that the Lord gets angry. However, be clear in your thinking as to who He avenges. He avenges His enemies, not His children.

———————

God loves me enough that He gets angry at individuals and things that would destroy me.

Through the Lord's mercies we are not consumed.
Because His compassions fail not.
They are new every morning.   —LAM. 3:22

The Lord told Noah to build an ark. It was years later that the floods came. Abraham was called out of Egypt with the promise that God would make of him a great nation. It was years before that promise was fulfilled. Sarah desired a child so that God's prophecy could be fulfilled. She ended up the mother of a teenager at age 103. Isaiah prophecied that Jesus would be born of a virgin. Years later, Christ was born to Mary in Bethlehem. What God promises, He delivers!

If life is a process, then patience must not be an enemy. If the really important things in this world take time, then it is patience we must learn.

Patience isn't passive. Rather patience is the invisible work we do inside while we hope. Patience is active. While Noah waited, he built an ark in spite of his neighbors' jeering comments. Abraham and Sarah waited and prayed for the fulfillment of God's promise. The Israelites watched for and anticipated the arrival of the promised Messiah.

Is it time for you to trust God to take over in some situation of your life? God is far more concerned about your welfare than you are, for you are His child. The fulfillment of God's promises does not depend on your actions or character but on His character.

On this Christmas day, thank God for sending love incarnate to earth. Go to the Scriptures and find a promise that God wants to make a reality in your life.

> *For I testify to everyone who hears the words of the prophecy of this book: If anyone adds to these things, God will add to him the plagues that are written in this book; and if anyone takes away from the words of the book of this prophecy, God shall take away his part from the Book of Life, from the holy city, and from the things which are written in this book.*
>
> —REV. 22:18–19

Revelation contrasts the serenity and blessings of believers to the severe plagues and pain that will come to those who refuse to accept Christ. There is also a final warning to all people not to mess with God's Word.

The Bible is under attack in our world, even by very "religious" people. Some discredit it completely, but others are more subtle. Does your own pastor believe in the inerrancy and inspiration of the Bible? Even seminaries often belittle God's Word. Cults crop up every day. Manipulative men want to control others' minds. Some claim to have written new books to the Bible. They take advantage of the naive.

God's Word is complete. It is God's inspired love letter to us. It guides us to recovery from our negative tendencies, sins, and addictions. It teaches us to reach out to God and our peers. It teaches us our significance and promises a glorious future. It is God's completed gift and our personal path to joy and peace.

May God grant us the serenity that comes from trusting His Word and not being fooled by those who would discredit it or add to it.

> *Do not fear any of those things which you are about to suffer. Indeed, the devil is about to throw some of you into prison, that you may be tested, and you will have tribulation ten days. Be faithful until death, and I will give you the crown of life. He who has an ear, let him hear what the Spirit says to the churches. He who overcomes shall not be hurt by the second death.* —REV. 2:10–11

Some people think Christians should be free of all troubles. However, this is false advertising; Scripture does not support it. The Bible honestly and realistically states that Christians will experience suffering and be tested by circumstances in life.

Jane entered therapy frustrated with God. She had recently become a Christian hoping all her problems would cease. She said the church she went to promised prosperity, but she claimed she was in worse shape now. She said she felt as if she were in a financial prison. John the apostle straightforwardly said that we would suffer tribulation and possibly even be thrown in prison. He said we will be tested. However, he encouraged us to be faithful, not to give up hope or to simply not give up! In a sense, he said to develop staying power. Hang in there tenaciously. Persevere. He promised that in the end God would reward us. If we can have hope and faith in God in the midst of trials, we experience life in a satisfying way. We can endure in the trial rather than running away from it.

The Christian life does not mean deliverance from trouble. It is deliverance in trouble.

> *Because he has set his love upon Me, therefore I*
> *will deliver him; I will set him on high, because he*
> *has known My name.*
> —PS. 91:14

Our responsibility is to set our love on Christ and trust Him to defend us. God's response is exultation. He will set us on high at the proper time. This is an incredibly freeing thought; no matter what happens we do not need to defend or glorify ourselves.

Our culture teaches us to respond defensively. It is a skill that each of us must learn and practice. Most of us assume that if we don't defend ourselves in a conflict, others will see us as weak. In reality, the opposite is true. Nondefensive responses such as, "Let me think about that," and "Why don't we talk about this when you're not so upset," keep conflict from escalating.

Christ is a perfect example of the truth of this passage. Christ was God. He didn't have to grasp for deity because He already had it.

Christ was so sure of His identity that He was free to lay aside His position. He willingly stepped from deity into humanity. Because Jesus set aside His human will in order to do the will of His Father, "God has highly exalted Him and bestowed on Him the name which is above every name."

Each of us needs to surrender our need to exalt ourselves. Our Lord will work out His perfect will in the details of our lives.

Lord, in the conflicts I might face today, help me to speak the truth in a loving, nondefensive manner.

I counsel you to buy from Me gold refined in the fire, that you may be rich: and white garments, that you may be clothed, that the shame of your nakedness may not be revealed; and anoint your eyes with eye salve, that you may see.
—REV. 3:18

One thing we all need the courage to change in our lives is our own naïveté. We also need to increase our intimacy with Christ. They are related.

As a psychiatrist, it has become easy for me to spot the dynamics of my patients while I often remain the last person to see my own sins and psychological "weights" that hinder me from intimacy with God.

In our passage for today, Christ (through John) told the Laodicean church members to purchase gold refined in fire. Laodicea was a rich, banking city and its citizens were immensely wealthy, but not spiritually mature.

Laodicea was famous for its black wool, but this church was told to wear the "white garments" of moral living. There was a medical school in Laodicea in those days, at the temple of Asclepius. They were known for a special eye salve they exported to the Middle East. But Christ says to put on the "eye salve" of spiritual insights.

God promises to "rebuke and chasten" those whom He loves, in order to shake them into reality.

Whether you are a believer or a nonbeliever, Christ said He is not willing that any should perish. He stands at your heart's door right now—this very moment. Please let Him in. He wants to love you for eternity.

> *For all that is in the world; the lust of the flesh, the lust of the eyes, and the pride of life; is not of the Father but is of the world.* —1 JOHN 2:16

This passage addresses the absolute futility of the human "rat race." We all struggle with it. We easily fall back into the rat race if we don't fight it with godly wisdom.

Everybody feels like a nobody sometimes. Many of us devote time, energy, and money to prove to others that we are somebody. People ignore their children, cheat in business, and generally ruin their lives to prove it, but they never find significance.

The ways we vainly try to prove our significance are known as the "ways of the world." Lust of the flesh implies illicit bodily appetites, including sexual, food, and chemical addictions. Lust of the eyes is the temptation of materialism. The Greek phrase for the pride of life literally means "the pretension of human life," pride, arrogance, ostentatious behavior, trying to control others.

Even if the ways of the world worked, they would be immoral and wrong. God says they can never fill the void in our souls. Only faith in Christ, and pursuing intimacy with Him and loving believers, can fill those vacuums and bring meaning to our lives. Only looking at ourselves the way God looks at us—as children who are in the process of being perfected in Christ—can bring true feelings of significance. Jesus is the answer.

May God grant us the wisdom to devote our energy to real gold—God and loving people—rather than fool's gold.

"Consider your ways!
You have sown much, and bring in little;
You eat, but do not have enough;
You drink, but you are not filled with drink;
You clothe yourselves, but no one is warm;
And he who earns wages,
Earns wages to put into a bag with holes."
—HAG. 1:3–6

A true friend says what is good for us, not just what sounds good. A good friend sometimes says the hard things because we need to hear them and make changes. A true friend cares enough to confront.

The prophet Haggai passed on God's loving confrontive words to the people of Israel. God had earned the right to confront. He was the Father of Israel and they were His children. He had supported them, provided for them, guided them, encouraged them. Now, however, in love He felt the need to confront them because of their choices.

It seems the Israelites had taken up poor spending habits. They were living beyond their means. They were not planning or saving. Whatever they made in wages was immediately spent. Even though they were spending, eating, and drinking, it was never enough. They always wanted more, but gave nothing to God.

Our God is a caring God. He cares enough to confront. He will, through His Word, show us areas of our lives that need to change, just as He did with the children of Israel.

Let God speak to you today through His Word and lovingly show you what you need to change. He loves you enough to confront.

ABOUT THE AUTHORS

Paul Meier, M.D., received an M.S. degree in cardiovascular physiology at Michigan State University and an M.D. degree from the University of Arkansas College of Medicine. He completed his psychiatric residency at Duke University.

Frank Minirth, M.D., is a diplomate of the American Board of Psychiatry and Neurology and received an M.D. degree from the University of Arkansas College of Medicine.

Dr. Minirth and Dr. Meier founded the Minirth-Meier Clinic in Dallas, Texas, one of the largest psychiatric clinics in the world, with associated clinics in Chicago; Little Rock, Arkansas; Los Angeles, Laguna Hills, Newport Beach, Orange, and Palm Springs, California; Longview, Fort Worth, Sherman, San Antonio, and Austin, Texas; and Washington, D.C.

Both Dr. Minirth and Dr. Meier have received degrees from Dallas Theological Seminary. They have also co-authored more than thirty books, including *Happiness Is a Choice, Worry-Free Living, Love Is a Choice,* and *Love Hunger.*

David Congo, Ph.D., is a practicing psychologist with the Minirth-Meier-Stoop Clinic in Laguna Hills, California. He received his M.A. and Ph.D. in clinical psychology from the Rosemead School of Psychology at Biola University. He and his wife, Janet Congo, M.A., a therapist, are codirectors of Free to Soar Seminars and have written two books, *Free to Soar: the Love of Power Versus the Power of Love in Marriage* and *Less Stress: The Ten-Minute Stress-Reduction Plan.*